# DREAMWORK
# AND
# SELF-HEALING

£21-99

# DREAMWORK
# AND
# SELF-HEALING

## Unfolding the Symbols
## of the Unconscious

*Greg Bogart*

**KARNAC**

Credit: Ouroboros illustration, from M. Maier, *Atalanta Fugiens* (published Oppenheim, Germany, 1618), reproduced with permission of Stadtbibliothek Mainz.

Cover design: Sophie Chery

First published in 2009 by
Karnac Books Ltd
118 Finchley Road
London NW3 5HT

British Library Cataloguing in Publication Data

A C.I.P. for this book is available from the British Library

ISBN-13: 978-1-85575-758-5

Typeset by Vikatan Publishing Solutions (P) Ltd., Chennai, India

Printed in Great Britain

www.karnacbooks.com

*For Diana Syverud,*
*the wise woman of my dreams.*

*Dream images appear as if purposive. They provide vital information which is necessary for an appropriate evaluation of the actual life situation and which is unavailable to consciousness through logical channels.... . In complementing and compensating, [dream] images seem as if bent upon altering and widening consciousness. We may say that they represent contents and impulses which demand to be allowed into conscious life.*

Edward Whitmont (1969, pp. 47–48)

*Just as the body possesses control mechanisms to keep its vital functions in balance, so the psyche has a control mechanism in the compensatory activity of dreams.... . [Dreams] provide a view of the dreamer's situation and mobilize the potential of the personality to meet it.... . As an efficient homeostatic system, the psyche possesses the capacity to heal itself, and it is in the compensatory function of the unconscious that this power for self-healing resides.*

Anthony Stevens (1990, pp. 49–51)

*The right way to wholeness is a longissima via, not straight but snakelike, a path that unites the opposites in the manner of the guiding caduceus.*

C.G. Jung (1968 [1944], par. 6)

# CONTENTS

# LIST OF ILLUSTRATIONS

xi

# PERMISSIONS

The author gratefully acknowledges:

Princeton University Press for permission to reprint selections from the *Collected Works of C.G. Jung*.

Spring Publications, for permission to reprint selections from *Individuation in Fairy Tales*, by Marie-Louise von Franz (1977).

Inner City Books, for permission to reproduce images from the *Rosarium philosophorum*, from *The Mystery of the Coniunctio*, by Edward Edinger (1994a).

Stadtbibliothek Mainz, for permission to reproduce illustrations from M. Meier, *Atalanta Fugiens* (Oppenheim, Germany, 1618).

Pierpont Morgan Library and Museum, for permission to reproduce an image from William Blake, "Illustrations of the book of Job": The Pierpont Morgan Library, New York. PML 30214, plate 18. Not to be reproduced without the express permission of the Pierpont Morgan Library.

Sony Music Publishing Group:

"I Am the Walrus," Lyrics by John Lennon/ Paul McCartney

© 1967 Sony/ATV Tunes LLC

Administered by Sony/ATV Music Publishing

All rights reserved. Used by permission.

# *PREFACE*

Dreams are potent catalysts of change. Their luminous images ignite the light of consciousness within us and become a source of energy and guidance, an axis of spiritual sanity. Dreams are transformative when utilized in psychotherapy, or by couples and friends who work with dreams together to assist and support one another, and to enhance their knowing of one another. Contemplating our own dreams through a journal or in silent meditation is also powerfully self-liberating. In all of these ways, we can inquire deeply into each dream image, drinking in its multiple meanings and messages, and the feelings each dream stirs.

This book explores how working with dreams enhances our emotional life, deepens our capacity for relationship, and helps us gracefully navigate change and transitions. *Dreamwork and Self-Healing* will interest all readers who wish to learn about dreams and their healing potential. It will be of special relevance to practitioners of counseling, psychotherapy, and spiritual direction. I recount stories that show how dreams aid us in personal metamorphosis, illuminating our life paths. I show you exactly how I work with dreams so that you can begin to do this work yourself—with your own dreams, and with those of your clients or loved ones.

A noteworthy feature of this book is the inclusion of extensive case examples. At times, the material is intense and carries strong emotional impact. This is not only a book about dreams but also a portrait of psychotherapy as a transformative emotional, relational, and spiritual process. I demonstrate the practice of dreamwork in highly focused and change-producing short-term therapy, as well as in long-term depth psychotherapy. I believe the human lessons drawn from these stories are relevant to everyone, not just therapists or those undergoing psychotherapy. Readers can follow the parallel movement between the symbolic events of the unconscious (dreams) and the courageous response of my subjects to maturational challenges and turbulent relationships, as they explore depression, anger, sexuality, and creativity, as they strive to be part of the deepest surges and cycles of the life force as it is evolving within them.

There have been many previous books on the physiology of dreaming, the history of dream interpretation, and the meaning of specific dream symbols. But there have been relatively few books exploring the step-by-step process of interpreting dreams. This book guides you through this interpretive process, and illustrates how dreamwork promotes emotional, relational, and spiritual transformation. I want to show how dreams produce practical and dynamic results; they are truly life-changing. You will gain a clearer sense of how to unfold dream symbols, and how to act upon the realizations each dream evokes.

Part I of this book introduces the methods and process of therapeutic dreamwork, and shows that dreams are a source of emotional and relational intelligence, carriers of immense and powerful meanings. I demonstrate how we can intensify the process of self-healing by working on dreams, especially with a therapist or guide to facilitate the process.

Part II presents a Jungian approach to dreamwork, discussing some core Jungian concepts—such as archetypes, complexes, shadow, persona, and individuation—which provide a context for the examples that fill this book. I discuss passages by C.G. Jung, Marie-Louise von Franz, Edward Edinger, James Hillman, and other luminaries whose ideas have influenced me. I demonstrate a form of dynamic process work that allows us to unfold and embody the mythic-archetypal symbolism and energies of dreams. I introduce a technique I call the *Dream Mandala*, which promotes wholeness and self-healing through the circular mapping of dream imagery.

Part III presents an extended case study exploring animal symbolism and male sexuality, and demonstrates the clinical practice of dreamwork. The subject of this chapter does some deep inner work that transforms a pattern of sexual compulsions and infidelities into a capacity for mature love. This case study illustrates principles discussed throughout the book, shows the kind of change that is possible, and contributes to our understanding of human sexuality.

The best preparation for practicing dreamwork with others is to be deeply involved in our own work with the unconscious. To illustrate this, the book includes a number of personal anecdotes about my own dreams. I hope you'll consider it a benefit that these stories convey some sense of me as a person and allow you to see me as I really am. These examples show the inner foundation from which I approach dreams.

I believe dreamwork has never been more relevant. As our current planetary upheaval deepens, with its complex problems of military conflict, environmental degradation, and moral confusion, we need to access the wisdom of the unconscious to find inner truth, inner guidance, and inner wisdom. By unfolding dream symbolism, we find a lamp that lights our path.

This book invites you to explore dreams with energy, humour, and a feeling of inspiration. The journey is endless, and the interpretation of a dream is never complete. Always a work in progress, it is an infinitely creative process.

# ACKNOWLEDGEMENTS

I'd like to thank the following beloved teachers, mentors, and colleagues: Robert Bartner, Margo Chapin, Betsy Cohen, John Conger, Marion de Coudreaux, Wayne Detloff, Vern Haddick, Arthur Hastings, Gareth Hill, Robert Hopcke, Karl Knobler, Mark Ludwig, David Lukoff, Gayle Peterson, Donald Rothberg, Stuart Sovatsky, Robert Steele, Bryan Wittine, and Jeremy Zwelling. I also thank Stanley Krippner for his encouragement and guidance.

I warmly thank my students and colleagues at the California Institute of Integral Studies, especially Brendan Collins, Brant Cortright, Daniel Deslauriers, Lise Dyckman, Jorge Ferrer, Judye Hess, Nathan Lupo, Gary Raucher, Bahman Shirazi, Joseph Subbiondo, Richard Tarnas, and David Townes. I also thank my colleagues Mary Gomes, Laurel McCabe, and Geri Olson of Sonoma State University.

I began work on this book during seven years of teaching at John F. Kennedy University and would like to express my gratitude to my colleagues: Clover Catskill, Michele Chase, Harvey Cohen, Marilyn Fowler, Ray Greenleaf, Penny Harrington, Gary Hoeber, Brian Lippincott, Maria Mattioli, Peter Rojcewicz, Theresa Silow, Vernice Solimar, Ann Stillingfleet, and Mary Tuchscherer.

The publication of this book would have held special meaning for my father, Leo Bogart, who was deeply affected in his youth by Freud's *Interpretation of Dreams*. He completed a year of psycho-analytic training before opting to become a famed sociologist. We shared and discussed many dreams together in the final years of his luminous life. And loving thanks to my mother, Agnes Bogart, my first writing teacher, for her strength, determination, and sense of humour. My parents offered unflagging encouragement during the nine years it took to complete this book, telling me to "go for it" and "never give up."

I also offer thanks to my sister, Michele Bogart, the late Philip Pauly, and Nick Pauly, and my aunt, Joanne Powers; to my brilliant editor, Nancy Carleton; to John Beebe, for his helpful comments and suggestions; to my chiropractor, Richard Robertshaw; to Meredith Sabini, Jennifer Privateer, and the Dream Institute of Northern California; to Marianne Morgan, Librarian of the C.G. Jung Institute of San Francisco; to Don Michael and Chakrapani Ullal for their wise counsel; and to my friends Sid Aaronson, Chris Abajian, Rick Amaro, Cathy Auman, Ken Bowser, Nick Campion, Kaleo and Elise Ching, Linda Cogozzo, Cathy Coleman, Robert Forte, Jennifer Freed, Richard Gale, Michael Gliksohn, Ray Grasse, Dennis Harness, Shelley Jordan, David Kesten, Joe Landwehr, Ian LeCheminant, Michael Lutin, Colleen Mauro, Leah Mazel, Charles Mintz, Martien Nielson, Robert Powell, Claude Palmer, Pat Russell, Laura Shekerjian, Kate Sholly, Elizabeth Spring, Claire Stone, Tem Tarriktar, and Stuart Walker. Loving thanks to one and all.

I'm indebted to all of the individuals whose dreams and stories are recounted here. Their deep inner work has been an inspiration to me. I've changed names and identifying details to preserve their anonymity.

Portions of Chapter Two previously appeared in *Dreamscaping: New and Creative Ways to Work with Your Dreams* (Krippner & Waldman, 2000). Chapter Four was first published in *Dream Network Journal*, Spring 2004. Chapter Thirteen appeared in *Dream Network Journal*, Winter 2008. I'd like to thank Roberta Ossana, Editor of *DNJ*, for her kind support. I also warmly thank Oliver Rathbone and Karnac Books for their skillful stewardship of this book.

# ABOUT THE AUTHOR

Greg Bogart, Ph.D, MFT is a psychotherapist in private practice in the San Francisco Bay Area, and a professor of Counseling Psychology at the California Institute of Integral Studies (CIIS). He also teaches in the department of Psychology at Sonoma State University. Greg is a graduate of Saybrook Institute (Ph.D., Psychology), CIIS (M.A., Counseling Psychology), and Wesleyan University (B.A., Religious Studies). He is the author of numerous books, including *The Nine Stages of Spiritual Apprenticeship; Finding Your Life's Calling;* and *Astrology and Meditation: The Fearless Contemplation of Change.* His writings have appeared in *The Journal of Transpersonal Psychology, American Journal of Psychotherapy, Journal of Humanistic Psychology, California Therapist, Journal of the Society for the Study of Dreams, Dream Network Journal,* and *Yoga Journal.*

# PART I

## THERAPEUTIC DREAMWORK

# CHAPTER ONE

# Introduction

Dreams are healing symbols of the unconscious. They make emotionally charged material accessible to consciousness quickly and safely, give focus to inner work and the therapeutic process, and provide clues about the origins of symptoms and core life issues. Dreams activate our capacity for intrapsychic and behavioural change. They have a unique capacity to promote healing from within.

Dreams are like icebergs rising out of the deep waters of the unconscious. Some are icebergs of the past, helping us understand early traumas and undigested memories, and thus are *retrospective*. Dreams are *integrative* when they enable us to perceive and reconcile our many conflicting feelings and subpersonalities. Dreams can also be *prospective* or anticipatory, harbingers of the future, depicting what is emerging, and what we have the potential to become. Looking backward and forward simultaneously, the dream's function is to expand the aperture of consciousness, the circumference of perception, the sphere of identity. The often humorous and paradoxical messages revealed by dreams jog loose new perceptions. Received reverently, each dream becomes a pearl from the depths of the ocean of the unconscious. Reflection on the dream's mystery often evokes a feeling approaching religious awe; we become filled with amazement at the psyche's capacity to portray its own condition.

The founders of depth psychology, Freud and Jung, both believed in the value of working with dreams. They viewed dream interpretation as a primary tool for psychotherapy and a source of transformative insights that breathe life into the therapeutic process. My own work has taken shape within this tradition. I explore the symbolism of each dream that my clients tell me, contemplating the dream's imagery and their associations to it, allowing the unconscious to portray its very personal meanings. I view each dream as a symbolic representation of the inner world, revealing a person's developmental issues, inner conflicts, and emotional states. Each dream also reflects the relational, interpersonal world of the individual, including issues related to the therapeutic transference.

The technique of dreamwork I practice is simple. I utilize free association and amplification of dream imagery. I ask questions about every image and every person appearing in the dream. I inquire into the current significance of every character, place, and action in the dream—each of which refers to the dreamer's inner state, interpersonal relationships, and current life situation. I ask questions about important figures in the dream:

- What does he or she look like?
- Who does this remind you of?
- Why is this person, place, or object in your dream?
- What does this place, action, or feeling in the dream remind you of?

I often ask clients to enact dialogues with dream figures. Rather than imposing my own interpretation, I work with the client to develop a shared interpretation of the dream. I avoid foreclosing the meaning of dream imagery and remain open to alternative meanings and multiple interpretations. At times I also suggest that a client "incubate" a dream by reflecting deeply on a pressing issue and asking the unconscious for a dream that will provide clarification or guidance.

## Jung's Approach to Dreams

This book presents a way of exploring dreams that has its roots in the work of C.G. Jung, who wrote:

> Every interpretation is a hypothesis, an attempt to read an
> unknown text.... A relative degree of certainty is reached only
> in the interpretation of a series of dreams, where the later
> dreams correct the mistakes we have made in handling those
> that went before.... I ... urge my patients to keep a careful
> record of their dreams and of the interpretations given.... At a
> later stage I get them to work out the interpretations as well.
> In this way the patient learns how to deal correctly with the
> unconscious without the doctor's help. (Jung, 1966 [1934a],
> par. 322)

This is the approach I follow. I ask my clients to record all dreams,
including small fragments, even if they appear to make no sense
whatsoever. I get the client actively involved in the process of deci-
phering the dream text. If possible, I work with a series of dreams
over time, noting how the dreams parallel changes occurring in the
person's life.

Jung believed that dreams convey the transformative wisdom of
the unconscious, which leads us forward in our individuation, the
process of unfolding our uniqueness and becoming who we really
are. Jung himself is the prototype of the person healed by dreamwork. He worked through a difficult psychological crisis by self-
interpreting a series of dreams. He also showed how to ground and
contain the unconscious through art, journal work, and amplification of dream symbolism. Through these methods, he found that we
discover mythic depth in dreams, which are structured by recurring
patterns of organization called archetypes. For example, dreams
show us images of the hero, mother, and death-rebirth. I'll describe
the archetypes in Part II.

Jung noted the *compensatory* function of dreams, the way that
dreams communicate insights, feelings, and perceptions that compensate for what we consciously know, feel, and believe. In other
words, dreams correct one-sided attitudes, and show us a different
way of seeing ourselves and our relationships. Jung wrote, "[T]he
unconscious does not simply act *contrary* to the conscious mind but
*modifies* it more in the manner of an opponent or partner" (Jung,
1968 [1944], par. 26). In dreams, we encounter an inner intelligence
that reveals the light, prods us onward, and invites us to change
and grow.

In Jung's view, the relationship between the ego and the unconscious occurs through symbolism, through what he called the "uniting symbol" (Jung, 1969 [1939], par. 523). In symbols, he wrote

> the union of conscious and unconscious contents is consummated. I have ... called the union of opposites the "transcendent function." This rounding out of the personality into a whole may well be the goal of any psychotherapy that claims to be more than a mere cure of symptoms. (Jung, 1969 [1939], par. 524)

Many of the dreams discussed in this book illustrate vividly the union of opposites and the rounding out of the personality into a whole. Indeed, these will be central themes of our discussion. To enhance awareness of the opposites in the personality, I sometimes portray dreams through circular diagrams that I call *Dream Mandalas*, explained more fully in Chapter Ten.

I believe that in this era of pharmacology and medical management of psychological symptoms and suffering, we greatly need a depth approach to the psyche. Dreamwork provides a vibrant alternative to long-term use of psychoactive medications and lives of misery and unhappiness. It makes possible a structural reorganization of the inner world that awakens joy and vitality. Dreamwork is a safe and effective basis for transformative process work, as I hope to demonstrate throughout this book.

A number of noted authors have presented comprehensive surveys of Jung's core ideas, including Jacobi (1942), von Franz (1975), Stevens (1990), Fordham (1990), Stein (1998), Storr (1973), and Bennet (2000). My goal here is to illustrate Jungian dreamwork in practice, to show, through detailed examples, how dreamwork can profoundly change us, promoting enhanced relationships, resolution of trauma and persistent symptoms, and a renewed sense of spiritual meaning and life purpose.

Edward Whitmont and Sylvia Perera beautifully presented the practice of Jungian dream interpretation in their book *Dreams: A Portal to the Source* (Whitmont & Perera, 1989). Five core ideas in that book serve as the foundation for this present volume. According to Whitmont and Perera:

- The dream is a symbolic statement about the dreamer's psychological situation, exactly as it is. Dreams are symbolic messages from the guiding and ordering centre of the personality, the Guiding Self—director of the individuation drive, the innate urge to become what one is.

- The only correct interpretation of a dream is one that meets the dreamer's assent, which comes from the person's embodied "gut sense."
- Dreams communicate through images and metaphors, which we decode by exploring the dream's web of associations. We enrich the dream through associations and amplify it to the point of intelligibility. We carefully examine each image and strive to understand its relevance to the dreamer's current life situation.
- Associations are ideas, memories, or whatever else comes to mind as we consider the dream and its images. We explore associations until they reveal their emotional core and psychological significance. When a powerful feeling emerges, we can assume that we've reached the essential core of the dream. Associations and amplifications form a unitary field with the dream itself, along with emotional reactions of the dreamer and witness(es) that arise as we tell and discuss the dream.
- The reactions of a therapist or other witnesses are also relevant. The listener's own unconscious is activated and provides relevant material about the meaning of the dream.

These ideas are my starting point. I'll describe how dreamwork can aid us in exploring depression, anger, childhood trauma, sexuality, bereavement, alcohol abuse, and relationship conflicts and impasses. Dreams initiate a process that transforms our suffering, touches our deepest emotional core, and helps us find our own paths to freedom.

*CHAPTER TWO*

# Dreamwork and Psychotherapy

Dreams are a potent force for change when we explore them in the context of psychotherapy—or when we explore our own dreams with a therapeutic attitude, seeking healing and emotional truth. Approached in a sacred manner, with an open mind and heart, our dreams begin to guide us, one step at a time, through the labyrinth of change. Dreams illuminate developmental tasks and stir up rich, juicy material for deep exploration. Dreams pinpoint what we need to revisit from the past, what we are feeling right now, and what new directions and possibilities are emerging. They move our lives forward with a powerfully healing influence.

### The Dream of the Cactus Plant

Bob, a man in his mid-forties beginning a course of psychotherapy, had this dream:

> *I'm six years old. I'm with my mother and we're cleaning out the closets.*

As Bob's therapist, I was immediately drawn to the emotional significance of events in the client's sixth year and the need to sort

9

through whatever had been hidden in the closet. Many family secrets came out of hiding in subsequent therapy sessions. I learned about the domestic violence and alcoholism that were closely kept family secrets. Bob was currently in a deep depression after the break-up of a relationship. As he began to examine his anger, his tendency to act abusively toward women, his sadness, and his need to accept his solitude, he dreamed:

*I'm on my hands and knees in front of my bed potting a cactus plant.*

The cactus plant represented Bob's prickly personality. When I asked what the further significance of a cactus might be, he said, "A cactus can live in a desert for a long time with very little water, and it finds its juice within its own body." The cactus was a symbol of his need to find juice or aliveness in the desert of his solitude, rather than looking to women and relationships for excitement. Bob was learning to live with himself, to care for himself. Being on his hands and knees suggested the emergence of humility. The dream of planting the cactus illustrates that each dream image, even the smallest fragment, is significant and meaningful, revealing a cross-section of the unconscious.

## The Dream of the Missing Money

A simple dream often carries deep emotional meaning. A woman named Jill reported:

*I dreamed that I'm in the store where I work, counting a stack of money. A bunch of money is missing.*

Jill offered this interpretation: "Being robbed in the dream reminds me of how I was robbed of my childhood. I never got a chance to be a kid, to be cared for and pampered. I was short-changed." Jill recounted to me the ways she'd been parentified, forced to function as a little adult in her family from the age of six. She began to understand how much grief and anger she still carried from her lost childhood. But the dream had another meaning: Money is missing. Jill was grappling with serious money issues. She was not earning much, and her self-esteem was very low. When I asked for her associations to "money is missing," she said, "I feel like I'm not worth anything." Each dream image is a hologram of the inner world, full of condensed meanings.

## The Dream of the Wildcat

A woman named Wendy, with an extensive history of childhood abuse, had trouble expressing anger and standing up for herself, and was frequently victimized by others. She dreamed:

> Some friends take me to an animal rescue place with wildcats, bobcats. They show us around, demonstrating how they talk to the animals and handle them. A big lioness or wildcat jumps me and puts her claws into my leg. I talk to her and try to stay calm.

When I asked for her associations to the wildcat, Wendy said, "It's powerful, untamed. Anger and aggression are hard for me. The lioness is a creature that knows how to show its claws." The dream suggested a need for Wendy to rescue and shelter the fierce, animal part of herself. Where previously she'd been like an innocent lamb or a victim, with little ability to stand up for herself, this dream heralded the emergence of a positive capacity for aggression, will, self-defence, self-protection. A week later Wendy reported standing up to a friend who had wronged her, detailing her grievance, and expressing her anger. The dream coincided with the emergence of her inner wildcat.

## The Dream of the Wall

Tanya, a woman in a sexless marriage, dreamed that there was a massive wall between the living room and the bedroom of her home. The wall symbolized her resistance to sexuality, her need to maintain boundaries to defend against physical and emotional injury. Contemplating this image proved helpful not only to Tanya but also to her husband, James, who was able to better understand the depth of Tanya's fear of sexual intimacy. Tanya was able to recognize how her body had become frozen in fear, creating an impenetrable barrier to any sense of closeness. Working with this dream helped Tanya and James begin to dismantle the wall between them.

## The Dream of the Sleeping Wolf

An ex-priest dreamed that he entered a cave where he found an altar, in front of which lay a sleeping wolf. The wolf symbolized not only his feelings of being a lone wolf, fending for his own survival now that he had left the Church, but also his long dormant (sleeping) animal nature, his sexual desire, his hunger for embodied, passionate life. The wolf in front of the altar suggested that rediscovering his sexuality was sacred. It was associated with a place, and feeling, of worship.

## Six Dreams of a Depressed Woman

Dreams provide important insights into the therapeutic relationship. A fifty-four-year-old woman named Ann presented several dreams that referred to her transference. In one dream, Ann said:

> I sat in the back of a lecture hall as you [Greg] gave a lecture. I couldn't decide whether to stay or leave.

This dream revealed her ambivalence about the therapeutic process. Should she stay or flee? As Ann's therapist, the dream informed me that Ann perceived me as overly intellectual or "preachy." In another dream, I (the therapist) disappeared unexpectedly, reflecting Ann's fear of being abandoned by me.

Dreams deepened Ann's treatment immeasurably. Later, she dreamed:

> I'm a flightless bird.

Ann's flight and freedom of spirit were inhibited. She was dysphoric, chronically depressed, and unable to find any pleasure in daily living. When I asked her to explore this further, she described how caged in she felt in her marriage, how her husband actively thwarted her efforts to gain greater autonomy, and how little fun they had together.

Then Ann dreamed:

> A man is at my window, angry and menacing. There's something wrong with him. I feel concern for him, for he's in desperate need of help.

Ann had a history of incest, so issues of boundary intrusion (angry man at the window) were central. She herself was desperate for help. But the dream also reflected conflicted feelings toward her child-hood abuser, including fantasies of helping or rescuing him. Ann had suffered from a phobic aversion to sex and had been unable to make love with her husband for many years. This dream helped Ann understand how her refusal of sexuality started out in her childhood as a self-protective measure, to keep out the intruder. The man in the dream reminded her of her husband, who had become increasingly angry with her. She was able to see that while she wasn't attracted to her husband, she was also terrified at the prospect of leaving him because, she believed, he needed her to take care of him.

Dreams illuminate relational issues that may be re-enacted in the therapeutic transference. Ann dreamed:

> A little girl is playing innocently on a lawn, running around and catching fireflies in her hands, laughing and shrieking with joy. Then a small buffalo comes over and starts bumping his head against her. She's not in danger, but she feels anxious and wishes he would go away. She wishes there were someone around who could make the buf-falo go away, but there isn't anyone to help her.

Ann's dream of torment by a buffalo evoked childhood memories of sexual violation by her stepfather, her inability to protect herself, her sense of being abandoned by her mother, her longing for protection. The theme of innocence—its loss and recovery—became a central thread of our discussion. The buffalo also reminded Ann of her hus-band's insistent sexual demands and his angry frustration with her unresponsiveness.

This material became the focus of the next several sessions. When I asked for further associations to the buffalo, Ann was reminded of me, her therapist. She said, "The hairy buffalo reminds me of your beard and long hair."

I said, "You and I have been butting heads the last few weeks about some things."

She laughed and said, "Actually, it was a very skinny, scrawny buffalo!" We both laughed. This dream opened up new space in our intersubjective field. Now she could talk about feeling anxious about whether she could find comfort and protection in therapy.

We could talk about our therapeutic relationship and what it felt like when at times I challenged and confronted her.

Several months later, Ann dreamed:

> *I was wearing the red dress I wore the night before my wedding.*

This dream evoked the expectancy and excitement of marriage, and feelings of being young, beautiful, sexy, and desirable. Later she dreamed that she was pregnant for the third time. Ann was pregnant with herself; the dream portended inner rebirth and renewal. This dream coincided with her beginning sex therapy with her husband.

## Dreams as Intensifiers of Emotions

Dreams reveal and intensify our emotional states. A man named Lonnie dreamed:

> *I went to a Thanksgiving party, but there was no substantial food there, only a few pieces of fruit and some small snacks. Some children arrived at the party and were disappointed that they weren't going to eat.*

This dream encapsulated an emotional experience of deprivation and lack of nurturance that Lonnie had felt since childhood.

A woman named Sandra dreamed of a dilapidated mansion of an "old family," a family with a long tradition. She said, "They used to live in grand style, but the house hasn't been kept up and needs repair and renovation." This dream evoked sadness about her estranged relationships with her children and a longing for restoration of her sense of family.

A woman named Laurie dreamed that she was lying in a hospital bed. This reminded her of being sick, convalescing, being weakened. The dream depicted Laurie's wounded self, her depression, which she needed to allow herself to feel.

A woman named Linda dreamed:

> *I was up on a stage wearing a frock my mother forced me to wear when I was a kid. It was very tight in the collar.*

The dream clarified several emotional truths: Linda felt that her mother was always trying to show off her daughter, to validate her own self-worth; and Linda felt she had to comply with mother's wishes, despite the way this was choking her emotionally. She felt suffocated by her mother's expectations.

## The Dream of Mother and the Grisly Murders

Dreams allow us to recognize and reveal our most disturbing feelings and memories. Cindy, an incest survivor, had this nightmare:

> My mother was accused of several grisly murders. Part of her ritual in these killings was taking pictures of the bodies. I was looking through the pictures. I didn't know the people. Out of the corner of my eye I saw a poorly exposed photo of a bloody face wearing a football helmet. I looked at her and said, "Mama, did you do it?" I shook her. She didn't answer me.

The grisly murders and bloody faces suggested that people had been bludgeoned, representing the way Cindy felt she'd been assaulted emotionally. The dream was also a message to me, her therapist, to take seriously that what happened to Cindy as a child had been brutal. The dream initiated a discussion of her troubled relationship with her mother, and the buried rage Cindy felt toward her. Previously Cindy had done extensive therapy exploring her relationship with her stepfather (the perpetrator of sexual abuse), but this dream voiced the question, "Mama, did *you* do this?" In other words, "What was *your* role in what happened?" This dream brought to the surface Cindy's feelings of not being able to trust someone who supposedly loved her and would take care of her. The dream also portrayed a transference issue: Could she trust me, her therapist? In the dream, a football helmet, which should have provided protection against injury, hasn't worked. This insight enabled Cindy to verbalize her core disappointment—"that my mother abandoned me and left me in the hands of this terrible man."

## The Dream of the Pig

In stating that dreams are intensifiers of emotions, I also mean that the feelings evoked by dreams can be quite intense. I've found that the most intense, disturbing dreams are often powerfully healing, if we're able to unfold their underlying emotional content. Once I was leading a group in which one of the members, a woman named Terri, dreamed:

> I'm in a bathtub. I had to slaughter a pig. I sliced its arm. The pig was bleeding, slowly dying, passing out. I sat in the tub with the pig and held it under a faucet, stroking its head, comforting it.

Terri commented, "I was born in the Chinese Year of the Pig. People who eat too much are called pigs. A pig is a glutton. That brings up all my issues about food."

I said, "It reminds me of being a glutton for punishment."

Terri said, "Cutting the pig reminds me of a suicide attempt I made some years ago, when I cut myself." When Terri said this, the other group members grew tensely hushed; it was a highly charged moment.

I said, "Don't be afraid of all the feelings in the room. Terri, your dream provides an opportunity to resolve your feelings about this episode, and to bring into awareness the feelings that led you to do it. Only then can you really begin to heal. Washing the bleeding pig is a symbol of your healing."

Terri said, "In the dream I felt love for the pig." Her dream of holding the pig evoked a powerful experience of self-love and self-forgiveness.

## Dreams and Illness

Dreams sometimes make us aware of emerging physical conditions or needs. Dream researcher Harry Hunt calls this the *medical-somatic dimension* of dreaming (Hunt, 1993). A woman who had been a vegetarian since childhood dreamed that she went to a restaurant where she was served a turkey sandwich. This dream coincided with a time when she was aware of physical depletion and lack of energy, and it seemed to communicate that her body wanted something that her mind resisted.

## The Dream of the Staircase

Dreams can provide new meaning for those grappling with chronic illness or major injuries. A man named Warren was grappling with the onset of a crippling disease and the fact that his fiancée had broken off their engagement and left him. He dreamed:

> *I'm living in a white suburban house with my sister and her hus-*
> *band. We find a button on the wall that we've never touched before,*
> *and have never been curious about. My sister pushes the button and*
> *the ceiling opens up and a staircase opens from the upstairs. Wow!*
> *There's another floor to this house! We've lived here for twenty*
> *years and never knew this was here. I ran up and down the stairs*
> *excitedly.*

In the dream the staircase opened up, suggesting ascending, climbing, finding a higher perspective or viewpoint. This dream evoked the sense of a previously unknown dimension revealing itself. It heralded Warren's discovery of the vertical dimension of spiritual experience and meaning that complements the horizontal plane of linear time and everyday life. In medieval alchemy, one of the central procedures is *sublimatio*, the rising up of vapour from a heated substance. In *sublimatio*, one experiences the rising up of spirit, symbolized by a white bird, or by a ladder, connecting earth and heaven. Warren's dream of the staircase up to a hidden upper floor pointed to the possibility of transcending some portion of suffering through discovering the archetypal dimension.

## The Dream of Being Flipped Upside Down

Later Warren dreamed:

> *Jane (my ex-fiancée) and I are on a couch, which flips over suddenly as*
> *if in an earthquake. We're dumped upside down.*

This dream reminded Warren of his recent break-up with Jane. He said, "The first thing that comes to mind is how I've been dumped by Jane. It also reminds me of how my world has been turned upside down by my illness. The dream reminds me of the Hanged Man, surrendering, having a new perspective, being on a cross, or experiencing a crucifixion. This illness is my cross." The dream suggested a need for Warren to live his suffering consciously and to make meaning from it.

## The Dream of the Rose

Dreams are the psyche's means of self-healing. Allen was very discouraged and depressed about his relationships with women, as his girlfriend had recently left him for another man. He had this dream:

> *I was swimming underwater. The water was very clear and warm, with a lot of rich plant life growing in it. I saw a rose that was my mother's. The rose was on the surface and began to sink down toward the bottom. I saw how deep and vibrant its red colour was. It had no thorns. I caught it before it reached the bottom. It came to rest in my hand, and when I touched it, it began to open up and blossom in my hand with a very powerful and loving energy. Later it began to rise to the surface again.*

Allen and I explored our associations to each part of the dream. Being underwater suggested being submerged, immersed in water, in his emotions, in the unconscious. The water is warm and life-giving, suggesting it is safe and life-enhancing to explore the unconscious. The rose is a symbol of the Self, flowering, individuation. Allen said, "It reminds me of deep, honest love—unshakable, unfailing love, like my mom's love for me." The red colour of the rose suggests heat, passion, smouldering with feeling. He added, "I'm angry about being derailed from being trusting and loving. I want to love someone with all my heart." The rose with no thorns evoked feelings of being defenceless, innocent, having no aggression.

I said, "The rose coming to the surface brings into consciousness the awareness that in your essence you're a man of deep, honest, open, abiding love." One month after having this dream, Allen met someone and fell in love. They quickly moved in together, and Allen completed his stint of brief therapy.

## The Dream of the Teenyboppers, Homeless Men, and Caretakers

Dreams help us understand the complex developmental challenges of a particular stage of life. Here are two dreams of a man in midlife (thirty-nine years of age). A long-time meditator, Karl longed to actively pursue his inner, contemplative journey but felt restricted in these pursuits due to the responsibilities of fatherhood and career. He sought psychotherapy to address marital stress, an obsession with viewing pornography, and sexual problems in his marriage.

*A woman is sitting on the floor meditating. A guy with a reputation for being inconsiderate of others is there making a lot of noise. I tell him I'll beat the crap out of him if he doesn't stop. Teenagers are playing a sound system really loud, playing CDs of contemporary teenybopper love songs, full of teenage angst. I wonder how to change this music to make it better for meditating. Then I criss-cross a river and see a shelter or lean-to where I find two guys in their early twenties. They look worn, as if they've been homeless for many years. Then a group of people in a room discuss how to care for the sick and elderly. They want to help but are afraid of not knowing what to say. They might offend someone or say something taboo. What if they make the person feel worse? What about diaper changes for the dying person, or what if they had to watch the dying person go through something deforming or disabling? Someone presses a button and an electronic Tibetan bowl starts to make a sound. It's meant to relax everyone, to get their minds to quiet down. The sound changes; upper harmonics gradually fade in. The overtones are opening. I go deeply into the sound, which takes me into a deep trance. I lose the sense of the room. As I come out of trance the people in the room are still in a quandary about what to do about the dying person. I suggest that they go and simply express their love. I realize I haven't visited my sick uncle in over a month. I feel bad about not visiting and decide to do so as soon as possible. Then I wake up.*

When I asked about his associations to the various dream figures, Karl said, "The woman meditating represents my desire for spiritual exploration and inner freedom." Indeed, the dream itself provides a taste of release in deep trance. The trance later in the dream could also indicate dissociation, a tendency to avoid painful feelings through entering altered states. Karl continued, "The inconsiderate man reminds me of a part of myself that snaps at my kids or wife. It's my temper when I'm reactive and inconsiderate, my way of being demanding of others, coming across as harsh and unpleasant." Here the dream focused on the integration of shadow material related to anger. Then Karl noted, "My statement in the dream that I'll beat up this man reminds me of how I beat myself up for snapping at my family, wasting time, watching junky TV, staying up late, not getting enough exercise, masturbating too much, and not being romantic enough with my wife." Here we uncovered a hostile inner critic for further exploration.

The teenagers in the dream reminded Karl of his twelve-year-old son and his peers, and of the noisy, disruptive quality of adolescents and adolescent culture. Asked about the homeless young men in the dream, Karl said, "They don't want to work hard. They have a degenerate quality I don't like, and it reminds me of the degenerate quality of how I fritter away time looking at pornography on the Internet or watching crappy TV shows." When I asked about how he feels "worn," Karl replied, "I feel worn out from carrying around my baby girl." Karl and I were now able to identify the pressures and fatigue of parenting (changing diapers) as central themes in his present life, quite in contrast to the pursuit of blissful meditative trance and inner journeys. Karl was feeling the weight of the earth, both in the responsibilities of caring for children, but also in his awareness, brought into focus by the dream, of the need to care for the dying. Karl said, "I haven't wanted to deal with the fact that my uncle is going to die soon. And I wonder, is it okay to talk with him about his own death?" As a man in midlife, Karl was both caring for new life and confronting the end of life. In the midst of it all, he was surrounded by teenagers full of sexual energy and longing.

## The Dream of the Prostitute-Mother-Transsexual

Karl's next dream further addressed the theme of adolescent sexuality:

> I leave a business meeting and go into the bathroom. I find a Playboy magazine and start getting really excited by it. Then a woman walks through the room, a prostitute who is just getting off work. She's holding her child and is taking him upstairs to go to bed. Another woman comes in, and I pay her $20 to remove her clothes. I see she has terrible surgical scars on her body, and then I'm shocked to see

*an erect penis. She is, in fact, male—a transsexual. I'm horrified and repulsed. Then I realize I've been absent from the business meeting for a while. My wife Jane shows up and ushers me back to the meeting. How will I explain my absence? Inside the meeting my colleagues are sitting around a round table in discussion. Several guys are older, in suits, with grey hair. Somebody makes a comment about a city planner. Another grey-haired guy says, "City planner? What are you talking about?"*

The dream portrayed the ongoing theme of Karl's distraction from work (the business meeting) due to his pornography obsession. The dream depicted a conflict between an adolescent type of sexual excitation focused on pictures of *Playboy* bunnies, and Karl's efforts to love a real woman with a child. When questioned about his feelings toward the prostitute, he said, "I feel compassion for her. She's a hard-working person trying to raise her child on her own. But the fact that she has a child makes me less interested in her sexually." The figure of the prostitute-mother was a symbol of woman as both whore and Madonna, a potent image of unified opposites. Karl quickly made the connection between this dream image and his wife, mother of his children. Karl was able to feel how deeply he loved and respected Jane, how much he appreciated her both as mother and lover.

The dream image of the transsexual reminded Karl of an aggressive, demanding, phallic quality he perceived in Jane. He said, "I respect her directness and assertiveness, but sometimes I find her anger overwhelming. That's when I feel like I have to get some space from her." This androgynous image represented Karl's need to come to terms with his wife's strength and power, her animus. But what about the transsexual's terrible scars? Karl said, "It reminds me of how my masculinity feels wounded. I feel ashamed of my desire to have affairs. It's like a scar on the purity of our marriage."

I said, "The scars remind me of the ordeals of an initiation or rite of passage."

"Our relationship has been both an ordeal and an initiation. There's a lot of love between us, but also lots of anger and hurting each other."

Working with this dream helped Karl explore a full range of feelings and perceptions about his wife and their marital relationship.

The older men in Karl's dream represented the archetypal *senex*, symbol of age and maturity, which sometimes also carries with it a sense of being trapped by responsibilities and obligations. These figures contrasted with the dream's *puer* (archetype of eternal youth) imagery (in the bathroom with the magazine). The men sitting around the round table suggested Arthurian knights, introducing a mythic dimension to Karl's need to accept his role as a mature, stable man, a provider, a "city planner"—an image which Karl believed symbolized his need to plan for his family's future.

These dreams illuminated a number of opposing elements in the psyche that were becoming unified: mother/lover, young/old (puer/senex), male/female, love/hate, birth/death. In these potent dream images Karl discovered material enabling him to discover a more spiritually meaningful life, one lived in the conscious tension between opposites, and in the awareness of how they are eternally intertwined. Dreamwork helped Karl understand some of the complex emotional and interpersonal challenges of his current stage of life, and led to noticeable gains in his capacity to find satisfaction in his work and family relationships.

## Fundamentals of Dreamwork

As the examples in this chapter have demonstrated, dreamwork offers a wealth of insights and messages that help us live more fully. You can begin to apply the principles of dreamwork described in this book by following these basic steps:

- Write down all remembered dreams and dream fragments. Even the smallest detail is meaningful, even if at first it doesn't appear to make any sense. When you record dreams in a notebook or journal, leave room to add notes, associations, diagrams and dream mandalas. Strephon Kaplan Williams noted:

    The core focus of journal work is the building of a reflective and active consciousness which sees as its task the forming of one's personality into a unified and passionate whole ... . If I have forgotten something I have wanted to forget it; we do not forget what we really want to remember. Without memory we can't bring the past into the future and transform both the past and the future ... . Write down any and all dreams, even the worst!

We are not good beings. We are total beings. Dreamwork reveals all! What we most avoid is what we most need to face ... . What we remember is what we live. Memory is life. (Williams, 1976, pp. 20, 80)

- Sense the emotional quality of each dream image. How does it make you feel? Pay special attention to images that are especially charged.
- Don't be afraid to explore dreams that are scary and disturbing. James Hillman wrote, "Far more dreams are unpleasant than pleasant" (Hillman, 1979a, p. 92). Disturbing dreams indicate that the unconscious is trying to get our attention, to make us conscious of a memory or a feeling.
- Ask questions about every detail of the dream, especially details that perplex you. Williams (1976) described some key questions for responding to dreams: What is the dream ego, the I, doing in the dream? What is the dream-ego's self-image? What are the issues, conflicts, and unresolved situations in the dream? What are the major contrasts and similarities? What symbols in this dream are important to me? What are the various feelings and actions in the dream? What relation does this dream have to what's happening right now in my life? Something in my future? Who or what is the adversary? What is the helping or healing force in this dream? What is being wounded? What is being healed? What would I like to avoid in this dream? What actions might this dream be suggesting I consider? What does this dream want from me? What questions does it ask of me? What choices can I make as a result of working with this dream? Who or what is my companion? Why did I need this dream? Why am I not dealing with this situation in this way? Why have I dreamed of "so and so" now? Where are my helpers in life and in my dream? What can happen if I work actively with this dream? What new questions come up from this dreamwork? Which questions do I avoid asking about this dream?
- Voice your associations to dream images freely, allowing bold interpretations that are provocative and reveal the unexpected.
- Remain open to alternative meanings. Don't be in a rush to find a definitive interpretation. As Edward Whitmont (1969) wrote, "Symbolism is not fixed. The same images may present different meanings in different contexts" (p. 52).

- Take your time with the process and explore your associations to each dream detail. Squeeze every drop of juice from the dream image.

- Look at the dream as a commentary on your current stage of development, your current maturational tasks and challenges. Working with dreams is an effective means of focusing and accelerating our personal growth. The dynamic symbolism of dreams can make each moment resonant with meaning and emotional nuance.

- If you are a therapist, also view the dream as a commentary on the therapeutic alliance and therapeutic process. Dreams provide important material regarding transference and a client's perception of the therapist. Talking about an initial dream or dreams with a client is a powerful way to access memories and feelings about crucial events in the person's life history. Dreams provide important clues about the origins of symptoms, recurring issues, or emotions that need further exploration.

## Dream Incubation

We can actively invoke the spiritual clarity and wisdom of the unconscious through dream incubation. This is useful when we need insight regarding a specific problem or concern. To incubate a dream, before going to sleep spend some time in meditation while thinking intensely about your question or personal issue, your goals, your longings. Ask the guiding intelligence within you for assistance in the dream state. Ask the unconscious for insight, for an answer to your questions. Affirm to yourself that you'll receive guidance while you sleep, and that you'll remember your dreams and write them down upon awakening. Sustain this practice until a dream comes. It won't necessarily happen the first night.

## The Dream of the Embroidered Gown

A thirty-six-year-old woman named Susan had been cleaning houses for eleven years and had her own business. She made good money, but her body was wearing out; she had bursitis in both shoulders. It was obvious that she needed to change occupations to preserve her physical health. But what was she to do? She had no clear idea of the path forward. I suggested that Susan practice dream incubation. On the fourth night she had this dream:

> *A group of people is standing in two lines forming a canopy like in a wedding. I walk through the canopy wearing a beautiful full-length gown covered with embroidery.*

I asked Susan her associations to the dream. She said, "Actually, I make embroidered clothing for my friends. It's sort of a hobby of mine." Could this have some relevance to her need for a career change? Two weeks later, a friend offered Susan a loan to start a business to make a line of embroidered clothing. She took the leap, and started to produce the clothes and sell them. The incubated dream provided an image of a significant personal task.

## The Dream of the U-Turn

Dreamwork is a process that asks us to do some deep work on ourselves, to actually change. Sam, a 54-year-old man who was questioning whether he possessed the capacity to change, had this dream:

> *I'm driving a truck and have to make a sharp U-Turn. I keep both hands on the wheel instead of my usual one hand, and make the turn safely.*

The dream was a message to Sam that he must turn his life around. The dream seemed to say that if he approached this task with his full attention, and with his whole being, rather than allowing himself to be distracted or half-hearted, he'd be able to complete the turn.

Dreamwork clarifies areas of our lives we hope to change, and it activates our feelings. Dreams also help us navigate transitions and mark pivotal thresholds. Dreams are like a fountain flowing from our inner depths that can be of inestimable value to the process of psychotherapy and self-transformation.

*CHAPTER THREE*

# Dreamwork and Relationships

Dreams provide a source of relational intelligence. As a marriage and family therapist, my work often involves working with clients experiencing stress and conflicts in their personal relationships. Dreams help us identify the origins of these conflicts, illuminate feelings and behaviours that we repeat in our interactions with others, and aid us in creating healthier relationships. Dreams also illuminate core issues and conflicts regarding sexuality, which I'll explore further in the case study in Chapter Thirteen.

Dreams provide healing insights about our relationships with spouses, children, parents, and friends. Abby, a woman whose teenage son was sick with cancer, dreamed:

> *I saw Chris's essential being, his Higher Self. It was luminous and unchanging.*

This dream helped Abby find strength as she saw Chris through his chemotherapy treatments.

A woman named Cassandra, who felt her boyfriend James was too physically clingy, dreamed:

> *A dog jumped on me and started biting me, and wouldn't let go.*

27

After this dream, Cassandra was able to ask James to be less smothering.

A man named Paul dreamed of meeting a famous musician who was distant, didn't listen to other people well, and seemed not to notice or acknowledge others. Paul said, "My girlfriend always says that I never listen to her when she talks to me. She says I never give her my full attention." The dream revealed a painful truth about Paul's way of relating, and allowed him to begin practicing new listening skills.

Dreams can make us aware of how our relationships are undermined by unconscious, pathogenic beliefs and attitudes. Debbie, a woman who had trouble sustaining relationships for more than a few months, dreamed:

> I'm in bed sleeping with my boyfriend and awaken to see my stepfather standing in the doorway.

I asked Debbie how her stepfather might be in the way, blocking passage (the doorway) in her relationships. She said that her stepfather always berated her mercilessly, and that now she was doing the same thing to her boyfriend. This insight enabled her to examine the ways she was undermining relationships with her criticism.

## The Dream of Nazis, Mother, and the Half-eaten Sandwich

A man named Terry complained that his wife was bossy, controlling, and didn't show him enough affection. Terry was aided by an unexpected dream suggesting that his problems with his wife were connected to feelings rooted in his relationship with his mother. He dreamed:

> I'm in a park where Nazis are rounding up a large crowd of people. Across the park I see my mother sitting on a bench with a half-eaten sandwich and a nearly empty can of soda.

Terry's associations to the dream were that his mother was bossy, rigid, controlling, and punishing—"like a little Nazi." The half-eaten sandwich and empty soda can suggested that she had no nourishment to give, and it reminded Terry of being undernourished. He realized that he had a deep emotional hunger, a longing for nurturing, and that he consistently experienced his wife as rigid, cold, bossy, and controlling, just like his mother.

## The Dream of the Condoms

Richard, a divorced man and a recovering alcoholic, dreamed:

> I visit a friend who is sick with a liver disease. The man's wife is very supportive and loves him very much. She rubs the man's distended belly. Then I go over and embrace the man and hand him some condoms.

The man with the liver disease was an image of Richard's shadow, his wounded self. When he was still drinking Richard had severe liver problems. The distended belly suggested starvation, the fact that he was starving emotionally. The woman in the dream was the wife he was seeking, the *anima* he hoped would heal him, and the love he wanted to extend to himself. The couple in the dream was a symbol of the *coniunctio,* the sacred marriage. Giving the man the condoms signified giving himself an affirmation of his sexuality, of his desire to connect with a woman, to date, to have an active relational life. The condoms signified being prepared to make love with somebody. Richard had this dream the same week he began dating a woman with whom he felt a growing intimacy.

## The Dream of the Bride

Kristine, a woman who was having a hard time finding a stable relationship, dreamed:

> I go to a wedding with my father as my escort. He is drunk and embarrasses me. I try to get away from him. Then I see the bride in her beautiful dress.

In explaining her associations to the dream, Kristine said, "It feels as if I'm married to my father." The dream indicated that something about her relationship with her father was an obstacle for her. The bride symbolized the wholeness she sought, the next station in life she hoped to reach. But her unconscious emotional union or entanglement with her father was making it difficult to find a partner and become the bride.

## The Dream of the Shivering Child

Dreams help us understand how our adult relationships are influenced by our early relationships with parents or caregivers. They also help us resolve our core wounds and earliest developmental traumas.

In his second psychotherapy session, a man named Alex was upset because his landlady was demanding that he pay his rental deposit, which was four months late. Alex became enraged and told her he was going to move out of the house rather than pay the deposit. It seemed that he was acting out some unconscious conflict. Being asked to pay the deposit money evoked memories of how his alcoholic father exploited him and stole money from his bank account. In addition, the fact that the landlady was a woman triggered an important realization: Alex (who is gay) told me he'd never had a woman in his life to take care of him and that he was unconsciously expecting this woman (the landlady) to mother him and show him special consideration. When I inquired about his mother (whom he hadn't mentioned in his first session), Alex revealed that she was institutionalized as a schizophrenic when he was three years old. He watched as she was taken away in a straitjacket, and she never returned home. This was a severe psychological trauma for him. Alex had received virtually no mothering in his life.

His lack of nurturing came into focus vividly during the following week's session, when Alex told me this dream:

> I see a small boy about three or four years old. He's cold and shivering and obviously wants to be held. There's a woman there, his mother, but she isn't doing anything to help the boy. She seems clueless and does nothing. Finally I grab a blanket she's holding, and I pick up the boy and cover him with the blanket and hold him close to me. It feels very good to be protective of him in this way.

The dream depicted a lack of what Daniel Stern (1985) calls *maternal attunement*. The adequate, competent mother can figure out what a child wants and needs, what the child is trying to communicate, and takes steps to address those needs. Here the mother was incompetent, not at all attuned to the boy. Alex's fright and anxiety were experienced somatically in the dream as shivering, and he felt that sensation in his body as he recounted the dream. Something that had been unconscious had come to consciousness. Alex said, "My mother was clueless, never knew what to do, and left me in states of intense distress and couldn't care for me or soothe me." Yet the dream also evoked and awakened the capacity to self-nurture, self-soothe. It felt good to take care of this scared, vulnerable part of himself.

In Chapter Ten, I detail a technique called the *Dream Mandala*, which enables us to visually depict the major characters, themes, and images of dreams. Here's a basic diagram of Alex's dream:

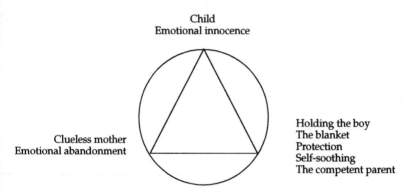

Child
Emotional innocence

Clueless mother
Emotional abandonment

Holding the boy
The blanket
Protection
Self-soothing
The competent parent

*Dream Mandala: The dream of the shivering child*

Notice how Alex's dream looked both *backward*, toward his childhood deprivation, and *forward*, evoking the emerging capacity for self-care. This illustrates one of the ways that Jung's understanding of the unconscious went beyond Freud. While Freud emphasized that the unconscious reveals material about childhood traumas and early developmental conflicts, Jung showed that the unconscious also leads us forward toward wholeness. This dream suggests that both perspectives are true.

## Two Dreams of a Man Who Suppressed Anger

Dreams helped me in my work with a man who had a great deal of suppressed and unexpressed emotions, especially anger and sadness. Ed was a fifty-year-old man in a stagnant, unsatisfying relationship. He came to see me because his girlfriend, Lucy, threatened to break up with him if he didn't get psychotherapy. He was depressed, dissatisfied with his job, and sceptical about therapy. He informed me that he never remembered his dreams.

Initially, Ed externalized the problem, insisting that it was Lucy who was "screwed up." I noted Ed's distant, unemotional demeanour, which I intuitively felt was masking something. I tried to get Ed to talk about his own feelings, but he kept talking about Lucy. He said that he and Lucy had been considering opening up their relationship to other sexual partners. In fact, she had already been seeing someone else. But Ed was unable to voice any feelings about this, although I sensed that he was quietly hurt and angry. He said, "I don't know how far things have gone, and I don't want to know."

"I find it interesting that you don't want to know."

"I just keep quiet and let her do what she's going to do."

"So you don't communicate to her how hurt and angry you are?"

"No." And so our work began.

Ed came to his second session and said, "I'm really surprised, but I remembered a dream."

> I was six or seven. I was in the kitchen of my parents' house. I wanted something to eat. There was stuff on the stove. Water drained from one pot to another. There was nothing to eat. My brother Ken was sitting there with a big pot of food. He was eating all the food, and I couldn't get any. I felt palpably what I felt as a kid. No one is taking care of me. I went to my room.

I asked Ed to tell me more about his family; the dream prompted me to inquire about family history and his childhood. Ed replied, "My parents were violent. I was beaten with sticks and hangers. I ran away when I was in high school. I survived my childhood by staying out of the house and becoming a great student."

I asked, "What do you remember about being six or seven?"

"I remember how afraid I was of my brother Ken. He was big and had a nasty temper. I stayed away from him. He ate like hell. My dad beat up both my older brothers, and they both became chronic alcoholics. I became the lost child of the family. I withdrew. There was no love in that family. It was like a civil war."

I said, "This dream takes you back to this formative time, and to feelings of deprivation in your childhood. But it also evokes your current situation where you feel neglected by Lucy; you don't feel taken care of. Your withdrawal in childhood, hiding out in your room, is just like your not saying anything to Lucy about her going out at night without you. Because of your experience in your family, you don't know how to reach out and ask for what you need, for love and affection. Instead, you withdraw as a self-protective measure. It's as if you're re-enacting your childhood experience in present-time deprivation in this relationship." This interpretation evoked from Ed an admission that he might have some strong feelings about Lucy's seeing other men.

In his next session, Ed reported another dream:

> I'm in a white room with four panes of frosted glass. I couldn't see through it. Then it became clear at the top so I could see through it. Somebody was looking in. I couldn't see who, but I could see the person there.

I inquired about the frosted glass in the dream. Ed replied, "It was grey. I think I'm looking at my own life. I was surprised when the glass cleared up so I could see through it." I noted the contrast between a feeling of obstruction, having no view, a window one can't see through, and the image of clear glass, suggesting transparency, and being able to see through something. Perhaps the window was a metaphor for consciousness. Something that had been clouded was now becoming clearer and more transparent; it was coming into consciousness. The image of someone looking through the window reminded Ed of being spied upon and being under observation by his boss, who was always keeping tabs on him. This reminded him of how he was keeping tabs on Lucy's comings and goings. Ed told me, "The feeling in the dream was threatening and malevolent. I wanted to scream, but I couldn't speak. I was so terrified."

"That's just like your relationship with Lucy. You're so angry you want to scream, but you can't. You keep quiet and don't protest or defend yourself."

I asked Ed about the person looking in through the window, and he said, "I wanted this person to go away. It seemed like some kind of male energy; it was red energy, anger, like someone was angry at me. It reminds me of my own anger."

"Yes, an angry part of you that hides and never shows its face."

"It felt like an angry man."

"So who is an angry man?"

"Me!"

"What is this angry person at the window looking for? What is he after?"

"He's after my life. He's life-threatening."

"So showing your anger and showing Lucy how much fury you feel inside could be life-threatening. Your family was violent and abusive. Your only strategy for survival was to retreat to your room and your books. Growing up, you never expressed anger, and you have a hard time expressing it now, even when you feel that Lucy is tormenting you." Discussing this dream helped Ed access his anger, and over the next few weeks he began to stand up for himself, protesting Lucy's behaviour, letting her know it was not okay with him.

I had Ed amplify the dream further. He said, "The room in the dream was white and the window had green trim—a deep forest green. It was soothing." Now Ed was retelling the dream with a different twist, emphasizing colours. The dream took place in a white room with green trim, a grey window, and a red, angry man looking inside. Ed noted, "The green trim reminds me of nature. I used to do a lot of nature photography. But I stopped years ago." He longed for the connection with nature and the creative expression he experienced during this period of his life. Was it possible to recover this part of himself?

I had my own associations to the colours in the dream. Seeing through a grey glass window suggested things looking drab and colourless—Ed's depressed mood and hopeless attitude. The red suggested fire, anger, and passion for life. It was hidden, but it was lurking behind the window; it was *there*. Ed had the potential to express the fiery, red energy—anger, self-assertion, being more passionate, letting Lucy know that he really *wanted* her, rather than acting detached and disengaged. I told Ed, "The deep forest green suggests an element of healing in the dream. Your attention to the colours and luminosity of nature has been missing recently. You haven't been seeing it through the grey, cloudy glass. But the glass clears up; now you start to see things more clearly."

Ed began to express his feelings to Lucy. He let her know her behaviour was unacceptable, and she, sensing his greater involvement in the relationship, stopped flirting with other men.

He reported better communication and greater satisfaction in the relationship. Dreams worked their subtle magic by helping Ed become more emotionally responsive.

## Three Dreams of a Woman in an Abusive Relationship

Dreams portray our basic structures of object relations, internalized patterns of relating to others that are formed in childhood and often re-enacted in adult relationships. Tina was twenty-two, a recent graduate of an Ivy League college, daughter of two alcoholics. She was involved in a tumultuous relationship with a woman named Beth. A few weeks before beginning therapy, she tried to break up with Beth, who became suicidal and threatened to kill herself if Tina left her. Tina relented, and their relationship continued. She asked me, "What should I do about this relationship?" Beth was demanding, intense, manipulative, and engulfing, yet Tina felt tremendous guilt for causing her pain and anguish. Tina's parents strongly disapproved of this relationship, and Tina was conflicted about wanting her parents' approval. She was financially dependent on them, and they were trying to influence her decisions and life planning, a major source of friction for her. She wanted to be independent and to make her own decisions.

Issues about lesbian identity had preoccupied Tina since childhood. Tina described how all her friends at school turned on her after she was caught kissing another girl. They began taunting her, calling her "dyke," and socially ostracizing her.

Tina told me this dream:

> I'm at a graduation, and people from my high school are there.

Graduation implied transition, a change of status, completion, growing up, a rite of passage. It evoked Tina's recent college graduation and her questions about what to do now. The dream also suggested the need to revisit some emotionally charged issues of her adolescence (high school).

In another dream:

> I'm living at home with my parents, flirting with Beth on the phone.

I said, "You're attached to your parents and want their love and approval. But you're also bonded with Beth, which causes clashes with your parents. Your dilemma is how to honour all the relationships that are living under the same roof inside you."

Beth said, "In middle school I started getting programmed: 'You have to be perfect, you have to go to Harvard.' I felt pressure to achieve. I believed that if I achieved enough, my parents would be fixed; they'd stop drinking. I began doing whatever I thought would please them. Now I'm doing the same thing with Beth, placating her when she's upset, coming back to her when she was desperate and suicidal."

Tina described how volatile and emotionally intense Beth was. "She rants and raves and is always demanding more and more of my time and my attention. She gets angry if I don't make her the centre of my life. She pressures me to separate from my parents, to not talk to them so much. She says she must not be that important to me because I'm so attached to my parents. She yells at me a lot. I'm afraid of conflict, and I just freeze up when she gets like this. I just want her to stop getting on my case. But I'm afraid she'll be devastated if I leave her."

In her next session, Tina reported this dream:

> At a family reunion. I'm with Beth in a glass elevator going up and down, repeatedly.

I asked, "What does a family reunion bring to mind?"

"My sense of obligation toward my family."

"You also have a strong sense of obligation toward Beth. The family reunion suggests that you're re-enacting family dynamics in your relationship with Beth."

"I'm always trying to match the family ideal—getting straight A's, doing everything perfectly. I tiptoe around trying not to set off Beth, and that's just like being with my family. She tries to make me feel beholden to her. She always tries to mould my behaviour, saying 'You have to be like this.' That's just like my parents too." Her relationship with Beth truly was like a family reunion.

I asked Tina about the glass elevator. "It reminds me of this awful shopping mall I used to hang out in as a teenager. I hung out there with my friend Chris, the sociopath."

I said, "I don't think you've told me about him before. Who was he?"

"He was this guy who was obviously gay and got harassed and called names all the time. So we had that in common and we started hanging around together, along with my friend Pat, another total reject. And that reminds me that I just had a nightmare the other night that Chris was going to find me."

"He must be an important figure for you if he's looking for you in your dream. Tell me more about him."

"I've always had a selfish person in my life who treats me like shit. Chris certainly played this role, and Beth plays this role in my life now. He was very abusive, physically and emotionally. He used to be really mean to me and Pat. He'd trick us, pull our hair, hit us, and roughhouse with us. He didn't have any guy friends to play rough with, so he treated us rough. He tried to strangle me once. He put his hands around my neck and started to laugh. He pushed me down another time, and I hurt my knee. I still have the scar."

"So Chris was a persecuting figure who tormented you. I also remember you telling me how kids in school rejected you, and taunted you. It seems you keep feeling rejected and persecuted."

"I was always the reject, the outcast."

"So there's this inner division between the figure of Chris, the abuser, the person who treats you badly, the rejecting mob, the friends that turn on you, and your own role as the reject, the outcast, the victim. Going up and down in the elevator with Beth, and going through the ups and downs of your relationship with her, reminds you of being with Chris, this persecuting figure from your past. The dream suggests that with Beth you again feel persecuted and under attack. The dream evokes this way of relating, symbolized by being at the mall with this cruel, abusive person who's supposedly your friend."

One month later, Tina broke off her relationship with Beth, moved away from her, and began dating other women. Her story shows how dreams increase consciousness by illuminating the tension of opposites within us. Tina recognized her tendency to assume the position of a persecuted martyr, and to let others control her, and this evoked a new capacity to assert her own needs, and set boundaries.

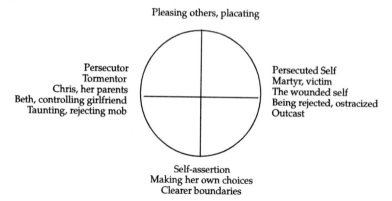

Pleasing others, placating

Persecutor
Tormentor
Chris, her parents
Beth, controlling girlfriend
Taunting, rejecting mob

Persecuted Self
Martyr, victim
The wounded self
Being rejected, ostracized
Outcast

Self-assertion
Making her own choices
Clearer boundaries

*Dream Mandala: Three dreams of a woman in an abusive relationship*

## Dreams of Separation and Endings of Relationships

Dreams can help us at times of break-ups, separations, the endings of relationships. Tim and Claire, a couple breaking up, had the following dreams on the same night. Claire dreamed that a silver chain, holding a pendant that Tim had given her as a gift, broke. Tim dreamed that a giant crane picked up Claire's car and dropped it into the ocean.

A week after the break-up, Tim dreamed:

> *I'm living in a slimy, fleabag rooming house in downtown Philadelphia. There are no lights, no security. It's dirty and dangerous.*

Tim was ready to move on from the relationship, but he was also in touch with feelings of loss and desolation.

In my own life I once found myself struggling because I wanted to break up with Lisa, a woman I was dating, but I couldn't find the words to do it. Weeks passed. Finally I dreamed of a voice singing these words: "God sees you. God sees you. Say it from the heart: 'We need to be apart.' God sees you." The next night I told Lisa, "We need to be apart." We separated gracefully.

Carol, a woman who was conflicted about her decision to end a relationship with a man named Craig, dreamed:

> *I was standing with a female friend on a bridge where I could see Craig. My friend noticed that I had a sore on my thigh. Suddenly I began to throw up violently over the side of the bridge. When I was finished, my friend looked at me and said, "Your wound is healed."*

*When I woke up I felt completely resolved about this relationship, and that I had let go of my bitter feelings toward Craig.*

Notice the somatic process in the dream, the way the emotions are felt viscerally, in the body, to bring about healing. The wound in her thigh reminded Carol that through this relationship she'd begun to heal a wound regarding sexuality. She was later able to express to Craig that she was grateful to him for that.

## The Dream of the Graveyard and the Garden

Gwen, a woman going through a divorce, dreamed:

*I'm in a graveyard that is also a garden. There are two square garden plots ready to be planted.*

The graveyard evoked feelings of sadness, loss, and desolation at the end of her marriage; it felt like a death. The garden ready to be planted represented the expectancy of a new stage of life, new beginnings. In one alchemical image of *mortificatio*—the experience of confronting death and mortality—grain grows out of a grave. We realize that within death there is transformation; the seed of life is present within death, endings, and the moment of suffering.

## A Dream about Death and Bereavement

Gwen, whose husband died of cancer twelve years earlier, hadn't remarried despite many proposals. She finally found a man she loved, but she couldn't bring herself to throw away her deceased husband's clothes and other possessions. In twelve years she still hadn't cleaned out his drawers and closets. Then Gwen had this dream:

*Jackson, my childhood dog—whom I loved and whose death I had long grieved—was dying. I felt guilty about it and responsible, but I couldn't do anything to save him. Jackson looked at me and said, "Hey, it's all right. I'm okay. It's not your fault."*

What Gwen could not accept from any human, she could finally hear from her beloved dog. Her husband's death was part of the flow of nature. It wasn't her fault. Reflection on this dream helped Gwen move on with her life.

## A Dream about Suicide

A woman named Donna consulted with me several months after Bob, her ex-boyfriend, committed suicide. She told me this dream:

> I see Bob in the afterlife, where he's in a nice room that holds and protects him. He doesn't have absolute freedom here. Something protects him from being in trouble.

In this instance I took the lead in the amplification of the dream. I said, "The fact that in the dream Bob is being protected suggests that what he did may not be a 'punishable offence.' But at the same time you don't win any points for it either. The dream suggests to me that he's now in a holding room, a probationary status where he must review and confront the impact of his action on other people and on his own soul's evolution."

After the session Donna wrote to me and said that she felt very comforted by this interpretation of the dream and felt more at peace and resolved about Bob's death. She said that before he died he had reached out to tell her how much she meant to him and how grateful he was for her love and friendship. I replied, "The circle of love between you is complete." This example illustrates how dreams can be helpful and healing in short-term therapy, or even in a single session of counseling.

## Four Dreams Regarding the Decision to Have a Child

Julie and her husband, Walter, were struggling with a decision about whether or not to have a child. Julie dreamed:

> An enormous chicken was walking through our living room.

This reflected their fear of parenthood. As Walter said, "We're both too chicken to do it."

Several months later, Julie dreamed:

> I'm standing by the fence looking over toward our neighbour's house (they have a big family). A bull with big horns silently comes up behind me. At first I'm scared he'll hurt me, but he just stands there nearby.

Julie wasn't aware that Walter was having fantasies about her becoming pregnant. In retrospect she was able to see that the symbol of the bull sneaking up behind her expressed her unconscious awareness of Walter's interest in having a child. The bull is an archetypal symbol of fertility. It's interesting how both of these dreams used animal symbolism to convey an instinctual perspective.

Soon thereafter Julie dreamed:

> A vase in our bedroom broke, and the whole room was flooded with light.

Julie and Walter began to talk about the luminous creative power that might be unleashed in their bedroom.

The fourth dream occurred the night before Julie went to a doctor's appointment. Walter dreamed:

> I saw a tiny circle join and become part of a rotating ring of circles, like a necklace. It reminded me of cells reproducing, of the circle of life. I woke up with the thought that Julie was pregnant.

That day Julie discovered that she was, in fact, pregnant.

## The Dream of the Red Silk Curtains

Leslie, a young woman who had recently become engaged, had this dream:

> I'm in my hometown with my aunt and my fiancé, looking for an apartment. All the houses and apartments look the same, except for one that has silky red curtains and wide open doors. I'm attracted to this apartment and think this must be the place we're meant to take. We walk through knee-deep snow to get to the building.

This apartment had wide-open doors, suggesting vulnerability and openness. Leslie said, "That reminds me of how I feel when I make love with my fiancé. I've been wondering is it safe to be this open and vulnerable with him."

The knee-deep snow reminded Leslie of a bright, delicate white. White reminded Leslie of purity, innocence, something virginal, entering virgin territory. She said, "That reminds me of regaining my innocence, and overcoming my jadedness, my feeling of 'been there before,' my cynicism about love."

I said, "It reminds me of a white wedding dress and your upcoming marriage."

The apartments that all look the same reminded Leslie of "conformity, hiding who I am, closing down, keeping up appearances." This was in contrast to the individuation implied by finding the apartment with red, silky curtains, suggesting passion, intimacy, sexuality and excitement. Clearly, this was the place for her to inhabit now. The dream evoked an inner union of red and white, passion and innocence.

## Dreamwork in a Case of Internet Pornography Addiction

Sometimes managed care companies send me clients for short-term therapy, and I have to try to accomplish a lot in just a few sessions. Dreamwork is a great aid in such work. A man named Steve, thirty-three, came to see me about problems he was having with his girlfriend Rita, who was furious at Steve because he'd had an affair. For several months they'd been dealing with the angry aftermath. Steve felt remorseful about hurting Rita, but he was still sexually restless, spending hours every night looking at pornography on the Internet. He felt that he couldn't stop himself. Now Rita was angry about that too. In this example, a brief dream fragment elicited my own associations and a spontaneous commentary on his situation. Steve dreamed:

> At a sporting event, maybe a bowling or pool tournament. The champ is retiring.

Bowling or pool reminded Steve of hanging out in bars with his buddies. The champ reminded him of bragging to friends about his sexual escapades. It also reminded him of the character of bartender Sam Malone (from the television show *Cheers*), who was a notorious, unattached Don Juan.

I said, "The part of you that identifies with the Great Lover needs to retire. Your whole relationship to sex and pornography seems out of balance. Our culture and mass media pump up everyone with constant stimulation so you feel like you're missing out if you don't experience hot, screaming sex every day. You feel like a loser if you're not out every night dancing half naked in a nightclub, throbbing like electric jello. But it's not realistic. The alternative is to deal with your disappointment and sadness about the relationship, about not having as much intimacy as you want with Rita. The question is, what will you grow in the garden of your disappointment? You can spend hours searing your eyeballs looking at pictures in cyberspace. That's okay, but I think you can do better for your life. Perhaps we can imagine other ways to feel a sense of aliveness."

Steve said, "Rita wants to put some energy into buying a house. That might be interesting."

"You have to decide whether the champ is in the ring or out of the ring. Because all the energy you put into thinking about other women becomes part of the field of the relationship. Rita picks up on it; she feels it. What if you eliminate that? It will change the home, and the emotional field around you. Disarm yourself so there's nothing for her to not trust. If you really want to make this relationship work, I think this is where you need to begin." The champ retiring was a significant internal event for Steve.

On my office coffee table that day, I had a book depicting the Rosarium series of alchemical illustrations. These pictures represent a sequence of recurring psychological events or archetypal situations. I showed Steve two pictures that I thought were of special interest. In the fifth image, the King and Queen are shown making love. This symbolizes how we embrace our object of desire, and seek union with it; we merge with our anima or animus (Edinger, 1994a). We are the lovers uniting.

*Figure 1. Fifth Rosarium image: Lovers unite.*

The sixth Rosarium picture then depicts the lovers lying together in a tomb. After making love, they lie next to each other, silent and depressed. They look as if they've died. The feeling of passion has ebbed. We undergo a psychological death, a loss of connection with the energy of desire. Edinger commented:

> [T]his is an image of the mortificatio: ... It's the theme of marriage and death, marriage being followed by death or someone being married to death, or linkage between the two one way or another. ... It is the typical fate of lovers to die. ... [T]he opposites die in the course of giving birth to the higher totality that transcends them. ... [T]he ego has been united with the desired object and then experiences disillusionment, ... [or] failing to get what one wants, [or] being frustrated. (Edinger, 1994a, pp. 68, 70, 72)

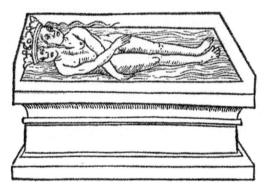

*Figure 2. Sixth Rosarium image: In the tomb.*

This depicts how we need to tolerate the depressed phase of the relational cycle, the experience of disillusionment with our spouse, lover, or therapist. In a therapeutic relationship, negative transferences occur. This disillusioned phase has to be endured until something is reborn—a renewed feeling of excitement, desire, and connection. In our relationships we experience the pulsating cycles and tidal movements of nature, rising and falling tides, waxing and waning sexual energies. Steve learned to accept the limitations of his partner but also tried to focus on enhancing their relationship. He began to read books on purchasing a home, which made Rita very happy, and they became more closely knit as they began discussing this shared goal and how they could realize it. Facing the moment when we feel that love has died, sometimes it springs back to life like wildflowers.

## The Dream of the House at Lake Tahoe

Dreams often bring into focus a personal ideal, aspiration, or a central life task. In the next example, working through obstacles in relationships was a central task of maturation.

Nicki, a forty-four-year-old single woman, had retired from a successful career that was financially rewarding, yet she felt emotionally and spiritually unfulfilled. She began therapy to explore her problems in relationships. She told me she never had dreams, but within several weeks of beginning therapy she remembered one:

> I'm going to a friend's house at Lake Tahoe. The departure is at night. I'm driving on a big road around the lake. I'm blinded by the light of oncoming cars. This road isn't safe; I have to get off. I thought I knew where I was going—to a shopping mall—but I never make it. I'm driving along a gravely driveway and come to the end. I find parked cars and can't go any farther. There's a way to get through if I turn to the right. I see an auto repair lot. Someone is working on the cars. I drive around to the back. There's a two-story brown house. I come to a fence with a gate, a gate with a door. There are trees around the fence. I need to get through, to get someone to help me through. I'm trapped with a bunch of parked cars. I see a door that's ajar and I peek in. I see the mechanic. I say, "Excuse me, can you help me?" He's about to get into his twin bed. He reminds me of a bachelor. He's wearing a long white night suit with a night cap. He's a grouchy, sleepy guy dressed like someone out of the eighteenth century, right out of a fairy tale. He looks at me with a look that says, "Give me a break." He wants to go to sleep.

The friend's house in Lake Tahoe reminded Nicki of a vacation house, a retreat, an escape, a place to hang out and have fun with friends. The departure at night suggested the mythic theme of the night sea journey, the journey into the underworld. This implied that Nicki's quest was comparable to the mythic Hero or Heroine's Journey. The lake reminded Nicki of a recent period when she used to drink and party a lot with friends. Now that period of her life was over. She had grown more quiet and introspective, and her intellectual interests were stronger than her urge to drink and party. Nicki said, "The house by the lake is serene and beautiful. It's an ideal for the future, but I've given up on it. It represents people who have it all, married people who have kids, and a vacation spot in paradise that they can enjoy with the family."

I said, "The house at Lake Tahoe represents the ideal life and family you fear you'll never be able to achieve."

The shopping mall reminded Nicki of "a place that is safe and homey and comforting, where I can browse at my own speed." Browsing reminded Nicki of checking out men with an unhurried attitude. She could browse without needing to buy right away. But Nicki was concerned that, in checking out her options thoroughly, she was forever searching for the right match but was unwilling to commit to a "purchase," to bringing a man home and fully into her heart.

Being blinded by the oncoming cars in the dream was frightening. When I asked what was frightening in her life, Nicki replied, "Uncertainty about my future. Should I continue my quest? Should I go back to my old career and keep making a lot of money?" Her relationships with men also felt unsafe. She had recently broken up with a man named Gary because the emotional intensity of their relationship caused her to cry a lot, and she often found herself angry with him.

In the dream Nicki arrived at a gate with a door. A gate implies a portal, a transition point, a threshold of initiation. Usually in myth, where there's a gate there's also a gatekeeper. To get past the gate there's some kind of a test. I said, "The search for someone to help you through the gate represents your need for a guide, a shaman. By coming to therapy you're allowing me to guide you, and in this dream you find inner guidance that is helping move you through a life passage."

Small details of a dream often open up significant feelings and memories. Peeking into the auto repair place reminded Nicki of spying on her parents when they were fighting and drinking. Her witnessing of marital discord had formed an internal impression of what a committed relationship would be like. Nicki so feared ending up in a discordant marriage like her parents' that she tended to break off relationships as soon as anger emerged. We discussed how fear of conflict undermined her capacity to love somebody. Peeking into the auto repair place also reminded her of learning from watching other people, including those who are able to successfully couple and make beautiful lives together. It was an act of envious voyeurism, but also an act of emulation. She wanted to be like those people who could find love and form couples and families.

The House at Lake Tahoe was a symbol that evoked envy and a feeling of defeat, "the sense that I can't have it all." But the house was also the mythic destination that would make her whole, the goal of her heart's longing. The theme of the house was repeated later in the dream when she found the two-story brown house where the bachelor mechanic lived. The mechanic reminded her of Gary, her ex-boyfriend, his pyjamas, and his sleepiness. "Gary was tired a lot. I used to find that annoying. Now it seems really cute and endearing to me, like it would be nice to curl up and sleep next to him." She felt some sadness about ending their relationship.

Nicki said, "The look that said 'Give me a break' reminds me of looks I've gotten from guys who say 'Don't talk so much,' people who disdain me and my interest in books and ideas." This reminded Nicki of her father's disdain for her ambitions, and a part of her that minimized the value of her quest for knowledge and meaning. She needed to address this self-critical, disdainful inner male figure before she could have a healthy relationship.

Two years later I heard from Nicki. She was living with a man and making plans for the future. Here's an illustration of the opposing and complementary forces present within her dream:

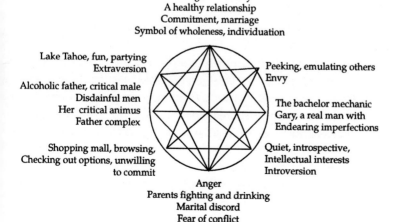

*Dream Mandala: The Dream of the House at Lake Tahoe*

## The Dream of the Scorpion

Dreamwork is a potent practice for couples, allowing partners to recognize feelings and perceptions from each other's unconscious. I call the practice of dreamwork in relationship counseling *couple's dream yoga*. Ed and Janet were a couple at an impasse. They'd been arguing frequently, and both of them expressed a high degree of marital dissatisfaction. Janet felt Ed's guitar was more important to him than she was. She complained of a lack of closeness and sexual intimacy. Ed felt the walls were caving in financially and was highly anxious about the future. They were seriously considering divorce. Janet had this dream:

> *Ed and another man are sitting on the floor playing a game, involving moving around a game piece—a scorpion. Ed loses the game. The scorpion now gets to bite or sting you. The scorpion stung him, so there was immediate risk for losing the game. There could be long-term, chronic danger.*

I said, "The dream depicted playing a game of chance or risk. I think the unconscious is commenting on your relationship and the risks you're playing with."

She said, "The scorpion reminds me of my anger."

"The dream suggests that there's a scorpion, running loose in your home. It signifies your poisonous resentments, and the fact that these are a danger to your marriage."

Janet replied, "I resent that people like Ed. Ed takes me for granted. He lets me handle all of the household chores and doesn't lift a finger to help out. I have a lot of resentment about that. He never cleans the bathroom. But everyone thinks he's such a nice, great guy. If they only knew."

That was an important moment in couple's therapy because the scorpion allowed us to talk about Janet's anger and resentment and the validity of specific grievances. There was another message here for Ed. In the dream, he lost the game. He was able to acknowledge that he'd have much to lose if their marriage ended. Ed and Janet ended up staying together and became more closely bonded.

In this chapter I've noted how dreams illuminate and enhance our relationships—a theme we'll explore throughout this book. In the next chapter, I describe how dreamwork helped a man resolve his relationship with his father, form a positive therapeutic alliance, and prepare inwardly for marriage.

CHAPTER FOUR

# Twenty Dreams of a Young Artist:
# A Case Study with Mythic Dimensions

This chapter describes how a series of dreams guided a psychotherapy treatment lasting three and a half years. The dreams illustrate the intelligence of the unconscious in addressing issues of prolonged bereavement, depression, sexuality, love, creativity, and vocational goals. I'll demonstrate how dreams promote individuation through the emergence of a personal, spiritual symbolism. The series of dreams feature the father archetype, the anima, several animal figures, Duke Ellington, and the symbolism of archaic male initiation rites. I'll note the significance of several recurring symbols, and show how each dream allowed the client to work through specific issues, memories, and feelings. This chapter illustrates the catalytic role that dreams can play in psychotherapy, especially when a series of dreams are viewed as a cohesive set of images fostering emotional healing.

These dreams were like an underground stream that irrigated the therapeutic process—nourishing, providing focus, and adding emotional depth. Through these dreams we encounter the intelligence of *psyche*—the unconscious, that living, breathing, self-organizing medium that is the focus of the work, and the object of fascination, of depth psychologists.

My client, Ken, began seeing me when he was twenty-eight years old, and I worked with him weekly for three and a half years. He was an artist, and the son of an artist. Ken had a college degree and was employed doing building maintenance for a large business firm.

In his first session, Ken informed me that, when he was six years old, his father died at the age of forty-one from cancer. His father was a follower of Christian Science and refused medical treatment. Ken said, "Dad's death was never dealt with. Mom was overwhelmed with four kids. There was no funeral. I saw shrinks throughout high school and college. I have problems with lack of focus. I lost the momentum to do art after college because of the pressure of working to support myself. I've been experiencing a total creative block. I want to unfold my creativity, but I'm stuck. That's making me very depressed. I have very few friends. I also have some issues in my three-year relationship with Ann. I'm confused about my sexual attraction to men." These were Ken's main presenting issues. I also learned that Ken was preoccupied with his father's death, and that his artwork was filled with material related to this event.

## The Dream of Boys on the Street

About a month later Ken brought me this first dream:

> I'm driving in a car in traffic in a suburban neighbourhood. A little boy runs in front of me, four or five years old. I jump out of the car. There are two kids there. I grab the younger child, being really tender. I hug him very close, and tell him he has to be careful or he could get hurt. The streets are dangerous; they aren't for kids to play in. The younger boy runs off, playing mischievously. I'm shocked by his fearlessness.

Ken commented, "The two boys were like a part of me, unsupervised, roving. I didn't have much adult supervision as a kid."

"What did these kids look like?" I asked.

"The younger one was four or five years old with a blonde Dutch boy haircut; he looked just like me. He seemed aloof, in his own world. I remember being very aloof."

I said, "Do you mean that after your dad's death you were numb?"

"Yes, I acted that way because I didn't want others to see I was in pain. I was totally unemotional. I forced back tears, and tried to be strong."

"In the dream you're looking at yourself as a little boy and embracing this part of yourself."

"It reminds me of how my mother gave me a watch and I deliberately destroyed it by throwing it against a wall. I had a lot of pent-up anger, and I took it out on this gift my mom had given me." Tears flowed as Ken recounted this episode. The kids in the dream also reminded Ken that as a child he always had imaginary friends; he remembered playing alone a lot. I asked Ken what it felt like to hug the boy: "I felt like a protective parent." In the dream Ken extended kindness toward this four-year-old part of himself.

The next dream highlighted Ken's anxiety about his desire for closeness with other men. Also, incidentally, it seemed to illustrate Freud's tripartite model of the id, ego, and superego. Ken dreamed:

> I'm in a park where I see lots of men around, hanging out together, sitting on blankets, some walking hand in hand. I'm interested in them, but I'm not a part of the group, just witnessing, observing. All of a sudden there's a thunderous roar of surveillance helicopters with pilots patrolling and filming everything. The men in the cockpit are taking photos or video of the men in the park, spying on them. The pilots are hooting and hollering at the men below, laughing like giddy little kids. They act as though they're in charge.

Ken commented that the men in the park holding hands reminded him of an incident when several gay men whistled at him in Golden Gate Park. The dream evoked feelings of sexual curiosity about men, a theme that would occupy several therapy hours. Freud would say these impulses emanate from the id, and are a cause of internal conflict for the dreamer. The men in the helicopter cockpit (the pun was no doubt fully intended by the unconscious) are surveying the scene, and seem uncomfortable and childish in their reaction to the other men being affectionate with one another. They're symbols of the superego, or internal judgment. They are homophobic authority figures who act like they're in control. Ken said, "They're hovering above, assuming a position of superiority, as if they're better than the men below. The pilots are like voyeurs, with cameras. They reminded Ken of "a part of me that watches, witnesses when around an openly gay environment." Witnessing suggested ego consciousness trying to mediate the conflict between id and superego, impulse and restraining judgment. The men hovering and watching from above contrasted with the men on the ground, who Ken said, represented community and overcoming isolation, not just men attracted to men. Ken was in the middle, trying to sort this out and gain some perspective.

I was interested in Ken's comment that the men in the park symbolized men having a good time together, developing a strong sense of community. This image reminded Ken of his loneliness and desire for friendships with other men. Since moving to the San Francisco Bay Area three years earlier, Ken still didn't have a single male friend. He felt isolated, and attributed much of his difficulty to the homophobia he faced, both in himself and in other men, living in the Bay Area, with its large gay community. He said the dream also reminded him of men working together, artists sharing studios, and also therapist and client working together. After working with this dream, Ken experienced an internal shift from homosexual fantasies to a longing for male friendship and mentorship by older men, as well as acceptance of the emotional support and nourishment he derived from his therapy sessions with me.

## The Dream of Eating Twigs and Thorns

Two months later, Ken had this pivotal dream:

> I'm in the woods in the middle of nowhere. I have not brought any food, clothes, a tent or sleeping bag. What should I do? I'm totally unprepared. I start eating sticks with twigs and briars and thorns.

Ken said, "The dream reminds me of feeling alone and unprepared."

I said, "Like a child without a father." I wanted to keep naming this for Ken.

He said, "I don't know how to cope with the world. I feel unequipped for my life."

"What does eating thorns remind you of?"

"It reminds me of Christ with the crown of thorns. It reminds me of my dad, and how he martyred himself for his beliefs in Christian Science. The strength of his faith carried him through cancer eating his body."

I said, "The dream also evokes the image of your own cross, your own suffering over the loss of your father. Jesus said, 'Father, why hast thou forsaken me?' The dream portrays your re-enactment of the Christ mythos, and the way you've been reliving your dad's suffering over and over again. There's a sense of your sharing or participating in his suffering. The dream is trying to unfold a resolution to this drama." This is an example of how the symbols emerging from the unconscious connect us to a mythic, transpersonal level of meaning. Ken was fixated on his father's death, and the dream helped resolve this predicament by revealing its archetypal core.

## The Dream of the Mentor-Father

Several weeks later, Ken dreamed:

> I'm walking through an underdeveloped part of town, on a dirt path. Paul Auster, the novelist, walks with me. He was like a mentor-father. I felt close to him. We may have been holding hands.

Here again are men connecting. When I asked his associations to Paul Auster, Ken said, "I had a sense of him as the greatest father in the world. He's an artist who is uncompromising, utterly dedicated. He found it hard to make a living from his art when he was younger. But he stuck with it and he made it. Father-son is a prominent theme in his writing."

Father and son was the central theme in Ken's healing journey. Here he met the Father-Artist, and experienced closeness with this figure. He spent many therapy hours recounting events he wished his father had witnessed and participated in. At the same time, Ken was establishing a positive bond to me as a trusted older man and internalizing the nutrient of my attention and interest in his development.

## The Dream of Mt. Fuji at Night

Ken's next dream repeated the theme of being unprepared:

> *I'm with friends from high school. We're climbing Mt. Fuji, at night.*
> *There's snow all around. We find a little cabin. I realized I'm wearing*
> *shorts and a T-shirt. I was unprepared for the climb. I decided to go*
> *back down.*

Ken said, "Mt. Fuji reminds me of climbing the mountain of life." I asked Ken about his friends from high school. He said, "Interestingly, one of these people recently got an editing job without much background in her field. She had guts; she put herself out. I admire that. I know I have a talent that I haven't tapped. I have the resources inside me, but I don't know how to make use of them effectively." Being unprepared on the mountaintop suggested lack of foresight and planning. Ken's dream posed the question, "What is needed to climb the mountain, to reach the pinnacle of success and achievement?" Daniel Levinson (1978) noted that climbing the ladder is a central metaphor and developmental task of adulthood. In the dream Ken retreated and climbed back down to safe ground. Ken wanted to make decisions about his career and life direction, but he wasn't quite ready. The path forward wasn't clear. It wasn't yet time to ascend the mountain. In fact, it would take two more years before Ken made the decisions that began to shape his life direction. He needed plenty of time to work through the past before new possibilities emerged. As so often occurs, the block, the complex, and the client's sense of frustration, often seem to get worse once treatment gets underway.

## The Dream of the Seesaw Train

The next dream shows the therapist's associations leading the dream interpretation forward. Ken dreamed:

> *Standing in front of a bridge. There are concrete walls as barriers at*
> *the outer edges of the bridge. I'm on the concrete wall hanging on to*
> *it. You got on a complicated contraption like a seesaw train from old*
> *movies; you pump yourself out to the bridge. Then you could cross the*
> *bridge. A little boy was next to me, about four years old. The boy was*

*leaning back, starting to fall. I caught him. He didn't know what was*
*happening.*

Ken was perplexed by this dream and didn't have any initial associations. I prompted him, saying that the bridge implied transition,
crossing a threshold. The pump suggested pressurizing a sense of
motivation; "priming the pump," building up a charge of intention,
purpose, desire, and ambition. I said, "Something about losing your
father thwarted your sense of ambition. You felt it's useless—what's
the point of trying?"

"Yes. The little boy reminds me of me. He was very serious and
troubled; he wasn't happy where he was. He reminds me of my
childhood."

I said, "To cross the bridge, you have to hold this boy and keep him
safe; you can't let him fall. To cross the bridge you have to prime the
pump, build a charge, get over the lethargy and hopelessness. The loss
of your dad left you feeling that there's no one to be proud of you."

Ken said, "The message I take from this is that I want to take
myself and my ambitions more seriously."

## The Dream of Riding in Circles

Sometimes the smallest dream fragment releases intense memories
and affect. Ken dreamed:

*I'm on a long bike tour in Connecticut. I rode around in circles.*

Ken said, "This reminds me of learning to ride a bike when I was
seven or eight. I was alone, I had training wheels. I rode around in
circles. A dominant memory of my childhood is riding a bike and
being alone. I had elaborate fantasies about who I was with, a motor-
cycle gang or a group of friends." The dream took him right back to
that time, to the feeling of loneliness.

I said, "This makes me think of a boy learning to ride a bike with
his dad watching, cheering him on, celebrating his son's achievement of autonomy. The dream evokes a memory of loss, the absence
you experienced, the loneliness of your childhood."

Ken replied, "I spoke to my imaginary friends a lot." He spent
the remainder of the session telling me the names of his imaginary
companions.

## The Dream of the Black Homeless Man

In his next session Ken told me this significant dream:

> In a café I went to the bathroom. When I return my art equipment
> bag is gone, and my meal has been eaten. A man is sleeping in the
> window. He gets up. He's a black man, dishevelled, covered in blan-
> kets. He had the bag. I say to him, "You've got my bag." He scowled,
> looked me in the eye, handed me the bag, and walked away. When
> I saw he hadn't put up a fight I felt sorry for him and wanted to give
> him something, and I followed him. I found him sleeping in a car.
> Another black man with grey hair was nearby watching. I ran away.
> The guy was just watching. No one was chasing me, but I wanted
> to run.

Ken commented: "The art equipment symbolizes my career change
issue, the whole issue of being an artist. It's stolen from me. The
dishevelled, homeless black man reminds me of the Other, someone
who is foreign to me. It reminds me of the only dream I ever had
about my dad."

## The Dream of the Homeless Wanderer

Then Ken told me another pivotal dream:

> My father is this homeless-looking guy with a poncho on. He has some-
> thing under the poncho. Is it a backpack or a hump? He's a mystery to
> me. Is he homeless or does he live somewhere? He's the Wanderer, the
> oppressed, a person the odds are against.

I asked Ken, "What odds are working against you?"

"My fear of failure and my concern that I lack talent or business
savvy."

I said. "You feel that the loss of your father stacked the odds
against you. His death seems connected to your lack of confidence
and your fear of failure. You felt a lack of paternal support to help
you out. I wonder what it means that the black homeless man in the
first dream gives you back the bag; the homeless father has stolen
your career but he also gives it back to you. In the dream you felt
sorry for the man. Who do you feel sorry for?"

"I feel sorry for me, and my mom. The homeless man reminds me of a man without a family, and a family without a man," said Ken. In other words, it reminded him of *his* father, *his* family. The homeless man also reminded Ken of feeling rootless, his fear of never having a career or a stable life. The wandering man's hump reminded Ken of "disfigurement, mystery, something concealed from me. I didn't know what it was."

I said, "Maybe your father's pain was hidden to you."

"Yes. And the black man represents for me the extremes of human potential. Men like Malcolm X and Bob Marley overcame poverty and became the best of all people. The black man in the dream represents being self-made, fierce, and overcoming adversity. He reminds me of fatherless children, broken families, and the struggle of women to keep it all together." Ken's feelings about his mother would soon come into vivid focus.

### The Dream of the Church, the Pagan Altar, and the Sacrifice

Nine months into therapy, Ken dreamed:

> I'm at work. My office has moved and now it's a church, which is empty, closed down. I walk through the pews. Light is coming in through windows. I go down to the basement of the church. I was in this ancient pagan place of worship. The floor was a cave, painted blue. There was a design in the centre of the floor, a pentagram or mandala, a large circle. In the back of the room was a sign that said, "Do not go beyond this point. This is where sacrifices are performed. They sacrifice sheep." It felt creepy. It was like the basement when I was a kid. I wanted to leave.

Ken said, "The scene reminds me of the Christian Science church. My dad died because he refused medical treatment. It also reminds me of a pagan worship site, a very personal, sacred place, connected to the earth and a rebirth of spirituality. I wondered, were they sacrificing sheep or children? That reminds me of the tremendous sense of loss I felt in my childhood."

I said, "The sheep reminds me of Christ as the shepherd, and also being meek, innocent. So the dream evokes the sacrifice of the innocent."

"That's what happened to me as a boy—the sacrifice of the innocent. My dad was innocent and helpless too."

"In the dream you're entering forbidden territory, approaching something that has been off-limits, perhaps your identification with your dad's suffering, and your own. You're getting close to the central mystery here. You're entering the inner sanctum of the church where disturbing truths are revealed and sacrifices are offered."

Ken said, "My childhood was sacrificed. Parents make sacrifices for their children. All her life my mom made sacrifices for us. She sacrificed her childhood to work during World War II. Her grandfather was sacrificed by the Nazis. Then she lost my dad. I used to be racked with guilt about all my mom went through. I always felt like anything I went though would be nothing compared to her life." Ken wept as he said this. The dream's motif of sacrifice jarred loose memories and emotions that had been long buried. These feelings emerged out of his associations to this dream journey down into the underworld, to a blue cave with a sacred circle where rites were enacted involving sacrifice of sheep, symbol of innocence and the need to be guided or shepherded. Perhaps this attitude of innocence and meekness needed to be sacrificed on this internal altar. Only then could Ken move beyond the grief and survivor guilt that afflicted him and his mother. Note the mandala painted on the floor of this sacred cave; an internal order was emerging within the psyche.

## A Dream about the Therapeutic Relationship

A few months later Ken dreamed:

> I was coming to therapy. I arrived at the curb and sat in the car. I heard you [Greg] calling. You were leaning out your window calling me. I'd been sitting in the car forty-five minutes listening to music. I said, "I don't know what happened. I'm really sorry." You said "All right, come on up."

When I asked his associations to this dream, Ken commented, "I'm having resistance to coming. I've been feeling like I don't have much to talk about. I'm in a dry spell."

"So you're asking yourself is it worth coming here? Is it worth the money? Perhaps you're concerned that I'd be annoyed with you if you were to stop coming."

"Yes, I have fear of how my decision would affect you, and of what conflicts would arise." This dream helped us discuss Ken's resistance to going deeper into treatment, as well as to making decisions and plans. This was also the beginning of discussions about his eventual termination of therapy—which, as Otto Rank (1978) emphasized, is a crucial horizon that makes a client aware of the urgency of making needed life changes. All dreams about the therapeutic process are opportunities to discuss the client-therapist relationship and goals of the therapy.

## The Dream of the Crossroads and the Dead Bear

A few weeks later, Ken had another potent dream:

> I got a phone call from Liz, my girlfriend from college. She tells me she misses me. Then I'm driving my truck. I come to a crossroads where I turn off the road, taking a left turn down a road I'd always wanted to go on. I stop my truck. It's the road less travelled. It's covered with leaves. No one has been on that road for a while. It was too steep for the truck so I decided to walk it. I walk on a dirt path in the woods. I realized there was an enormous bear lying on the path. At first I thought it was sleeping. Then I realized it was dead. It had been dead for a while. I thought I should get a camera and take pictures. I walked down the path. I got spooked and headed back toward the truck. I started running as fast as I could.

When I asked about Liz, his girlfriend from college, Ken noted that therapy had helped her. I said, "Maybe this is also addressing your feelings about being in therapy. Therapy can help you take control of your life, and to take the road less travelled, the road that only you can go on. Taking a road that you'd always wanted to walk on is a symbol of individuation, becoming who you really are. The dream reflects fear of walking the road less travelled. To travel the road that is uniquely yours, you have to deal with the dead bear first."

Ken said that the bear was enormous. "It reminds me of my dad's death, and of uncontrollable nature that can't be reasoned with."

I said, "Finding the dead bear and getting spooked reminds me of how frightened you must have been as a child encountering death for the first time. The dead bear is your father, but it could also represent a part of you that feels dead and defeated, that wants to give up. This dream suggests you're approaching crossroads, a turning point, and big choices about what road you'll travel in your life."

The symbolism of the dead bear was intriguing. Joseph Campbell wrote:

> Of the Paleolithic traditions that spread west-to-east, the bear cult is almost certainly the oldest, dating from Neanderthal Man's veneration of the cave bear.... The bear hears everything, even at great distances. He also remembers and will avenge himself for every hurt .... The killing of a bear is generally regarded as a ritual act, to be performed in a special way. (Campbell, 1983, pp. 147–148)

Among the Ainu people of Hokkaido, Japan, the bear sacrifice involved paying homage to the bear deity by sacrificing it and eating it.

> The bear festival is a kind of cultural feast—a feast of friendship—in which Bruin himself also participates. Indeed the bear is offered to himself and his worshippers in common.... Offerings are made of his own meat to his pelt, which has been placed, with head attached, in the seat of honor. Words of thanks and praise are addressed to him.... The Ainu ... refer to him as That Divine One Reigning in the Mountains. (Campbell, 1983, pp. 147, 152)

The Ainu believe that the bear returns to its spiritual mountain home after the ceremonial feast (Campbell, 1983). This reminded me of the Dream of Eating Twigs and Thorns, which could be seen as a bear like image, and which was also a dream concerned with the principle of sacrifice. In this sense, Ken's artwork depicting his father's death was a form of reverent homage, like the ceremonial offering of bear meat to the bear.

## The Dream of the Bear and Cub, the Gate, and the Path

The bear motif reappeared in Ken's next dream:

> I'm camping out with a friend. There are rolling hills, trees. A bear and a cub come running after me, growling, snarling. The bear was right there on me. Then it stopped chasing me. Walking together, we come to the edge of some woods. There was a gate where a path started.

Camping with a friend reminded Ken of bonding, intimacy, friendship, and his lack of male friends. The rolling hills reminded him of a golf course; golf is a social game where guys get together. When I asked about the bear cub, Ken said, "It reminds me of being my dad's shadow, following him around while he did his work." It reminded Ken of being a kid, a little cub.

I said to Ken, "Ask the bear, 'Why are you in my dream? What part of me do you represent?'"

Ken responded, in the voice of the bear, "I'm the part of you that is your power, your spirit, the force that gives you energy and motivates you. I came to show you that you have power and that you can run in the world."

"The bear is a powerful totem for you. The dream is telling you that you can have big presence, big power. You can grow up and become a bear, like your dad. Being chased by a bear suggests an initiatory theme, comparable to mythic stories about the young hero's initiation into manhood through encountering a power animal. The dream ends with finding a gate, suggesting crossing a threshold, passing through the gate, a passage in your life. Here, the dream tells you, you find the beginning of a path."

## The Dream of the Tall Man and the Sharp Stone

Six weeks later, Ken dreamed:

> I was in a small rowboat, tied to a dock. A killer whale came up from the depth, jumped up from the water, and swam underneath me. I was afraid he'd knock over the boat. I pulled the boat closer to the dock. I jumped onto the dock and ran inside a house. I was scared. Then I was in a big old Cadillac with other men. We drove to a pier at another shore. We arrive at the pier and got out of the car. We climbed down a ladder to get to a lower level of the pier. A tall man approached me with something in his hand, a sharp stone. He was going to circumcise me with this sharp stone. I climbed up the ladder. He grabbed me and pulled me down. He said, "I need to mark you." He got me in a bear hug. He said, "I'm going to hold you like a baby."

Being in the rowboat reminded Ken of drifting, having no oars. Being tied to a dock reminded him of being on a leash, but also of safety, being able to pull himself to shore. Ken said, "The whale reminds me of *Jaws*, a vicious predator, biting aggression. That reminds me of my relationship with Ann. We've been quite aggressive with each other lately."

I said, "The killer whale reminds me of the story of Jonah and the whale. Joseph Campbell views this myth as a variation of the hero's journey motif, where the hero goes down into the belly of the whale. The image of the man with the sharp stone also reminds me of male initiation. It suggests that you're ready to receive the marks of manhood. This inner male initiatory figure is present and is going to mark you."

In the book *Rituals of Manhood: Male Initiation in Papua New Guinea*, anthropologist Gilbert Herdt (1982) discussed how the tribal societies of New Guinea feature "the ritualized development of male gender identity" through various secret rites, including graded initiations for boys from ages seven onward (pp. 49, 53). They believe that ritual sparks, fosters, and maintains manliness in males. Maleness, unlike femaleness, is not seen as a biological given; it must be artificially induced through secret ritual. Herdt wrote, "Masculinization means the overall process of separating a boy from his mother, initiating him, ritually treating his body, biological attainment of puberty, and eventual reproductive capacity; boys must be activated by men" (p. 68). Masculinization comprises "maternal detachment, subordination, and then sexual domination." Boys become subordinate to men both socio-politically and sexually, through subincision or other physical trauma, or sexual domination by older males. Herdt called this a "culturally sanctioned trauma," which is "socially channeled, ritually reinforced, and continues to live on in a boy's sense of himself and maleness" (pp. 73, 77). Ritual utilizes "extreme aggressive behaviour, to redirect the child's attachment away from the preferred maternal figure and compel it toward male figures" (p. 79). Ken's dream of the man with the sharp stone suggested that the archetype of male initiation was active in his unconscious, moving him forward into the next stage of development.

## Reflection on the Anima

Several months passed. Ken and I engaged in work focused on Ann's attraction to another man and Ken's attraction to other women. One evening he saw a woman sing and play guitar in a nightclub, and that night he had a dream about her. He then became very moody for several days, depressed because Ann didn't inspire him the way this woman did. I explained to Ken, "This is a problem of the anima—the enlivening feminine. When faced with the anima problem, you can dump your girlfriend to pursue the inspiring woman—who may already have a boyfriend or who might be a free spirit unwilling to be tied down; or you can recognize the face of the anima as your own unlived potential. In meeting the anima, a man's soul is pierced by a longing for union. The enticing divine feminine that men long for, that we think will make us whole, carries intimations of our own wholeness. The vision of the anima often evokes a moody depression in a man, a surly resentment about the woman waiting for you at home, 'the old ball and chain.' But the depression comes because you think you lack something. The anima is really the unrecognized face of your own soul, your own creativity." Over the next several weeks Ken began painting and drawing again, ending a lengthy drought.

## The Dream of the Forklift and the Cinderblock

Several months later, Ken dreamed:

> I'm working construction, using a forklift moving a huge cement cinderblock, six or seven feet tall. I move it three blocks away and leave it there. I come back. The route cuts through a warehouse art studio. I'm dressed up in nice clothes with my wingtip shoes. Liz was in the room—an artist I worked with last year who is living in both New York and Los Angeles, commuting back and forth. I go back with the forklift to get another huge block.

I said, "Moving the block suggests moving something that's been blocking you. The construction site suggests that the Self is under construction; building and construction suggest ego development." Cinderblocks are used for walls, foundations.

This reminded Ken of his desire for a stable foundation. Doing construction work while wearing nice clothes contrasts doing "grunt work" and building maintenance with wearing nice clothes, which Ken said represented "the intellectual and artistic part of me."

I said, "The dream depicts a union of opposites. You're a man of culture and refinement driving around a forklift."

Liz represented success and sophistication. She enjoyed making art, and made good money, but she lived a bohemian life in an art studio. She was a positive symbol of making it as an artist. Here again Ken was trying to imagine himself as a viable artist in the world.

Wearing nice shoes and clothes reminded Ken of dressing up, going on job interviews, making a good impression, looking sharp, projecting an image of success. He said, "It's an image of the enterprising artist who has motivation and drive, and is charming and successful. They say that clothes make the man." Ken was grappling with the process of evolving his *persona*, his public image and self-presentation to the world. The focus of the unconscious shifted from Ken grieving his lost father to defining his own ideal: the enterprising artist.

## The Dream of the Old Homeless Man

Next Ken dreamed:

> I'm walking though an empty house looking for people. Then I'm down on a beach near the Golden Gate Bridge. There are cliffs behind me. I find an old photograph, one of my dad's. On shore, there's an old man on an inner tube. We're looking for a place to launch him off on his inner tube. He's dressed in slacks and a tweed blazer. He looks like an old homeless guy in an old, ratty suit. He gets out of the inner tube. I hug him and start crying really intensely. I didn't want him to go. I was sad he was leaving.

The figure of the homeless man emerged for the third time, clearly embodying a central complex. "The old man reminds me of my father, grown old. This reminds me of a homeless guy I used to see around town wearing a suit. He always looked troubled. I feel tenderness for him. His troubled look reminds me of how I feel a lot, my insecurities about the world."

I said, "Now it's time to launch this old guy off, and get on with your life."

"Hugging the old man reminds me of not wanting to let him go, to lose him."

"Like you didn't want your dad to go away." For a few moments we dwelled in the grief Ken felt as he sadly watched his father's life slip away. The intense crying in the dream felt cathartic to Ken; as a little boy he bravely fought back his tears. This dream allowed completion of the grieving process.

Later Ken said, "The old man also represents failure to me. He's not in a nice, crisp suit. He's a derelict, not having achieved anything and not trying to. He reminds me of addiction and weakness, wanting to be an artist but not knowing how to do it." The dream suggested Ken's need to compassionately embrace the old man, the feeling of despair about not knowing how to achieve his goals. His path to wholeness required embracing the regressive shadow, his sense of failure, his feeling of defeat.

## The Dream of the Maggots

A month later Ken had a dream that evoked some despair and negativity that occupied us for several sessions:

> I was in my apartment with Andy, a childhood friend. There were maggots coming out of the kitchen water tap. There was a dark trail of ants on the floor. And there were maggots in the sink. I realize I've been drinking water coming out of that tap. I woke up very disturbed.

Disturbing dream imagery usually carries great emotional intensity. The maggots reminded Ken of death and decay. He said, "They disgust me."

"What disgusts you in your life?"

"What's going on in the world politically, terrorism, the war in Iraq. I feel a sense of futility and hopelessness. I want to have will power and drive to overcome obstacles, but right now I don't have it. It's hard for me to focus on the future with these disturbing events."

I said, "The maggots also imply decay in the sense of not striving for clearly defined goals, a feeling of stagnation and decay."

Ken said, "The maggots got on my hand and were boring under my skin, like a leech."

"What's getting under your skin?"

"Frustration about my career. I used to feel a sense of adventure about my work. Now I feel that artists are even more irrelevant than ever. I feel fear and self-doubt."

"You said that the maggots remind you of leeches. What do leeches remind you of?"

"Leeches remind me of taking, not giving or sharing."

"How are you being a leech?"

"I'm goofing off on the job, being half-hearted, not doing much work at all."

"Do you think that contributes to your feeling of decay and weakens you?"

"Yes."

"Drinking the water filled with maggots symbolizes this despair and discouragement. You're drinking from this tap." The maggots were a symbol of the alchemical process known as *mortificatio*, which represents a stage of intrapsychic decay, putrefaction, and decomposition—the emergence of foul moods and deep discouragement. We descend into the dark valley before we reach the Mountain of Light.

Ken's childhood friend Andy was a successful entrepreneur who again symbolized Ken's desire to become a successful artist. "The ants are diligent workers, who can lift things five times their size." The dream depicted a contrast between the industrious worker ants and the maggots, which symbolized despair, decay, discouragement, negativity, feeling like "What's the use?," rotting away on the job, and not striving toward clearly defined goals. Through this mysterious insect symbolism, the dream helped bring about an inner union of opposites.

## The Dream of the Little Girl in the Living Room

Ken's next dream seemed simple, but in fact it held rich meaning:

> I'm in a house, a living room, dimly lit; it's a beautiful, idyllic setting with dark wood, lots of plants. I'm sitting on a couch. A little girl is sitting on top of me. We're playing, giggling, talking, hanging out.

Ken commented that the dream reminded him of intimacy and love, and of Ann and the playfulness of their relationship. This dream portrayed a childlike attitude, in contrast to Ken's recent heavy, dark mood. This image instructed him to contact this young, feminine, playful spirit inside him.

To understand the dream further, I introduced Ken to Gareth Hill's (1992) model of the active and dynamic masculine and feminine principles. In Ken's previous dream, the figure of Andy embodied the *dynamic masculine* principle, which represents the youthful *puer*, the emergence of heroic potential and possibility. The hero or heroine's drives and initiatives are gradually channelled toward acknowledged social accomplishments through *fiery initiations* that advance us in the social order and bring fuller commitment to the pillars of our life structures—job, relationships, responsibilities. This is the *static masculine* principle, the urge to meet the requirements of social adaptation and to function within hierarchical institutions. The old man/*senex* figures of Ken's recent dreams were static masculine symbols. The static masculine position eventually becomes dry, rigid, and overly serious and calls forth the laughter, joy, playfulness, spontaneity, and openness of the *dynamic feminine* principle, symbolized here by the dream of the little girl giggling. Ken said, "The dream reminds me of having a child. I think that could be fun."

What hadn't been touched so far was the ground of the *static feminine*, the emotional return to the mother, which Hill describes as a source of renewal and restoration of our intrinsic wholeness. Suddenly our work with this dream took an interesting turn. Ken said, "The room had a Japanese feel to it; it reminds me of Japanese gardens, that kind of consciousness about space and the atmosphere these gardens create. The room is lit ambiently by other rooms. It reminds me of a childhood memory: I was sitting in a dark room, the living room, while mom was in the dining room with the light on full blast. She was trying to figure out the bills, crying, hitting her head against the wall, feeling overwhelmed, as I sat in the dark room and watched her, helpless." Ken wept as he recounted this story. Here he connected to an experience of the static feminine: his mother's feeling of being trapped; and his guilt about his mother's suffering, grief, and despair. It was paradoxical: The little girl in the dream living room brought him back to the boy in the dark living room watching his frantic mother's grief. The dream helped Ken understand and release his unconscious identification with his mother. This is an example of how dwelling in the atmosphere of a dream allows the unconscious to spontaneously cough up memories and feelings that need to be experienced and discharged. Note how the dream linked together light and darkness, joy and sorrow, an example of how dreams promote the *coniunctio*, the creation of consciousness through the union of opposites (Edinger, 1994a).

## The Dream of the Silver Man

Then Ken dreamed:

> *I'm at my workplace. In the back there's a metal shop. A guy is dressed in work clothes with welder's goggles. He's silver, covered with aluminium dust from head to toe. There's a big oven behind me, or a forge. I turn to my right. I see Ted (a teacher from my college, head of the art department) shoulder to shoulder with me. He's so close that he pushes me off my course, nudging me. He says, "We're all going to start complaining about a general stiffness." He tells me that all the workers are going to start complaining about the same ailment so we can get workman's compensation.*

The silver man reminded Ken of musician Tom Waits in a similar costume on an album cover. Ken said, "Tom Waits is one of my heroes. He represents unbridled creativity." Here was another example of the artist archetype finding expression within Ken's unconscious. "Silver reminds me of guys doing mime in San Francisco in silver makeup, doing performance art; doing performances for spare change; doing art for very little money, just because they love doing it."

I said, "The oven or forge reminds me of fiery initiations, the tests that enable the youthful hero to prove himself worthy of acceptance and validation within the social order. The forge or oven also reminds me of the shaman or blacksmith melting solid metals to pour into moulds, to shape it and forge it." The blacksmith was the first *technician of the sacred*, as Mircea Eliade (1979) showed in *The Forge and the Crucible*. "The forge suggests to me alchemical themes: the fire of creativity, creation, transforming matter, the Promethean fire of art, innovation, and creativity. These fires are burning in you, Ken."

Mime reminded Ken of silent acting; silently doing your job, going through the motions. "In the dream the figure of Ted is influencing you, changing your direction, nudging you."

"He represents ingenuity; he was an important mentor, an expert at many things in art."

I asked Ken about "a general stiffness." He said, "It reminds me of a David Mamet films about scams, people trying to pull something out of nothing."

I said, "It reminds me of a creative block, a sense of inertia, a place you're stuck, a state of negativity. Your mentor is nudging you from inside to change your course."

"Ted would never complain about working hard. He'd always take pleasure in what he was doing, and he welcomed problems as something to solve." Another positive male mentor figure was emerging from within, encouraging Ken to prove himself by undergoing the fiery initiations that would enable him to find his place in the world.

## The Dream of Meeting Duke Ellington at a Funeral

After several years of work together Ken was on the threshold of some major breakthroughs. The final dream I'll discuss here was intensely catalytic:

> I'm at a funeral in a big cathedral, for Ellis Marsalis, father of the famous jazz musicians Branton and Wynton Marsalis. The service is over; everyone is outside, like a New Orleans street parade. The mood is sombre yet celebratory. Leaving the cathedral I'm walking with Duke Ellington. I also saw Danny Glover, the actor, and wanted to meet him. The cathedral was located on a big cliff on a Northern California coast. I walked toward the cliff. There was a chain-linked fence. I walked around it. I was feeling very emotional. I thought to myself, "The whole world is cold, stupid, and doesn't give a damn about anything." I was going to burst from the emotions inside me. Then I looked down and saw a patch of daffodils, colourful flowers. My emotions were released and everything made sense to me and I didn't feel overwhelmed anymore.

The funeral reminded Ken of his father, death and rebirth, celebrating life, letting go of the past, a ritual. I asked Ken about the current relevance of a ritual, and he said that he and Ann were planning their wedding. "I'm closer to where I want to be. I feel in motion.

Things are building momentum. With acceptance of my dad's death, I sense new possibilities for my future."

The dream contained death, but then an unexpected rebirth. I asked, "What is being born?"

"My ability to stand up for myself and value myself."

Ken continued, "The Marsalises remind me of the album they made called *Fathers and Sons*. The album is about making art, and going through the struggle of being an artist."

I added, "It seems to represent the continuity of generations and the commitment of artists—like you and your father. The New Orleans parade reminds me of Mardi Gras, a celebratory event of endings and new beginnings, a renewal of the profane world through a return to a mythic, sacred time." Deep within the unconscious there was a shift, a turning from mourning and death, toward life, celebration, and creativity.

When I asked about Duke Ellington, Ken said, "He's the archetypal jazz musician and artist, totally dedicated to his music. He sacrificed his life for the music."

I said, "He represents dignity and creative genius. The name Duke denotes royalty, the king archetype, the solar principle of confident self-expression. He's a symbol of your individuation and unfolding of potential."

Ken said, "Duke was like the king of the world, carefree but sombre. He's there to encourage me, and inspire me to dedicate myself to being an artist and to put the work into it and to put my faith in it."

Danny Glover, Ken said, is dignified, politically active, the successful artist who still has principles and speaks his mind. Here again is the artist archetype, dedicated and refined.

In the dream Ken walked from the funeral to the cliff, suggesting uncertainty, being on the precipice. The cliff reminded Ken of the Fool, innocence, walking on the edge of the cliff, the abyss, trusting the unconscious and the unknown.

The chain-linked fence suggested a barrier, something in Ken's way. The dream was speaking of the need to identify the internal barrier, perhaps his feeling that the world is cold and impersonal, and doesn't care about people. The dream portrayed the union of opposites: suffering and happiness, despair and hope, ugliness and beauty, the stupid, uncaring world and colourful flowers, the beauty of art and nature. The daffodils represent the golden flower of alchemy, a symbol of wholeness and rebirth. The dream ended with a sense of closure from the funeral, and with Ken's emotional response to the flowers. He told me, "I want to get married. I'm excited about it. That is something beautiful happening in my life."

This dream offered an epiphany and an emotional release. It depicted an internal movement from brooding over his father's death to being taken under the wing of Duke Ellington and Danny Glover, symbols of the male creative principle, embodiments of the artist with integrity, representing dedication to artistic craft, excellence, and achievement. Although Ken's father passed away long ago, the archetypal father was vibrantly present to guide and protect his development.

As I mentioned earlier, there was no funeral when Ken's father died. In the dream there was finally a funeral. This dream allowed Ken to bring closure to his prolonged bereavement, and put to rest his anxieties about having no male role model to emulate. He was able to find images of his own ideal emerging from deep within, from the mysterious centre of intelligence that scripts our dreams.

Soon after this dream, Ken made a major decision about his career that would require advanced training in a specialized art technique. While many uncertainties remained about his ultimate path, he had found a new direction. The flow of dreams subsided as Ken considered his options for training and education, and as he and Ann had their wedding and honeymoon.

In these initial chapters, I've described how dreams clarify and intensify our feelings and relationships. In Part II, I'll describe how we can enhance our experience of dreamwork by applying the principles of Jungian psychology. This approach allows our dreams to reveal their deepest emotional and spiritual significance.

# PART II

## JUNGIAN DREAMWORK

# CHAPTER FIVE

# Archetypal Themes

reams weave infinitely varied narratives, yet they're woven from the threads of recurring themes. In dreamwork, we not only access a wide range of feelings and personal memories, but we also access mythic, archetypal layers of the unconscious. The archetypal patterns of human transformation were brilliantly illuminated by the work of C.G. Jung, whose dynamic insights provide the basis for the chapters that follow.

In Jung's model of the psyche, the *ego* (seat of personal consciousness), and the *personal unconscious* (derived from forgotten or repressed biographical memories) both rest upon the deeper strata of the *collective unconscious,* a reservoir of timeless images derived from the universal experience of humanity, across cultures and historical eras. The collective unconscious is a matrix of *archetypes,* images of the typical experiences of humanity—primordial patterns of behaviour that are expressed in dreams, fantasy, free association, art, literature, and film. Archetypes form the deep structures of the psyche and the mythic background of our lives. We live, over and over again, the universal themes and primordial experiences—birth and death, mother and child, the hero's quest, the martyr, the king or queen. Jung wrote that "every individual life is at the same time the eternal life of the species ... . [T]he archetype ... reveals the hidden, unconscious ground-life of every individual" (Jung, 1969 [1938/1940], par. 146). Elsewhere, Jung said:

> There are as many archetypes as there are typical situations in life. Endless repetition has engraved these experiences into our psychic constitution, not in the form of images filled with content, but at first as only *forms without content*, representing merely the possibility of a certain type of perception or action. (Jung, 1969 [1936], par. 99)

Anthony Stevens commented:

> [A]rchetypes predispose us to approach life and to experience it in certain ways, according to patterns already laid down in the psyche. What is more, they also *organize* percepts and experiences so as to bring them into conformity with the pattern. This is what Jung means when he says that there are as many archetypes as there are typical situations in life. There are archetypal figures (e.g., mother, child, father, God, wise man), archetypal events (e.g., birth, death, separation from parents, courting, marriage, etc.) and archetypal objects (e.g., water, sun, moon, fish, predatory animals, snakes). Each is part of the total endowment granted us by evolution in order to equip us for life. (Stevens, 1990, p. 38)

## Central Archetypes: Mother, Father, Child, Hero

My purpose here is not to provide a comprehensive discussion of Jung's theory of archetypes (see Stevens, 2003), but rather to demonstrate the relevance of archetypes to the practice of dreamwork. In this chapter, I describe some of the archetypal characters and themes we're likely to encounter in dreams and personal complexes.

The mother is the primordial source, womb, and matrix, and represents the full cycle of gestation, birthing, sustenance, nurturing, and protection. The mother is our origin, the sustaining ground of existence. She appears as the nourishing, tender, patient, loving good mother, or as the cold, rejecting, withholding, or devouring terrible mother. The duality of the archetype reflects our experience of real mothers, who, in most cases, are "good enough" but not "perfect." Most women who become mothers strive, as part of their path of individuation, to embody the most nurturing, life-enhancing features of a good mother. This also applies to men striving to become good fathers.

The father is the archetype of generativity, protection, strength, power, and authority. The father is the guardian, provider, disciplinarian, bestower of kindness and blessing. He provides structure and socializes children into social norms and standards. The father represents choicefulness and taking responsibility for ourselves.

The child represents birth, beginnings, potentiality, innocence, vulnerability, resilience, and dependency. According to Marie-Louise von Franz, the child represents:

> youthfulness ... the naïve truth which puts everything right ..., spontaneity and genuineness ... . [Children symbolize] a renewal of life, a new personality ..., a symbol of the Self being constellated and activated in the unconscious not yet in any way integrated or realized in consciousness ... . [The child represents] a possibility, but not yet a realized fact. (von Franz, 1977, pp. 16–17, 19, 25, 27)

These three archetypes, mother, father, and child, are part of the experience of every human being, and are evident in many dreams. For example, see the Dream of Mother and the Large Mouth (Chapter Six), the Dream of the Mentor-Father, the Dream of Boys on the Street, and the Dream of the Seesaw Train (all in Chapter Four).

The hero/heroine/warrior represents a personal quest or initiative, the process of undergoing testing and trials, and exhibiting courage, valour, and a sense of honour. The hero/heroine heeds the call to adventure, overcomes obstacles, vanquishes enemies, and experiences both triumph and defeats. The hero (or heroine) courageously sets forth into battle, into the fray. Sometimes, like Arjuna in the *Bhagavad Gita*, he becomes weary and says, "I will not fight." von Franz (1977) notes that the hero possesses "a vocation which is carried through without any doubts" (p. 74). He represents "obedience to an ultimate inner authority" and possesses "*elan vital*, the certainty that the thing has to be done ... . [T]he Hero also personifies the Self, the One Man, the unified personality, with all its strength" (p. 75). In the Grail legend, "Gawain is the chevalier without fear, with complete honesty and courage. He personifies the Persian medieval idea of the hero: the man who fears nothing and whose shield of honour is without stain." But a hero may also experience vulnerability; for example, Perceval, who stumbles and fails to ask the Grail question. He breaks down, waivers, but "he is the one who eventually finds the Grail" (pp. 74–75). The hero archetype appears in the Dream of Clint Eastwood and the Evil Witch (this chapter); the Dream of the Desert and the House by the Water (Chapter Nine); and the Dream of Uriah Heap and the Kung Fu Fighter (this chapter).

## Persona, Shadow, Anima/Animus, and the Self

Jung emphasized four central archetypes, which I explore in later chapters: persona, shadow, anima/animus, and the Self.

*The* persona refers to the social mask, our conscious self-presentation.

*The* shadow represents forbidden, excluded aspects of the personality. The shadow appears in dreams of characters who are scary or repulsive, or who chase or confront us, knock on the door, or wait outside a window, demanding that we pay attention to their presence. I'll explore the persona and the shadow in Chapter Seven.

The anima and the animus are the archetypes of intensified feeling and dynamism. For men, the anima appears in the form of an enlivening female figure who arouses intense feelings of attraction, longing, or inspiration. She is the romantic ideal, the object of idealization and erotic fascination. The anima also refers to a man's unconscious femininity, commonly expressed in extreme moodiness and sensitivity. But men who consciously develop the anima exhibit emotional intelligence and nurturing behaviours. For women, the animus is an enlivening male figure who embodies charm, confidence, power, and persuasive convictions; he evokes admiration, idealization, and fascination. The animus also refers to a woman's unconscious masculinity, commonly expressed in intense wilfulness and dogmatic assertions. Women who consciously develop animus awaken determination, confidence, and strength of purpose.

Those figures in dreams and waking life who embody for us the anima/animus have a magnetic star quality. We're attracted to them, yet they're elusive and ephemeral; they evoke longing and embody our own dormant potentials. When the anima/animus is activated, we long for fulfilment through union with our beloved. At other stages, we discover the attractive qualities of the intriguing anima or animus emerging from within, expressing our own zestful life spirit. Chapter Eight explores these archetypes.

The Self symbolizes the centre, wholeness, goal of individuation, and is represented as Christ, the messiah, the divine child, the jewel, or as a circle or mandala. In *Aion*, Jung wrote:

> As for the Self, it is completely outside the personal sphere, and appears, if at all, only as a religious mythologem, and its symbols range from the highest to the lowest ... . The totality images which the unconscious produces in the course of an individuation process are ... "reformations" of an *a priori* archetype (the mandala) ... . [T]he spontaneous symbols of the self, or of wholeness cannot in practice be distinguished from a God-image ... . [L]ight and shadow are so evenly distributed in man's nature that his psychic totality appears ... in a somewhat murky light. The psychological concept of the self ... depicting itself spontaneously in the products of the unconscious as an archetypal quaternity bound together by inner antinomies, cannot omit the shadow that belongs to the light figure. (Jung, 1959, pars. 57, 73, 76)

In this passage, Jung tells us that the Self appears in dreams as a "totality image" that may contain light and shadow, fourfold imagery (quaternity), or symbolism unifying the conflicts and "antinomies" of the personality. Jung noted that two historically significant symbols of the Self are Christ and the alchemist's *lapis* (philosopher's stone), both signifying "the figure of the total man" (Jung, 1959, par. 123). The Self represents our wholeness and totality, which is experienced, and symbolized, as a union of opposites. The Self is the tendency of the psyche toward its own internal order.

## Teacher, Wounded Healer, Shaman

One of the characteristic representations of the Self in dreams and waking life is in the form of a great teacher, healer, or charismatic leader. The spiritual teacher, the sage, or the wise old man or woman embodies wholeness, wisdom, love, compassion, and tranquillity. This archetype appears in dreams of great teachers and wise beings who represent the centred wisdom of the individuating Self emerging within us. For example, see the Dream of the Old Aztec Sage (Chapter Nine).

In many instances, the archetypal teacher appears to us in a familiar form. A Christian dreams about Jesus. A Buddhist dreams about Buddha, Guru Rinpoche, or the Dalai Lama. We dream about our priest, rabbi, yoga teacher, or spiritual guide. I'll share a brief example here. In my book on *Spiritual Apprenticeship* (Bogart, 1997), I described my experiences with Swami Muktananda, a great yogi. Many years after his death in 1982, I had a powerful dream about him. It occurred at a time when I was in trouble at work and was called in to get 'chewed out' by my boss. I was afraid I might even get fired. That morning I dreamed:

> *Swami Muktananda was sitting in my dining room. He was there to express his love, his concern, and his reassurance. He was completely there for me. I felt inwardly blessed.*

It was comforting that he was thinking about me and that a guiding presence in the universe was apparently concerned about my situation. This strengthened my confidence and faith. I felt connected to a sustaining inner wisdom. I felt like he was actually there in the room with me. I tangibly felt his bodily presence, the current of his vibrational influence. The archetypal teacher may appear as a sage, guru, or initiator.

Often the teacher appears as a wounded healer, shaman, messiah, or a figure such as Christ or Chiron, the wounded centaur who mentored others and practiced many healing and esoteric arts. This archetype represents the way initiatory ordeals and our emotional woundedness prepare us to be healers of our suffering world. The unconscious may symbolically represent this process through shamanic or chironic imagery of wounds or injuries.

## The Dream of the Charred Old Woman

Cass, a woman who had gone through a painful divorce, had this dream:

> *An old woman with a charred body came into my bed and held me. It felt good.*

I asked Cass to describe the old woman's body. She said, "She had this big wound on her back; it looked as if she had been burned."

"It reminds me of the way you feel burned by your ex-husband. This woman has been through the fire, and so have you."

"It was a raw wound. It still hurt."

"It still hurts you too. But here the wise old woman appears as a wounded healer. She's wounded, but she also holds you and heals you. It feels good to be close to her." Here we see an archetype embodied in a potent personal symbol. The dream evoked the bodily feeling of being healed. The dream of the wounded healer is itself a healing.

## Messianic Inflation and the Mana Personality

The archetype of the king, saviour, healer, guru, or great teacher is frequently found in dreams. Occasionally people get into trouble due to their identification with these figures, if the individual literalizes the archetypal image, believing that he or she is actually a saviour or messianic hero, a person of great potential with a major world destiny. Jung noted how exposure of the ego to the unconscious can result in feelings of inflation, conceit, all-knowingness, or godlikeness (Jung, 1966 [1928], pars. 221, 224). "He will therefore feel it his duty ... to enlighten the world" (par. 223). People touched by archetypal energies can become charismatic, powerful and magnetic, forming what Jung called a *mana* personality.

> [T]he mana personality is a dominant of the collective unconscious, the well-known archetype of the mighty man in the form of hero, chief, magician, medicine-man, saint, the ruler of men and spirits, the friend of God ... . The figure of the magician has a no less dangerous equivalent in women: a sublime matriarchal figure, the Great Mother, the All-Merciful, who understands everything, forgives everything, who always acts for the best, living only for others, and never seeking her own interests, ... just as the magician is the mouthpiece of the ultimate truth. And just as the great love is never appreciated, so the great wisdom is never understood ... . [W]ithout a doubt it is a question of inflation. The ego has appropriated something that does not belong to it ... . [T]he mana personality ... corresponds

to a dominant of the collective unconscious, to an archetype
which has taken shape in the human psyche through untold
ages ... . Historically, the mana personality evolves into the hero
and the godlike being, whose earthly form is the priest ... . But
in so far as the ego apparently draws to itself the power belong-
ing to the anima, the ego does become a mana personality. This
development is an almost regular phenomenon. I have never
yet seen a fairly advanced development of this kind where at
least a temporary identification with the archetype of the mana
personality did not take place. (Jung, 1966 [1928], pars. 377, 379,
380, 388–389)

People identified with the messianic archetype may exhibit hubris,
arrogance, inflated self-value, and self-importance. We'll return to
this theme in discussing the Dream of the Animal Skin (Chapter
Eleven). Yet the saviour or mana personality represents our spark
of potential greatness, our urge to fully activate ourselves in service
to a conscious life mission. To unfold this archetype is to awaken
our creative powers and to become filled with excitement about our
calling or vocation (Bogart, 1995). Moving harmoniously with the
forces of nature, we strive in our own way to be world-transforming,
to radiate a positive magnetic influence. We'll return to this theme
in Chapter Six.

## Trickster

The trickster is the archetype of change, the unexpected, and divine
humour. The trickster appears at moments when we act like a fool or
a buffoon, or become a focus of controversy or dissension. Trickster
is present wherever there are unexpected mishaps or reversals of
fortune. When the trickster appears, life plays a joke on us. Sometimes a bright surprise awaits.

The trickster appears in unexpected forms, at unanticipated
times. Once, while travelling with a group in Alaska, one of my
friends caught a close look at a moose while walking down a road.
A few minutes later I wandered off down the same path looking for
the moose, but he was nowhere to be found. As I walked back to our
van, I noticed all my friends waving at me. I thought they wanted
me to hurry up and return to the van, but they all began laughing,

saying that the moose had come out of the woods and had been following me, walking just a few feet behind me. They were waving to tell me to quickly *turn around*! I was downcast at having missed the sighting, but everyone reassured me that clearly this moose recognized me as a kindred spirit, one of its own kind. Sometimes the moose we think we're looking for is right there behind us, even when we don't see it. The trickster follows, witnesses. It behooves us to remember that the moose is on the loose.

Jung's description of the trickster notes his affinity to "the carnival in the medieval Church, with its reversal of the hierarchic order"; and to the medieval figure of "the 'simpleton' who is 'fooled' or 'cheated'" (Jung, 1969 [1954], par. 456). But there are also strong connections between the trickster and the archetypal shaman or messiah, clarified in this passage:

> A curious combination of typical trickster motifs can be found in the alchemical figure of Mercurius; for instance, his fondness for sly jokes and malicious pranks, his powers as a shape-shifter, his dual nature, half animal, half divine, his exposure to all kinds of tortures, and … his approximation to the figure of a saviour … . Ability to change his shape seems also to be one of his characteristics, as there are not a few reports of his appearance in animal form. Since he has on occasion described himself as a soul in hell, the motif of subjective suffering would seem not to be lacking either. His universality is co-extensive … with that of shamanism … . There is something of the trickster in the character of the shaman and medicine man, for he, too, often plays malicious jokes on people, only to fall victim in his turn to the vengeance of those whom he has injured. For this reason, his profession sometimes puts him in peril of his life. Besides that, the shamanistic techniques in themselves often cause the medicine-man a good deal of discomfort, if not actual pain. At all events the "making of a medicine man" involves, in many parts of the world, so much agony of body and soul that permanent psychic injuries may result. His "approximation to the saviour" is an obvious consequence of this, in confirmation of the mythological truth that the wounded wounder is the agent of healing, and that the sufferer takes away suffering … . He is obviously a "psychologem," an archetypal

psychic structure of extreme antiquity ... . [T]he trickster is represented by counter-tendencies in the unconscious, and in certain cases by a sort of second personality, of a puerile and infantile character ... . On the civilized level, it is regarded as a personal "gaffe," "slip," "faux pas," etc., which are then chalked up as defects of the conscious personality ... . [H]e is in many respects stupider than the animals, and gets into one ridiculous scrape after another. Although he is not really evil, he does the most atrocious things from sheer unconsciousness and unrelatedness. (Jung, 1969 [1954], pars. 456, 457, 465, 469, 473)

The Dream of the Charred Old Woman illustrates the principle that "the wounded wounder is the agent of healing." This describes the transformative potential of allowing ourselves to feel the painful aspects of our experience. This insight is a foundation of psychoanalysis, as expressed in Wilfred Bion's emphasis on learning to face pain rather than avoid it (Symington & Symington, 1996).

The most crucial decision on which mental growth depends is whether frustration is evaded or faced. Encountering a painful state of mind, does the individual immediately engage in one or more of the numerous defence mechanisms readily available for the purpose of getting rid of the awareness of the frustration, or is there an attempt to remain open to it, to tolerate it and to think about it? (Symington & Symington, 1996, p. 67).

Dreamwork allows us to get closer to our pain and woundedness, to tolerate and think about it, and also to gain a sense of humour about our own scrapes and mishaps—those injuries or defeats that we may accept as initiatory ordeals along our path to wholeness.

## Crone, Virgin, Witch

The Dream of the Charred Old Woman represents the archetypal crone, the wise old woman, the elder who has lived through many seasons, who has learned from suffering. The crone also appears in the Dream of the Pregnant Horse and the Grey-Haired Woman, later in this chapter.

The Crone is the polar opposite of the virgin, symbol of innocence and purity. See the Dream of the Red Silk Curtains. The dream of a little girl catching fireflies in Chapter Two also portrayed the state of innocence.

The witch is described by von Franz (1977) as "the destructive side of the archetypal feminine principle . . . . They generally intrigue, poison, kill, or eat people, or they slander them so that they quarrel with each other" (p. 30). In fairytales, the evil witch is an archetypal symbol of malevolent intent, negativity, and resentment. Yet, encounter with the witch is necessary and may in time reveal her other face, which is a wise healer.

## The Dream of Clint Eastwood and the Evil Witch

The next example combines the archetypal figures of the witch and the hero. A young man named Silas had just broken off a relationship with a woman named Debbie because he felt unready to meet her intense emotional needs. Silas dreamed:

> Clint Eastwood and a bunch of his "good guy" companions have been captured and are forced to go into a mine in a volcano, where they will die. At the last minute something major happens, akin to Frodo destroying the ring, which saves them. The evil witch, a bad person, is stopped.

The setting of the dream was a mine within a volcano, which reminded Silas of "a scary place where you can find treasures and resources through hard work. Volcanoes remind me of unstoppable transformation and surfacing something that's buried, and expressing your power."

I said, "It suggests to me that perhaps some fiery emotions have been surfacing in your relationship with Debbie. The dream seems to be about an unstoppable transformation that involves awakening your inner strength and power."

The dream pits the heroic figure of Clint Eastwood against the evil witch, a symbol of the devouring mother. The image of the witch made me wonder whether this relationship was bringing up some unresolved issues with Silas's mother, fear of Debbie's anger, or a sense of smothering engulfment. I noted von Franz's statement that the witch manipulates and pits people against one another.

Silas, an accomplished student of depth psychology, then offered this insightful analysis. He said, "I manipulate people by being nice or acting very supportive so they won't abandon or reject me. I try to control people by acting like a 'good guy,' as a way to hide my neediness and exert some power over them. In the dream the evil witch is going to kill Clint and the good guys. But then they're saved by Frodo destroying the ring. That's a reference to The Lord of the Rings trilogy, where Frodo undertakes a hero's journey to destroy the 'ring of power' and thus rid the world of evil."

In the archetypal story of the hero's journey, the hero or heroine leaves the normal world and goes into the underworld to face challenges. Eventually the hero vanquishes a dangerous foe and is rewarded for it. The hero then returns to the everyday world, where the reward he received helps replenish his community. The theme of the hero's journey is apparent in this dream. Clint descends into the mines (the underworld) to face his own death. Yet, he's saved and emerges victorious, having defeated the evil witch, just as in many myths the hero defeats the monster, representing the smothering aspect of the mother. The image of the witch stirred Silas's awareness that he was frightened about surrendering to sexuality with a woman and the emotional obligations this might entail.

We both had many associations to Clint Eastwood, an actor who embodies his own unique archetype through his roles in classic spaghetti westerns such as High Plains Drifter and The Good, the Bad, and the Ugly. Clint always plays a rugged individualist, an outlaw, a man who goes his own way and doesn't do what other people want him to do. He makes his own decisions and lives according to his own law. In The Outlaw Josie Wells, Eastwood's character lives on the margins of society and follows his own moral code. In many of his roles, he attracts women easily, but generally keeps his distance from them, treating them respectfully but also remaining free of entanglement with them. This resonated with Silas's current need to go his own way, free of strong emotional commitments. Silas's associations to Clint Eastwood were specifically to his character in the movie Unforgiven, in which Clint mourns the memory of his deceased wife and spurns the attention of other women, burdened by guilt for past misdeeds. This reminded Silas of unresolved sorrow about the break-up of his previous relationship, which he hadn't fully grieved before getting involved with Debbie. He was also concerned about whether Debbie, or her friends, would ever forgive him for breaking up with her, or if he'd always remain unforgiven.

Silas added, "The characters Clint often plays are cold, violent, and aggressive, qualities I resist by holding back my power and not speaking up for myself. I don't want to be destructive. Yet, Clint is a well-respected alpha male, and there's a part of me that wants the respect of others. In many of his movies, such as *Unforgiven*, Clint is self-sufficient and is comfortable being alone. I want to cultivate these qualities. I've always depended on a best friend or partner to feel secure. I'm learning to be comfortable with aloneness and nurturing myself. Clint represents empowerment and self-sufficiency. He takes decisive action in the face of criticism or judgment." At the present time, the balance of the psyche required that Silas take a stand for his independence, choosing to go his own way, rather than deferring to other people's needs and expectations. This dream portrayed a central phase in the unfoldment of this young hero's journey, in which he gained power and self-sufficiency through his encounter with the archetypal witch.

## Puer and Senex

A young man such as Silas who is unready to be tied down by responsibilities is expressing the archetypal theme of the *puer aeternus*, which represents the uncommitted youth, full of possibilities and inspiration. The puer corresponds to the attitude of many young adults who make provisional life choices without prematurely making binding commitments (Levinson, 1978). However, in a more extreme expression, identification with the *puer*, or *puella aeterna* in the case of females, manifests as "a constant inner refusal to commit oneself to the moment.... a savior complex, or a Messiah complex.... The one thing dreaded ... by such a type of man is to be bound to anything whatever" (von Franz, 1970, p. 2).

According to James Hillman, puer merges with the archetypes of the hero, divine child, Eros, king's son, son of the great mother, Mercury-Hermes, trickster, and messiah. "In him we see a mercurial range of these 'personalities': narcissistic, inspired, effeminate, phallic, inquisitive, inventive, pensive, passive, fiery, and capricious" (Hillman, 1979b, p. 23). The puer represents an adolescent attitude, and lack of connection to reality. Hillman noted the "crippling, laming, or castration of the archetypal puer figures" (p. 23). This is vividly portrayed in the Dream of the Emasculated Batman (Chapter Six). The puer is characterized by weakness and helplessness, and is often depicted flying or falling. The puer isn't at home on the earth, gives up easily, avoids restriction of his possibilities and thus resists development.

> Its wandering is as the spirit wanders, without attachment and not as an odyssey of experience. It wanders to spend or to capture, and to ignite, to try its luck, but not with the aim of going home. It has a pose—phallic warrior, pensive poet, messenger—but not a persona of adaptation.... From the puer we are given our sense of destiny and mission, of having a message and being meant as eternal cup-bearer to the divine. (Hillman, 1979b, pp. 24–26)

In short, the puer represents the freedom of the youthful soul to pursue its wandering journey of self-discovery. The puer sparks a feeling of excitement and, when joined with the maturity and wisdom of the senex, it engenders a sense of focus, passion, and life purpose.

The senex is the archetypal Old Man, symbol of work, discipline, responsibility, and maturity. It represents settling down, in contrast to the puer's need for freedom and exploration of alternatives. According to Hillman, the senex represents structure, order, time, hierarchy, limits, and borders, and is also associated with sadness, depression, and melancholia. The senex is the archetype of order and meaning, and represents the hardening process of consciousness, symbolized by the old king; also states of petrification, "consequent of the absent feminine, resulting in dryness and coldness." As the principle of coagulation, the senex "makes solid and square and profitable, overcoming the dissolving wetness of soulful emotionality" (Hillman, 1979b, p. 19). The senex represents commitment, egobuilding, all that's gained by repetition and consistency (p. 24). The senex appears as the old wise man, father, elders, the chief or medicine man, all figures who carry authority and wisdom.

Hillman observed that the puer and the senex represent eternal youth and Father Time, eternity and temporality, youth and maturity, the first and second halves of life.

The senex as well as the puer may appear at many stages and may influence any complex.... . The second-half is with us from the beginning, ... just as the little boy and his question 'why,' the child Eros, and the winged angel are with us to the last. The puer inspires the blossoming of things, the senex presides over the harvest. (Hillman, 1979b, pp. 10–11)

Many dreams in this book contain puer-senex imagery. For example, see the Dream of the Desert and the House by the Water (Chapter Nine); and the Dream of Uriah Heap, the Cathedral, and the Kung Fu Fighter (Chapter Six). Chapter Four also explores the archetypal dynamics of father and son, puer and senex, childhood and adulthood. In medieval alchemy, the senex and the puer appeared as the old king of power who was killed or replaced by his son, the young king.

## King

The king symbolizes "the dominant conscious attitude of the ego" (Edinger, 1985, p. 48). Dreams of important, powerful people, of presidents and celebrities, represent the archetypal king (or queen), symbol of conscious individuality. The king often appears as the wounded king, representing the state of depression, alienation, and unredeemed suffering that often precedes individuation. A recurring motif in alchemy is the bath of the king: The king is renewed by immersion in a bath, with a white dove hovering above his head. This symbolizes personal renewal through a descent into the unconscious. The king or queen occupies the throne of pride, resolve, and will, seeking to rule or dominate a situation, to be firmly in command. But the path of the king or queen also involves yielding to that moment when our rule is overthrown. In ancient civilizations, the king's death through ritual sacrifice renewed the social order. Something must die for something new to be born. We'll return to the king in Chapter Nine.

## Death-Rebirth, and Initiation

Death-rebirth is the process of transformation from one condition into another. When considering dreams containing imagery of death or dying, I like to ask, "What in me is dying? What is ending?" Dan, a man who had recently stopped smoking marijuana, dreamed:

> I found a wall of fossilized horses. I thought to myself, "Pegasus has died."

Pegasus was winged steed of the heroes in Greek mythology. The dream helped Dan accept the death of his need to get high. Instead of taking flight, he needed to walk on the earth—not as a hero but as a man. The death of Pegasus signified death of the hero.

Death imagery in dreams leads us to reflect on dying, loss, and mortality. Joseph Henderson and Maud Oakes wrote:

> [T]he subject of death and resurrection … is a subject which defies our ever finding the ultimate truth but one around which cluster a variety of symbolic representations by which the living have sought to approach the end of life in a meaningful way…. If we may postulate that the fear of death is basically fear of the unknown, there would seem to be no limits to the images of foreboding or hope which can be projected by a fearful ego into it…. Whenever we find the theme of death, we find that it is never seen to stand alone as a final act of annihilation. Apart from extreme forms of pathological depression…, death is universally found to be part of a cycle of death and rebirth, or to be the condition necessary to imagine transcendence of life in an experience of resurrection. Somewhere between the myths of death and rebirth and the myths of death and destruction, we find abundant evidence for another theme—the theme of initiation. Initiation provides the archetypal pattern by which the psyche … is enabled to make a transition from one stage of development to another…. (Henderson & Oakes, 1963, pp. 3–4)

We observe death-rebirth themes in the Dream of the Graveyard and the Garden (Chapter Three); A Dream about Death and Bereavement (Chapter Three); the Dream of the Crossroads and the Dead Bear (Chapter Four); the Dream of the Speakeasy and the Knife Fight with Desmond (Chapter Six); the Dream of Isidor, the Heart Attack, and the Competent Woman (Chapter Nine); the Dream of the Black Skull (Chapter Eleven); and the Dream of Radiance (Chapter Twelve).

Initiation is the experience of separation, liminality, and reintegration. We pass through transformative ordeals involving courageous endurance of trials that generate new vision and renewed sense of purpose. Jung noted the significance of rites of initiation, transformation mysteries, mystery religions, and how "modern men have absolutely nothing to compare with this." However, "The whole symbolism of initiation rises up, clear and unmistakable, in the unconscious contents" (Jung, 1966 [1928], par. 385). From this, I infer that dreams impart to us a series of initiation symbols marking progressive stages of our evolution in consciousness.

## Journey

The quest or journey is a central theme in many dreams. The journey depicts our movement forward into the future, and is evident in symbols of winding roads, ascending a mountain, crossing rivers and streams, and travelling by car, bus, train, bicycle, or other vehicle. It may appear in images of vacations, pilgrimages, and quests, or in images depicting aging and the course of time. These images heighten awareness of our passage through the life cycle, and reflect how our life structures are forming and changing. The journey depicts the process of transformation.

Arthur, a 62-year-old divorced man, was re-entering the world of dating. He dreamed:

> I'm crossing a street in Manhattan, walking awkwardly, wondering if cars will stop. I observe donkeys and horses riding on a bus. On the bus there's also a man who looks like Sean Connery or Harrison Ford, an Indiana Jones type. A young couple is also on the bus.

Walking awkwardly reminded Arthur of not being graceful or confident with women, and feeling clumsy. Donkeys and horses reminded him of being a workhorse in his profession. Donkeys are beasts of burden and reminded him of drudgery; they also reminded Arthur of the child's game "pin the tail on the donkey," in which you're blindfolded and must find your way without being able to see. This is an apt metaphor for the journey, where we must at times walk blindly, in the dark about our direction. Movie celebrities Sean Connery and Harrison Ford, and the adventure heroes they portrayed, James Bond (agent 007) and Indiana Jones, were action figures, representing the dashing, debonair, sexy, heroic side of Arthur he was trying to get in touch with. The young couple reminded him of his longing to return to the state of married union. Donkeys, workhorses, lovers, and action heroes were travelling within the same vehicle, part of Arthur's journey forward.

The Dream of Isidor (Chapter Nine) begins with this image:

> I'm travelling in a foreign country and don't know where I am or what my destination is. I get off a bus somewhere and walk around the streets.

This example captures the disoriented quality of many dreams, the feeling of being on a journey, in transition, lost, searching for something that is still unknown.

## The Dream of Submerged Cars

Luke, a 46-year-old man, dreamed:

> I'm at work. I go outside a parking lot, but I can't find my car any-where. I have to go give a presentation so I need to find my car. I notice some people driving cars off a steep ramp into deep water. Some resur-face; others do not. As I continue searching for my car, I get lost. I run down a steep hill and start sliding as if I'm on skates. Then I'm lost on a street. I stop in a house where I know some people.

Sliding downhill reminded Luke of reaching midlife, accompanied by concern that he was "letting things slide" in his life, and fear that he was on "the downward side of the slope." This reminded Luke of aging and the urgency of making needed changes. Being on skates portrayed loss of control, a recurring experience during an extended journey. Driving cars into the water reminded him of delving deeper into the unconscious, and doing so deliberately. Some cars don't resurface, suggesting the need for prolonged immersion. The feeling of being lost is again portrayed vividly. In dreams, we're like Odys-seus on his long journey, his seemingly endless wanderings.

Homer's Odyssey is the story of a series of ordeals, but it's also "a return, a coming back to where one started" (Edinger, 1994b, p. 104). Odysseus passed through various "confrontations with the unconscious ... that he had to meet and deal with effectively if he was to reach his home in Ithaca" (p. 104). He faced battles with fluctuating triumphs and defeats, becoming inflated by victory, at other times humbled, recognizing the limits of his ego's power in a world of competing individuals. Odysseus visited the realm of the Lotus Eaters, which represents the way we vegetate with food, drugs, or television, or become ensnared in the enchanting, slothful ease of the unconscious, fascinated by dream imagery for its own sake, without dynamic action in our waking lives. Odysseus also vanquished the one-eyed Cyclops, a symbol of overcoming single vision, an inflexible viewpoint, and learning to see with multiple perspectives. Odysseus visited an island where the enchantress Circe used drugs and magic to turn men into pigs. Odysseus avoided this fate when the god Hermes appeared and gave him an antidote to Circe's drug, a plant called moly, representing salvation, akin to the golden flower of alchemy (Edinger, 1994b, pp. 108–109). The spiritual medicine of the unconscious helps us develop the better parts of our nature, aiding us when we wash ashore on Circe's island and encounter pigs, or find ourselves transforming into someone obstinate or greedy.

A pivotal scene of the *Odyssey* is the Nekyia, Odysseus's journey through the underworld, the land of the dead, where "he was to consult the spirit of the dead sage Teiresias as to how to make his way safely home" (Edinger, 1994b, p. 110). Through dreamwork, we journey deeply inward to find our emotional and spiritual compass. Dreams bring the guidance of Teiresias, the blind oracle and seer, the truth teller, symbol of night vision, the clarity that shines brightly from within the unconscious. The theme of the journey to the underworld is found in literary works such as *The Divine Comedy*, *Faust*, and *Moby Dick*, and it's also found in many dreams—for example, the Dream of Catacombs, Bugs, and the Steady Firemen (Chapter Seven); the Dream of the Bunker and the Psychotic Killer (Chapter Seven); and the Dream of the Church, the Pagan Altar, and the Sacrifice (Chapter Four).

## The Dream of the Lost Wallet and the Border Crossings

Paolo, a teacher going through a contentious job loss, dreamed:

> *I'm at school teaching a class. Students start to drift away and I try to draw the class together—to no avail. Everybody drifts off. Nobody*

*is coming back to class. I walk around trying to round the students up. I also notice that I've lost my jacket and some spare shoes that I left somewhere. It starts to rain. There are huge pools of water everywhere. I pass through a portal. Now I'm lost on the trails, in the woods. Next thing I know I'm outside the school property and have crossed the border into Canada. I have only $40 cash in my pocket, no wallet, ID, or credit cards. Prostitutes on the street are trying to hook up with me for cash. It's a Hades-like scene, a hell realm of hustlers and penniless people. I see a guy wearing my tweed jacket but he denies stealing it. A blonde woman listens to my story and takes me up to a desk or gate. An old, leathery-looking man, very ancient and small, looks at me. He looks like Yoda from Star Wars. His eyes become mystical and he says to me, "A beautiful soul." He seems to want to help as he hears my plight. He tries to read the lines on my foot like a palmist. I pull away and say, "I don't have time for this. I have to get back across the border to find my students and explain what happened to me and why I suddenly disappeared." Suddenly, the old man transforms into a beautiful, blonde, Russian woman. She is crying, saying that I rejected her. I say, "No, I really appreciate what you've done for me." We hug each other, and she gets me over the border. I end up in a grocery story where I find that I now have my wallet and cell phone and can call my principal to tell him what happened to me.*

This dream depicted a journey over the border, into the seedy underworld, where Paolo was stripped of his persona, and separated from his students. Crossing the border is a symbol of liminality, being betwixt and between, in the transitional state of uncertainty and role confusion of an initiate going through a rite of passage. Losing his shoes, jacket, and wallet represented losing his income, his identity, and his security. It represented Paolo's fear of being indigent, of losing his house if he couldn't make the payments. Finding a man wearing his tweed jacket reflected heightened anxiety about job loss; in the dream Paolo was replaced by someone, who assumed his teacher persona. The rain and pools of water represented waves of sadness and grief. Yoda, the wise old man, was psychopomp and gatekeeper, validating Paolo's beautiful soul, voicing the inner support of the unconscious in the face of his defeat. Paolo then actively stated his desire to return to his work and his students. At that moment of Paolo's commitment, the old man transformed into the blonde Russian, the anima, who aided Paolo's second border crossing, his return from liminality. She represented a drive for emotional connection. The dream suggested that by embracing his rejected feeling function, Paolo would return from the underworld and recover his identity, and there would finally be a homecoming. Love, Eros, and passion accelerate the evolutionary journey. These are the gifts we can bring back from the underworld.

> The purpose of the descent into the Underworld is to gain something that is missing in the upper world, some piece of information, some wisdom... . Once the ego has had an encounter with the transpersonal standpoint it is transformed. (Edinger, 1994b, p. 116)

Odysseus's journey seemed endless. At one point, his soldiers stole the cattle of the sun, and their punishment was furious storms that stripped Odysseus down to nothing as he lost his last ship and all his men. We see this stripping down portrayed in imagery of homelessness—for example, in the Dream of the Homeless Wanderer (Chapter Four), and the Dream of the Teenyboppers, Homeless Men, and Caretakers (Chapter Two).

Odysseus received hospitality from the Phaeacians, who "agreed to help him home by providing one of their miracle ships that guided themselves" (Edinger, 1994b, p. 120). The Phaeacians asked Odysseus to proclaim his name, his country, his people and his city, so their ship could take him there. Then, with no further delay or impediment, Odysseus swiftly reached Ithaca, landing at a harbour with a long-leafed olive tree and a pleasant, shadowy cave containing jars of stone where bees stored honey, and with ever-flowing springs. Proclaiming our identity is an act of self-definition, setting our own course, choosing our destination. We saw this in the Dream of the Lost Wallet and the Border Crossings, where Paolo proclaimed his desire to return to his students. Eventually we dream of homecoming, to the cave with jars of honey and healing springs. We'll see this in the Dream of the Rundown Shack and the Cosy Cottage (Chapter Nine). Also, recall how Luke's Dream of Submerged Cars reached closure when he arrived at a house with familiar people.

## House

The rites of passage of the wandering hero eventually conclude with a return home to a specific place, symbolized in dreams by a house. Dream images of a house, home, building, or apartment represent the personality, our inner structure, our life edifice. A house represents organization within the self, and elements of stability and continuity over time. The house unifies spirit and matter, connecting our potentiality and aspirations to our actual, embodied experiences and memories. The house or home also represents the emotional atmosphere of the person, couple, or family that dwells in it. I often ask, "What does this particular house or home remind you of?" It's very common to dream of the family home of our childhood, representing our deepest roots and origins, a place that always exists inside us, our core structure. Our childhood home symbolizes the formative environment from which we emerged, and often represents central inner attitudes and values. See the Dream of the House at Lake Tahoe (Chapter Three); the Dream of the House, the Spider's Web, and the Old Man's Daughters (Chapter Nine); the Dream of the Desert and the House by the Water (Chapter Nine); and the Dream of a Wildcat in the House (Chapter Six).

Specific areas of a house are meaningful. The ground floor of a house represents the conscious ego state. Upper floors imply mental life, thinking, and the higher planes of existence. In the Dream of the Staircase (Chapter Two), set in a white, suburban house, a man discovers an upper floor symbolizing emergent spiritual potentials.

## The Dream of the Apple House and the Saloon

Osha, an unemployed business executive, was struggling with her lack of motivation to look for a new job.

> It's night. I'm going to the apple house. I'm lost. Then I find the entrance. I see a two story apartment complex, a big building and a smaller one behind it. On the ground floor there's a saloon, an old-fashioned place full of people well dressed, men in aprons. It's not a cosy place like the place in back, the apple house. This is a place for men.

Osha said, "I've dreamed about the apple house several times before. It reminds me of a place of wisdom and retreat, a hideaway. It's a place where you go to leave the world. It reminds me of the way I never fit in. It's important to me that I don't fit in. I have a certain disdain for the world. I don't *want* to be part of the world. "

I said, "You keep returning to the apple house; it's comfortable and safe. It represents an attitude that's preventing you from finding a job, your fear that there's no place where you'll belong and feel accepted. The saloon with well-dressed people reminds me of having a job and working in a corporate environment."

She said, "It's a loud and raucous place where people are always bumping up against each other. It reminds me of how I feel spit on by men in the workplace."

"This saloon is formal, not a cosy place. It's a place where working women have to compete in a man's world. I think the dream is saying that you can inhabit both houses, your place of introspection, and the saloon, where you find your place in the world." Several weeks later, Osha received a job offer and returned to work.

## The Dream of Tiny Dinosaurs

Dreams occurring in a cellar or basement of a house often portray unconscious contents that need integration—emotions, memories, anger, or sexual feelings and impulses. For example, Jeffrey, a young man who had been celibate for several years, dreamed:

> *I'm in the basement of a house. I find a bag filled with tiny, miniature fossilized dinosaurs. They're starting to come back to life.*

Primal reptilian energies that Jeffrey had minimized were beginning to stir, heralding renewal and rebirth.

## Animals

Each animal is its own archetype, a different expression of instinctual wisdom. Think of lion, raven, giraffe, eagle, rhino, shark, monkey, donkey, gorilla, vulture, mouse, ostrich, spider, stingray, bear, piranha, wolf, elephant, snail. In medieval alchemy, the dog was a symbol of fierce, aggressive libido. For me personally, a dog represents loyalty, humility, protectiveness, and a pack-oriented wisdom.

## The Dream of the Pregnant Horse
## and the Grey-haired Woman

Laura, a woman with several children, dreamed:

> *I'm helping a black, pregnant horse. It is not giving birth yet. It's sick*
> *or injured and needs help. An older woman with grey hair helps me*
> *put hot packs on its back. We give it an injection, and it calms way*
> *down. We put it out in the meadow. The woman says, "We have to*
> *look out for ivy, and deadly nightshade." I realized there was deadly*
> *nightshade in the meadow. She said the horses were in danger and*
> *needed to be moved. We got in the car. A large ram stepped out in front*
> *of the car and wouldn't move. It stood looking into the car at us. We*
> *drove on, and the ram was following us. It was going to charge. She*
> *and the ram looked at each other. There was an understanding that the*
> *ram needed help. She put her hands on it. I woke up.*

The pregnant horse reminded Laura of possibility, newness, burgeoning life. The sick horse symbolized the wounded self, her depressed, discouraged feelings. Healing the sick pregnant horse reminded her of healing her own conflicted feelings about motherhood. She said, "The older woman is me in the future. She has wisdom; she's experienced, calm, a crone."

I said, "She puts her hands on the depressed horse, like a healer. You are healing from within."

I asked Laura about ivy. She said, "I hate it. It reminds me of aversion, and feeling powerless. Nightshade is a poisonous plant. My anger is poisonous. It represents my unexpressed anger."

The ram reminded Laura of an animal that can get into tight places and walk a narrow ledge. She said, "It won't budge; it's stubborn. That reminds me of how I need to change my parenting style. I tend to be obstinate and inflexible."

I said, "The ram may also represent being firm as a parent, holding your ground. The ram is a symbol of dynamic self-assertion. The horns of the ram also remind me of an evolutionary spiral."

Laura was stirred by this interpretation, saying, "I've been stuck on the horns of a dilemma. I feel like I'm so bossy and stubborn, but sometimes as a parent you just have to be that way. The spiralling horns remind me that my consciousness as a parent is constantly evolving."

## The Dream of Skinny Snakes and a Python

A 44-year-old man named Evan was depressed about his slow corporate career advancement and was somewhat angry at the world, but he was striving to remain motivated. He also complained that his marriage lacked sexual aliveness. He dreamed:

> I've returned to my parents' house where I'm staying in a room out in back, maybe a basement room. Someone else had been staying here and the place is a mess, a pit. As I look around I see rotting food and a pile of magazines. It's a magazine for snake enthusiasts called Python Owner. Nearby, I see a cardboard box filled with snakes. Some are small and skinny. At least one is larger, maybe a python.

The snakes discarded in a box represented Evan's feeling that his sexuality had been discarded in his marriage. But he became aware that he himself was a snake enthusiast. Small and skinny snakes represented the part of him that felt puny and deflated. A python is a large snake with a lot of life force. It represented an evolutionary power, an awakening libido, his striving for more connection with his wife, as well as the activation of energetic professional initiative. The python also represented his resentments toward his wife and several predatory business rivals and competitors—resentments that were becoming venomous, consuming him, swallowing him whole. Evan said, "The python reminds me of my perception that other people are trying to devour me, and that they have all the power. But if I'm a python owner, then I also have power."

## The Dream of Two Lions

Several months later Evan dreamed:

> I'm in my house where I notice that there's been an add-on outside our bedroom window. Jutting out from the house there's a long wooden sealed cage for two large cats, a male and female lion or puma. They're fairly large cats. One of the cats gets out, and I press an intercom button trying to call my dad for help.

The two big cats were a mating pair that represented an instinctual, mammalian intelligence. Edinger (1985) noted that the lion represents "fiery energies of instinct" (p. 19). According to von Franz (1977), "Wherever the lion appears you know that the personality is confronted with strong passionate impulses, desires, passions, and affects.... A lion can also represent rage" (p. 38). This last detail was relevant to Evan, who had faced some issues of anger management in his workplace. He also felt angry that he wasn't as financially successful as his father, a prosperous dentist. Yet, maybe he could be a powerful lion, just like his father. In alchemy, there's a recurring theme in which "Two lions are joined into one.... Conquest of the lions is difficult and full of dangers, but ... it should nevertheless be carried out" (Fabricius, 1994, p. 48). The lion is a symbol of "male strength and ferocity" (p. 54). It represents

> a crescendo of persecutory anxiety and fear of being destroyed, but also the imminence of rebirth.... . The lion's mane is the same as the beard of the old father king.... . The aggressive position of the old lion father defending his throne is seen from the position of the advancing son, whose aim is to kill the lion and eat him up, thereby acquiring leonine strength and magical powers.... . Strength is the essence of the lion.... . His authority and independence are undisputed. The strength of the lion expresses the energy of a fire now under control and harnessed to useful ends.... . In alchemy, the lion symbolizes the father-king." (Fabricius, 1994, pp. 61–62)

Another theme noted by Fabricius is the "alchemical drinking of the lion's blood to gain his strength" (p. 62). Evan's dream symbolized initiation through gaining the strength and authority of the lion-father, and awakening the fire of his own passions. Over the next several years, Evan's energy, hard work, and initiative were noted by his employers, and he was eventually promoted to a position in senior management. He integrated the python and the lions.

The personal meaning of animal figures appearing in dreams is always worth exploring in depth. von Franz wrote:

> One must never hurt the helpful animal in fairy tales.... . Disobedience leads to trouble. You may temporarily disobey the advice of the helpful fox or wolf or cat. But if you basically go against it..., if any animal gives you advice and you don't

follow it, then you are finished... . [O]bedience to one's own inner instinctual being is ... more essential than anything else. (von Franz, 1980a, pp. 119–120)

Recall the Dream of the Wildcat, the Dream of the Sleeping Wolf, and the Dream of the Pig (all in Chapter Two), and the Dream of the Crossroads and the Dead Bear (Chapter Four). Also see the Dream of the White Rabbit, the Black Cat, and the Black Snake in Chapter Seven. Chapter Thirteen features a series of dreams with animal symbolism. For more on this, see Neil Russack's book *Animal Guides in Life, Myth, and Dreams* (Russack, 2002).

## Elements of Nature

*Elements of nature* are archetypal, including tree, ocean, spiral, storm, fire, cave, nest, mountain, lightning, volcano. Each carries a unique and essential meaning. For example, the tree is a central archetype, symbolizing development, and the process of becoming conscious, the urge toward individuation, and toward the gradual unfoldment of potentials. It signifies the Self, that within us which is greater than the ego (von Franz, 1980a, pp. 38–39). In mythology, the symbol of the world tree represents the *axis mundi*, a point of access between earth and heaven, the profane and the sacred. Like a shaman, we can ascend and descend the world tree during visionary flights or journeys to the underworld (Allen & Sabini, 1997).

### The Dream of the Potted Tree

Serena, a single mother and graduate student, had this dream:

> I own some land in a beautiful canyon with platformed cement. There are big drops between steps; some of them are rotten. I'm going to repair them. Then I'll plant into the cement. I want to put a huge tree in. Someone gives me a cutting; it's very leafy and green. I know where I'm going to dig out the cement and plant it. It'll be gorgeous there, the centrepiece. This plant doesn't have many roots yet. It has some roots from the mother plant, but it's not strong enough yet to grow here; it's feathery, not strong. It needs to stay in a pot. A woman is making diagrams that are off centre. I'm not drawn to her plans.

The land in the beautiful canyon is a big spread and represents having room to grow. But Serena said, "Someone else made decisions here that I wouldn't have made, putting in the cement walls. That reminds me of men in my life making decisions, and not including me. It also reminds me of how I often make choices other people don't agree with—like the way I used to go swimming in a freezing-cold aqueduct. Other people thought I was crazy, but I just loved to dive in."

Cement walls reminded Serena of an unnatural way to control nature, to protect land from erosion. I said, "Cement walls interfere with your connection to the earth. But in the dream you're going to see what's really there under the cement."

She said, "There may be loss involved; it's not tidy. There could be a hollow shell."

I said, "You're peeling back hardened defences, seeing what's underneath. It's going to be lots of work, a chunk at a time—a metaphor for therapy."

The rootless tree reminded Serena of men who aren't rooted and grounded, who don't want to do housework or live with children.

I said, "You feel you have no roots in your relationships. Some of the men you've been seeing have a flashy, showy veneer, but your roots aren't being watered."

The rotten steps reminded her of feeling that "accessibility is difficult. Going down these steps is not for everybody. You have to really want to go there. That reminds me of relationships with men who aren't emotionally accessible, who only want me when it's convenient for them. I want to stop making myself so accessible to those relationships."

I said, "In that sense the cement walls represent having firmer boundaries."

Serena said, "I want to settle down, but I'm still developing my roots."

"The tree of life is present here, but it's not ready to be planted yet."

She said, "The tree wants to go in the ground so it puts out showy leaves, but it's not ready. It's so sad to see that. The plant here has put its energy in the wrong place. All my life I've put my energy into some other person, trying to win their love and approval. When I was a kid, I always had to be a straight-A student. What was I trying to prove? My greatest nightmare is to be a potted plant, languishing root bound and dying from lack of water and room. But this tree *needs* to be in a pot. It's not ready to be transplanted."

I asked, "Tell me more about feeling rootless."

"To be rooted is to belong, to contribute, to be part of a community. That's what I've never really had."

"I think the dream is saying that your tasks are to find your roots, and to find out what's underneath the hardened crust of sorrow and disappointments."

"I'm afraid it could be dead under there."

I said, "I'm interested in the dead parts of you, the deadened feelings, the parts of you that never had a chance to grow."

Serena said, "The steps are rotten, not functional. That reminds me of how I'm still dependent on the mother plant."

"It's true that you're not yet financially independent. But that's why you're going to school, to prepare yourself to work and make money. The dream also comments on your therapy; we're going down into some inaccessible areas. We need to get out our pick-axes, find the depressed parts of you, and bring the soil back to life. The dream says that this tree will be fine if its roots are cared for." The tree that will become the centrepiece was a symbol of the Self's wholeness and totality, and Serena's growth of personality. It also represented her dream of becoming the centrepiece of a man's affection, not an afterthought.

## Water

Many dreams contain imagery of water, another archetypal element of nature. We dream of swimming in the ocean, riding waves, moving at great speed across the water, dissolving into water, riding rough seas, or watching large tidal waves coming in. Each of these is an archetypal situation. We dream we're far out at sea, or heading toward shore. We swim though stormy tempests, wade in shallow water, test the waters, get our feet wet, nearly drown, float blissfully, immerse ourselves in water like baptism, or barely keep our head above water. Each of these images has different connotations. Water dreams portray our present inner condition, our current emotional experience, and the state of the unconscious. See the Dream of Immersion and Spiritual Cleansing

(Chapter Nine); the Dream of the Rose (Chapter Two); the Dream of the Blind Date and the Shy Weightlifter (Chapter Thirteen); the Dream of Submerged Cars (this chapter); the Dream of the Maggots (Chapter Four); and the Dream of the New Year's Eve Party, Rolondo, and the Lake in the Desert (Chapter Six). For an example combining animals and the elements of fire and water, see the Dream of the Salamander (Chapter Seven).

## Planetary Archetypes

In astrology, planets are viewed as archetypal symbols.

Sun symbolizes the king and queen, the solar self, conscious personal identity and self-expression, our creative emanation.

Moon symbolizes the mother, feelings, nurturing, emotional attachment, cycles and phases of change.

Mercury symbolizes thinking, language, speech, communication, Hermes, the Messenger.

Venus symbolizes Aphrodite, the anima, love and beauty, art, music, harmony, graceful form.

Mars symbolizes the hero or heroine, the warrior, athlete, competitor, or adversary. Mars signifies dynamic will, self-assertion, initiative, and motivation.

Jupiter is the archetypal teacher, guide, priest, philosopher, and pilgrim. Jupiter is also fortuna, symbol of blessings and fortunate opportunities.

Saturn symbolizes the father, work, structure, responsibility, the senex archetype. Saturn represents the reality principle, social adaptation and conformity, and manifestation through concrete form.

Uranus symbolizes the trickster, rebel, revolutionary, inventor, scientist, Prometheus, revealer of fire and innovation. Uranus is the archetype of change, scientific discovery, technology, and social or systemic reorganization.

Neptune symbolizes the seer, mystic, visionary, suffering saviour, or martyr. Neptune can also appear as the addict or alcoholic, or the delusional madman or madwoman.

Pluto symbolizes death and rebirth, endings and renewal. Pluto is Hades, lord of death. He can appear as the dictator, the control freak, or in images or acts of violence or brutality. Pluto is Shiva, deity of irrevocable change. Pluto is the awakener of depth power, *kundalini*, the regenerative energies of the unconscious. Pluto often manifests as the shadow, the encounter with evil, immorality, criminal elements, impersonal power, or scary dream characters.

Awareness of the cyclical movement of the planets makes it possible to anticipate the periodic appearance of specific archetypes in dreams and in waking life. This is the basis of personal evolution through the study of astrological transits (Bogart, 2002). I'll limit myself to one brief example. Some years ago the planet Pluto was closely conjunct my natal Mars—the planet of warriors and gladiators doing battle, clashing, and sometimes being injured. At that time I tore a ligament in my foot while playing basketball and hobbled around on it for more than a year. I had to consciously live the Mars experience of pain, swelling, and inflammation. Simultaneously, a small planetoid called Chiron approached conjunction to my natal Sun. Chiron was the wise centaur whose injured foot made him a symbol of the wounded healer. My sore, swollen foot and limp were symptoms of Chiron's wound. I tried to receive the injury as an initiation. I couldn't run, but it made me sit still and meditate more, and continue my writing. I felt deeply touched and imprinted by the Chiron archetype. It's fascinating to note the correspondences between planetary transits and the appearance of archetypal characters and experiences.

## Temple, Gods, Monsters, Mythical Creatures

There are countless other archetypes:

Structures such as a temple, church, cathedral, or pyramid represent "the place of vision and power" (Metzner, 1998, pp. 223–248). Dreams with these symbols evoke a feeling of wholeness, integrity, a sense of connection to our personal centre and to the centre of the universe. Each of these is a place of the sacred, a citadel, a sanctuary. For example, a man named José decided to resign from a job involving long-distance auto-commuting to work closer to home and to devote himself to completing a novel. He dreamed:

> *I'm in the commuter's lane, stuck in traffic. I pull off the road and turn into a driveway where I notice a cabin in the woods. A crew is excavating an underground church that has just been unearthed. Beautiful stained-glass windows are visible.*

The dream affirmed José's decision to leave the commuter's lane to discover a new road, where he found a church representing the edifice of his own creative work.

Gods and goddesses of various religions are each archetypal symbols—for example, Yahweh and his judgment, revelations, and commandments; or Dionysus, symbol of freedom, ecstasy, wildness. We'll encounter Dionysus in Chapter Eleven.

Hindu gods and goddesses each represent specific archetypal qualities: Brahma, the creator; Vishnu, the sustainer; Shiva, the destroyer and god of change; Ganesh, remover of obstacles; Rama, the virtuous king; Sita, Rama's loving wife; Hanuman, the devoted, selfless servant. Each is a unique archetype, as are the many Buddhas and bodhisattvas, such as Guatama Buddha, Tara, Guru Rinpoche (Padmasambhava), Manjushri, Milarepa, and Kuan Yen (bodhisattva of infinite compassion).

Monsters and mythical creatures are archetypal, for example, werewolves, vampires, Frankenstein, and Medusa—the Gorgon, the devouring monster who turns to stone anyone who gazes upon her face. We meet the cold, rejecting Medusa in others, or we ourselves may become possessed by this archetype. Both men and women have an inner Medusa. Another example is the Hydra, a many-headed water monster, which represents a situation with many facets and complexities that can't be easily subdued. The mythical unicorn is a symbol of limitless possibilities.

## Rumplestiltskin

Rumplestiltskin is a notable character from fairytales. He's similar to a leprechaun or troll, but he's a very unpleasant and boastful figure, a manipulator. He's meddlesome, and makes shady bargains; he's always up to mischief. A miller brags that his daughter can spin straw into gold. The king demands that she prove this claim and locks her in a room with a large pile of straw. The daughter doesn't know what to do, but she's visited by a little man who offers to help her with the spinning, in exchange for her necklace, and the ring from her finger. When she has nothing left to give, he demands later delivery of her first-born child. The king is impressed by the girl's ability to weave gold, and offers to marry her. When the young queen soon gives birth, the little man shows up to claim the child, and gives her three days to guess his unusual name. Otherwise, she'll have to give him her child, a hideous thought. The queen sends out a messenger, who eventually learns the little man's name and rushes back to tell the queen, so that on the third day she's able to say Rumplestiltskin. This infuriates the little man, who storms off in a huff and steps into a hole, and pulls on his legs until he tears himself in two. When we say the magic name that frees us of enslavement to anyone who controls or torments us, not only do we dispatch with the little pest, but in the process we also learn to spin the straw of our lives into gold.

## Celebrities and Artists

Certain celebrities and historical personages are particularly strong carriers of archetypal presence—for example, Napoleon Bonaparte, Richard Nixon, Humphrey Bogart, Abraham Lincoln, Winston Churchill, Mahatma Gandhi, Jimi Hendrix. They are human beings who achieve a mythical status that makes them archetypal. The individuated person fulfils his or her own archetype. For example, the Dream of the Silver Man (Chapter 4) evoked the figure of singer-actor Tom Waits, whose sly, chironic personality exudes humour, wounded heart, and pathos.

The artist archetype has been embodied by Michelangelo, Pablo Picasso, Vincent Van Gogh, William Shakespeare, James Joyce, Georgia O'Keeffe, Jack Kerouac, Ingmar Bergman, Andrés Segovia, Joni Mitchell, and other geniuses. See the Dream of Meeting Duke Ellington at a Funeral (Chapter Four); Two Dreams of a Promethean Artist (Chapter Nine); and the Dream of the New Year's Eve Party, Rolondo, and the Lake in the Desert (Chapter Six). The Dream of the Silver Man (Chapter Four) depicted a shimmering Mercurius figure representing identification with the artist archetype and a capacity to merge with the creative principle.

## Sacred Marriage and the Syzygy

In alchemy, *hierosgamos*, the sacred marriage, symbolizes the joining of opposites. In the second Rosarium picture, the king meets the queen with a dove hovering above them (Figure 3). The dove is a symbol of the goddess Aphrodite, and represents the kindling of "an ardent desire" (Edinger, 1994a, p. 47). A spiritual impetus

*Figure 3. Second Rosarium image: The royal marriage.*

draws two people together, sanctifies the relationship, and bestows an enlivening Eros. The image of a king and queen meeting depicts how two wilful individuals—crowned and entitled—meet and try to realize their union. In this book, we've seen several examples of how dreamwork aids couples trying to achieve this divine marriage; for example, see the Dream of the Scorpion. This Rosarium image also depicts the process of *separatio*, "the original act of creation that separated light from darkness.... [C]onsciousness has been born" (Edinger, 1994a, p. 44). Many creation myths describe the separation of earth from sky, sun from moon. The Sun and Moon archetypes in human consciousness represent *all* pairs of opposites.

The *androgyne*, the union of male and female, appears frequently in dreams, as we'll see later. The *syzygy*, an image of lovers or a divine pair, is the archetype of paired opposites. The syzygy represents the path of achieving wholeness through love, partnership, and marriage. Syzygies include king and queen, Tristan and Isolde, Shiva and Shakti, Lennon and McCartney, Sartre and de Beauvoir, John and Yoko. All couples are divine syzygies in the making. But to accomplish this goal, both partners need consciousness of the opposing forces within themselves, within their spouse or lover, and the interplay of opposing forces between them. In most couples, there's a union of opposites such as thinking/feeling, introvert/extravert, sensation/intuition, financial-worldly/spiritual-mystical, orderly neat freak/disorderly slob.

The syzygy represents the union of paired opposites. Thus, this archetype governs the process of achieving wholeness in the personality through formation of conscious polarities. We can achieve this through the Dream Mandala technique, discussed in Chapter Ten. From the tension of opposites, the spark of consciousness ignites. Jung wrote:

> The syzygy is immediately comprehensible as the psychic prototype of all divine couples... . Although "wholeness" seems at first to be nothing but an abstract idea (like anima and animus), it is nevertheless empirical in so far as it is anticipated by the psyche in the form of spontaneous or autonomous symbols. These are the quaternity or mandala symbols, ... *symbols of unity and totality*... . Wholeness is thus an objective factor that confronts the subject independently of him, like anima or animus... . [W]holeness lays claim to a position and a value superior to those of the syzygy. The syzygy seems to represent at least a substantial portion of it, if not actually two halves of the totality formed by the royal brother-sister pair, and hence the tension of opposites from which the divine child is born as the symbol of unity. (Jung, 1959, pars. 59, 64)

## Feminine Archetypes: Daughter/Lover, Mother, Amazon, and Medium/Wise Woman

The varied aspects of our experiences of ourselves as men and women, male and female are symbolized as archetypal gods and goddesses. At the inception of analytical psychology, a rich panoply of male and female archetypes was identified, beginning when Toni Wolff, Jung's muse, lover, and colleague, defined four aspects of the archetypal feminine: maiden/daughter/lover, mother, amazon, and medium/wise woman (Wolff, 1956). Here are brief descriptions, drawing on Edward Whitmont's account of Wolff's typology (Whitmont, 1969).

The eternal experiences of women can be represented as a fourfold grouping of feminine archetypes consisting of two pairs, one contrasting youthful and mature approaches to relatedness (maiden and mother), the other contrasting introverted and extraverted attitudes (amazon and wise woman). These constitute a powerful family of archetypes describing two syzygies that together form a quaternity, a fourfold totality.

The maiden represents the orientation to love and relationships, flirtation, and difficulty in commitment to permanence in relationships. She appears as the love goddess, priestess, seductress, nymph, harlot. A central symbol is Aphrodite, goddess of sexuality, beauty, romance, Eros, pleasure.

The mother embodies a collective orientation, protective behaviours, sheltering, nurturing. A central symbol is Demeter, earth mother, goddess of nature, fertility, childbirth, and raising children. In her form as the terrible mother, she may be destructively devouring, rejecting, emotionally withholding, or punishing.

The amazon or heroine represents a woman's emphasis on strivings and ambitions, cultural values, and external performance. The amazon is self-contained and independent; she's a comrade, a competitor. She can also take the form of the career-oriented woman "who is insensitive to relationship needs and emotional values" (Whitmont, 1969, p. 180). A central symbol is Athena, goddess of wisdom, who values education, career, intellectual pursuits, and social justice. Another amazon goddess is Artemis, who is practical, athletic, adventurous, and loves nature, animals, and the outdoors (Woolger & Woolger, 1994).

The crone, wise woman, medium, or prophetess symbolizes immersion in the inner psychic atmosphere. She's open to the intangible, but may be oblivious to concrete reality, and absorbed in subjective visions. Whitmont (1969) noted that the medium "may be a source of inspiration or confusion" (p. 180). She mediates the inner world, but "she is in danger of inflation and of losing her own individuality and ability to discriminate"; she has difficulty pushing herself into external activity (p. 180). The wise woman is spiritual, mystical, clairvoyant, and is a source of healing for self and others (Woolger & Woolger, 1994, p. 120). A central symbol is Persephone, the maiden abducted into the underworld who became the consort of Hades. She represents awareness of the spirit world, the occult, and matters associated with death

(p. 120). Persephone is a symbol of transformation through suffering. She accepts her destiny of living half the year in the underworld with Hades, but she also spends half the year free in the world of the living. She represents initiation through the wounding of our virginal innocence, and allowing the bonds of love to be freely chosen. She brings the wisdom that love is loyalty to a power greater than the ego. We all have to make some accommodation to Hades, as we'll likely be visiting his domain from time to time.

Two other notable female archetypes are Hera (also known as Juno), goddess of monogamy, fidelity, and feminine power in marriage; and Vesta (also called Hestia), goddess of the hearth and the sacred fire, symbol of personal sacrifice, dedication, and altruism. Hestia is also the temple prostitute, goddess of sexual healing and mysteries; she appeared in Karl's Dream of the Prostitute-Mother-Transsexual (Chapter Two).

These archetypes represent complementary aspects of the feminine principle. For example, let's compare the paths of the maiden and the amazon, embodied by Aphrodite and Artemis, or Diana, the huntress. Aphrodite is the woman defined by love and the play of attraction. She is the eternal innocence and pristine beauty of the divine feminine, its attractive radiance and openness. Diana is the goddess who roams in the forest, and represents breaking the shackles of constricting, civilizing forces, fighting oppression, and finding renewal through relationship with the earth, animals, and all living things. In Chapter Eight, the Dream of the Bed, Princess Fergie, and the Child contains symbols of all four archetypes—maiden, mother, amazon, and wise woman.

Men, as well as women, can be carriers of these goddess energies. They can be playful and erotic. They can be nurturers and caregivers. Both men and women need to cultivate independence, value education, seek healing in nature, and explore inner spiritual mysteries.

### Masculine Archetypes: Son/Lover, Father/King, Hero/Warrior, and Wise Man/Philosopher

Jungians define a comparable fourfold typology of male gods and archetypes: son/lover, father/king, hero/warrior, and wise man/philosopher. This male typology was discussed by Whitmont (1969) and by Moore & Gillette (1994).

The son or lover is a man searching for relationships and his own individuality. The lover represents the youthful male unconcerned with authority or permanence. He appears as Adonis, Peter Pan, the knight errant, the puer aeternus. The lover experiences both the joy and painfulness of life and love. He also signifies the unconventional, artistic, creative part of a person, living with passion and feeling, and a quest for sensual experience (Moore & Gillette, 1994).

The father/king is the symbol of structure, order, *logos*, reason, and an emphasis on hierarchy and law. He's the leader, lord, and protector, appearing in myth as Kronos, Zeus, Odin, the primordial man, Anthropos, Adam. The father maintains order, manifests fertility and blessing, and represents feeling calm, centred, and a sense of inner authority (Moore & Gillette, 1994). The king may also take the form of an abusive father or tyrant.

The hero/warrior/soldier fights, battles, strives, and exercises his will and drive for power. The Warrior symbolizes instinctual energy, intense experience, outpouring of life force, and awareness of imminent death and the fragility of life. He symbolizes decisiveness, aggressiveness, training, skill, power, bravery and valour, self-control, loyalty to a cause, a people, a task, or a nation, and activity organized around central commitments, ideals, and a sense of duty (Moore & Gillette, 1994).

The wise man/philosopher/magician often appears as shaman, healer, or medicine man. This is the scholar, teacher, sage, seer, philosopher, embodied in such figures as Teiresias, Moses, Socrates, Merlin. The magician is an initiate of secret, hidden knowledge and is the wise ritual elder who guides processes of transformation, initiating others.

These four male and female archetypes represent the eternal experiences of men and women as we evolve through stages of the life cycle, from childhood to old age. The symbolism of these archetypes appears frequently in dreams.

### The Dream of Uriah Heap, the Cathedral, and the Kung Fu Fighter

A gay man named Conrad had a dream containing this fourfold male symbolism:

*My friend Jessica bought a new house. I told her where to put things.*
*Some people were dancing, and one guy saw me and was embar-*
*rassed. I had several remote controls and was turning the music up*
*and down, messing with the maid. I asked, "Do you have an attic?*
*We have to go to the attic!" We go up. People follow us. There's*
*a huge cathedral with white pillars, a rectangular hall. Everybody*
*sits. I have to fight somebody. We're kung fu fighting. It's exhila-*
*rating. He made a lot of superfluous movements. I punched him,*
*and he fell. A cloaked figure appeared; he had red hair and red eyes*
*that burned through you. He was like a Uriah Heap character from*
*Dickens. He was dangerous, but I wasn't afraid. I pulled up next*
*to this other small guy; he was so cute. Suddenly he turned around*
*and kissed me.*

Telling his friend where to put things reminded Conrad of his gay
persona, being very talented at decorating, having a good sense of
aesthetics. Buying a house reminded him of becoming stable, settling down, commitment, something he longed for. Conrad had
many transient relationships but had never experienced settling
down with somebody. The people dancing were doing synchronized
dancing, which reminded him of line dancing at a gay country bar,
where he once had a horrible date. That reminded him of his long
history of awkward relationships.

I asked about the man who was embarrassed: "He had a self-
conscious look on his face. It's hard for me to let myself go around
other people. I'm very self-conscious. Embarrassment is how I feel
every day." Here dreamwork allowed us to touch a core feeling.

Conrad described the scene where he changed the volume of the
music, saying, "I was joking around, messing with the maid, enjoying myself, being the joker, a playful trickster."

"You were expressing your natural joy. But it makes me wonder if you tend to use humour as a defence against that sense of
embarrassment."

The kung fu fighting evoked the warrior archetype. Conrad said,
"As far as fighting, anger, and self-defence, I couldn't do any of this
when I was a kid. I was often called a sissy. I've always needed to
learn how to fight. I used to get beaten up and called names all the
time. I've been harassed by gay bashers. I've always been timid.
I still walk in fear that someone will attack me."

I said, "Yet in the dream you're able to assume the stance of the warrior and defeat your enemy decisively. You express the dynamic warrior energy of self-defence impeccably. I think the dream is asking you to develop the warrior part of you, and to unify it with the sensitive gay persona. In the dream, your capacity for aggression, confidence, and strength is linked to Eros and attracting love. But what about the man who is making superfluous moves?"

"He's showing off, something I'm careful not to do. But occasionally I do notice myself showing off a bit; I actually enjoy it."

"So there's a part of you that is naturally fun and extraverted that you've had to shut down because you were so afraid of people."

In the kung fu scene, Conrad said, "The man's face was menacing. It reminds me of someone who wants to beat me up. In the dream I was afraid that if I let myself get angry I could destroy the world."

"That suggests you've been suppressing your angry, aggressive drives and feelings. Who were you afraid would be destroyed by your anger?"

"My mother. I always protected her from my anger. I was everything to her. I didn't want to ever hurt her."

Conrad continued, "The smaller guy in dream was a good, clean, all-American cute guy. I wouldn't expect him to be attracted to me." The cute guy was the *male anima*, the lover, Eros, a feeling of love that appears suddenly.

The cloaked figure symbolized the shadow and the negative father. Uriah Heap is a character in Charles Dickens's book *David Copperfield*. Conrad said, "He's creepy, evil, surly, twisted. He reminds me of my family and my stepfather, who was always watching me." The dream evoked Conrad's disappointment about not receiving the blessing of his stepfather; he felt only his disapproval, never cherished or accepted. In Dickens's novel, David Copperfield is a displaced orphan; thus, he represents the vulnerable child, the archetypal son, and innocent possibility.

The cloaked figure in the dream also reminded Conrad of druids, evoking the presence of the archetypal wizard or wise man. Integrating the powerful and the vulnerable facets of himself formed the basis of a wise inner perspective, an awareness that he, the kung fu warrior, was passing through his own form of internal male initiation.

In the dream, Conrad climbed up to the attic, where he found a cathedral. This reminded him of Sacred Heart cathedral in France, "a place I felt safe and where I felt connection to all that is past." It's promising that the dream takes Conrad to this place of safety and the sacred heart. It's on an upper floor, suggesting the attainment of a higher level of consciousness, an elevated perspective. The rectangular hall is a symbol of the quaternity, symbol of emergent wholeness, balance of opposites, and individuation. "[Q]uaternity symbols ... signify stabilization through order as opposed to the instability caused by chaos" (Jung, 1959, par. 382). Thus, a new internal order was emerging. The presence of the four primary male archetypes is readily apparent in Conrad's dream, as is evident in this dream mandala.

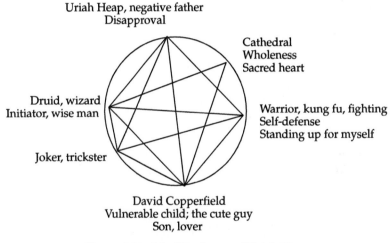

*Dream Mandala: The dream of Uriah Heap, the cathedral, and the kung fu fighter*

## Archetypes as Patterns of Transformation

Archetypes are not static entities. They are living patterns of transformation that manifest as dream symbols and shape our development. It's not enough to simply identify the archetypes in our dreams. We need to work with them, merge with them, and let them enhance our lives with their eternal meanings.

We undergo transformations in accordance with the archetypes. For example, after the birth of his first child, a man named Dennis, who had always seen himself as "a party animal," had two dreams about fathers. His developmental path was within the archetype of the father, which provided a blueprint of new protective, family-oriented roles, feelings, and behaviours that Dennis needed to integrate.

The archetype is part of our human inheritance, an instinct, an inborn tendency. It's also a guide, a signpost to change. When an archetype appears in life or in dreams we sense that many people have faced the same situations before. We feel how we're part of "the eternal life of the species." In the next chapter, we'll see how these recurring patterns of experience are embodied in dream characters and symbols that represent our personal complexes.

# CHAPTER SIX

# Unfolding the Complexes in Dreams

Dreams portray images of our central problems and conflicts, which Jung called *complexes*. Complexes are recurring feelings, thoughts, behaviours, memories, or patterns of relationship with others that become highly charged, points of maximum intensity, and "emotional preoccupations" (Storr, 1983, p. 33). A complex becomes a point of fixation and may be a source of repeated problems or suffering in our lives. When we repeatedly become angry and belligerent; when we practice and rehearse tasks but always fail to perform under pressure; when we're possessed by a need to criticize our loved ones mercilessly—we're in the grips of complexes.

Jung described a complex as "a conglomeration of psychic contents characterized by a peculiar or perhaps painful feeling-tone, something that is usually hidden from sight" (Jung, 1976 [1935], par. 99).

> What then ... is a "feeling toned complex"? It is the *image* of a certain psychic situation which is strongly accentuated emotionally and is, moreover, incompatible with the habitual attitude of consciousness. This image has a powerful inner coherence, it has its own wholeness and ... a relatively high degree of autonomy,

so that it is subject to the control of the conscious mind to only a limited extent. (Jung, (1969) [1934b], par. 201)

Early in his career, Jung used the Word Association Test to discern a person's complexes. He also found that dreams reveal these patterns of emotional organization, these autonomous personalities. Complexes are often the result of traumas or crises that we've faced, and are carriers of the most personal and wounded aspects of our life histories. Complexes become problematic when they cause us to react from past conditioning, rather than with mindfulness in the present moment, with all of its fresh possibilities. Nonetheless, a complex can resolve and unfold itself in ways that foster wholeness and aliveness. Identifying complexes shows us areas where deep transformation is needed, and possible. A complex is like a pressure point that can be lovingly touched and released, making possible a freer range of choices and behaviours. For example, in the Dream of Uriah Heap, the Cathedral, and the Kung Fu Fighter (Chapter Five), we saw Conrad's David Copperfield complex, which confined him within a victimized, persecuted self-experience. But this complex transformed within the dream into the emergence of a warrior, transforming the victim into an empowered hero. Resolving a complex, we feel the unfolding of an energy potential within us, like a great serpent releasing its coiled energy and becoming more fully expanded.

At the heart of each complex we find an archetypal pattern of transformation, which is enacted and expressed in our personal lives. James Hall explained the relationship between the archetypes and complexes:

> Archetypes themselves are not directly observable, but like a magnetic field are discernible by their influence on the visible contents of the mind, the archetypal images and personified or imaged complexes. The archetype in itself is a tendency to structure images of our experience in a particular fashion, but the archetype is not the image itself ... . There is a universal human tendency, for example, to form an image of the mother, but each individual forms a particular mother image based on this universal human archetypes .... Archetypal images differ from the images of complexes in having a more universal and generalized meaning, often with numinous affective

quality .... [E]ach complex in the personal sphere (conscious or unconscious) is formed upon an archetypal matrix in the objective psyche. At the core of every complex is an archetype. The ego is formed upon the archetypal core of the Self; behind the personal mother complex is the Great Mother archetype; the imago of the father and mother together has at its centre the archetypal image of the divine parents; and there are deep archetypal roots for the shadow and for many persona roles .... [A]ny complex that is penetrated to sufficient depth will reveal its archetypal associations. (Hall, 1983, pp. 10–13)

The primary complexes are mother and father complexes, rooted in our earliest experiences of attachment and relationship with parents. For example, recall the Dream of the Shivering Child (Chapter Three). Chapter Four featured several dream characters representing a complex about the father-son relationship: the homeless man, the lonely child, the dead bear, and the man eating thorns. Other examples include power complexes, characteristic of dominant, authoritarian, tyrant personalities; failure or inferiority complexes; somatization complexes, explored in Arnold Mindell's (1982) work on the emotional and spiritual meaning of bodily symptoms. In Chapter Seven, I describe an example of a homophobic complex, personified in the Dream of the Frenchman and the Dream of the Black Transvestite. The Dream of the Snake Woman and the Sheriff (later in this chapter) illustrates a complex related to alcohol abuse. Some people have complexes about not being able to find or sustain love; for example, see the Dream of the Bride and the Dream of the House at Lake Tahoe (both in Chapter Three). Others experience a martyr or victimization complex, repeatedly feeling hurt, abandoned, or abused by others, as the next example illustrates.

## The Dream of the Mobster

A woman named Peggy, who had many angry conflicts with people and often felt persecuted, had this dream:

> I'm lying on the ground. A man with a gun fires three shots into my leg and trunk. I say, "I'm still alive." He puts the gun to my head. I wake up.

The man reminded Peggy of a stereotypical mobster with hat and trench coat, a Mafioso. This reminded her of organized crime, a cold-blooded killer, someone who kills for money and has no feelings. I asked, "Who in your life is cold-blooded? What part of you has no feelings?"

"Part of me is judgmental, critical, and cruel, just like my mother was cruel and cold-blooded. There was no warmth in her. That's the way I feel—numb. I'm afraid to feel anything."

Being shot in the dream reminded Peggy of being a target, feeling marked or attacked by others. I asked if the fact that a man was treating her with such aggression reminded her of anything. Peggy became tearful as she told me how her father had verbally and physically assaulted her. The mobster reminded her of how much they used to hate each other. The wound around her father's violence and cruelty was the original trauma that was reactivated by her recurring interpersonal problems. This aggressive mobster personified a complex encapsulating Peggy's feelings of persecution. The mobster symbolized her abusive father, and he was the embodiment of everyone who had ever hurt her. But the mobster also represented her own dangerous, aggressive shadow. Peggy reached the pivotal insight that maybe one reason she often felt rejected was that her own belligerent behaviour caused other people to not like her. When gripped by the complex, she herself became the angry mobster who antagonized others. Underneath all of her anger, I always saw in Peggy a beautiful person longing to be loved and accepted; but her tendency to overreact made her prickly and kept others at a distance.

The mobster also embodied the archetypal animus. As we saw earlier in the chapter, the animus is a woman's complex concerning her unconscious masculinity, just as the anima is a man's complex regarding his unconscious femininity. The anima or animus complex is activated when we experience love, projection, and attraction toward a captivating other who makes us feel alive, who stirs our soul. The anima/animus is the experience of the enlivening feminine and masculine. It is felt as a fascination with a male or female figure who embodies unconscious energies that excite us and awaken the spark of aliveness, intensified feeling, or confidence and certitude. The unconscious anima/animus can also manifest as animosity that interferes with relationships and intimacy, as illustrated by the Dream of the Mobster. Anima-possessed men are grouchy and reactive, touchy and overdramatic, always feeling misunderstood. Animus-possessed women are angry and domineering, feeling that their opinions and intelligence aren't valued. I'll explore these themes further in Chapter Eight.

## The Dream of Mother and the Large Mouth

Here's a story of two dreams that were catalysts of a major life transition and aided the resolution of a mother complex. A fifty-year-old woman named Jennifer and her husband George were considering selling their house and buying a home in the country. They started to discuss the expenses and complexities this move would entail. Jennifer was fearful and hesitant, but it seemed like the right next step to take. Jennifer had two dreams that cleared the way inwardly for her to move forward with these plans.

> My mother is attacking me, sabotaging my home and office. I recall that in the dream she has no nose, only a large mouth. There are some homeless street people there who validate her attack on me. I want to get rid of her, but my husband George feels guilty about sending her away. He yells at me in front of her and treats me rudely. There's a large TV that won't turn off because the off button is broken. The plug is damaged and dangerous, so I throw the TV away. Then my brother Vince comes in, looking like he did as a teenager. I tell him mom is going to be upset about the broken TV, but he says not to bother him, he's too involved with his own depression. Then I'm sleeping in a run-down, depressed room that was arranged by my ex-husband, Fred.

The context for this dream was that Jennifer's mother had died within the previous year. She always had a difficult relationship with her mother, who was dependent on Jennifer in her final years. I asked Jennifer for her associations to the image of her mother with no nose, only a big mouth. She replied, "No nose reminds me of asthma, which I've been suffering from lately."

I said, "The big mouth reminds me of an oral type of person with intense need and emotional hunger, perhaps your own needs, but also your mother's neediness and dependency."

Jennifer said, "My mother only cared about herself. She always undermined me; she never really saw me. She was insatiably needy. She always needed more, more. When I was younger I tried to get emotional support from my mother, but eventually I realized I'd never get any. And sometimes I feel that I don't get any support from George. Meanwhile, my grown children are still very needy and depend on me financially. All around me are big mouths, people needing me to support them. But I have needs too, especially as I go through this huge transition in my life." It was interesting how George was allied with mother in the dream, and how Jennifer experienced both of them as emotionally draining. The core of the complex was the feeling of unmet emotional needs.

When I asked about her brother, Jennifer said, "Vince was a jerk. He beat me up when we were kids. The rundown place and my brother's depression remind me of the depressive atmosphere of our family when I was growing up. The broken TV I can't shut off reminds me of my mother's non-stop complaining."

The rundown, depressed room reminded Jennifer of her current emotional state. This rundown room was a place arranged by Fred, her ex-husband, with whom she originally purchased her house in the city, a place that had now become depressing to her. This detail about her ex-husband Fred was significant, because selling the house would mark the final symbolic ending of her first marriage. The homeless street people reminded Jennifer of her transition out of San Francisco, where she had lived for thirty years, and her fear of leaving and being "homeless."

## The Dream of a Wildcat in the House

The following week Jennifer had a dream in which animal intelligence illumined her path:

> A wildcat is in my house. I realize it is too large an animal to live in this house as a pet.

This dream affirmed Jennifer's plan to sell her house and relocate. The wildcat signified boldness, courage, the instinct to take a risk, to do something wild. She had outgrown her house in the city; she could no longer live here. Soon after dreaming about the wildcat, Jennifer and George sold their house and purchased a new home in the country. Dreamwork helped Jennifer overcome her fears and prepare to make this important transition.

## Reaching the Mythic Core of the Complex

According to Edward Whitmont (1969), a complex such as the mobster or the needy mother makes itself felt by a strong emotional charge, such as strong enmity or displeasure, or intense excitement. The complex is like an autonomous psychic entity or character, carrying a noticeable emotional intensity. Whitmont emphasized that everyone has complexes; it's not something that we can avoid. Rather, we should try to discover "the mythological core of the complex."

> The core of the complex ... consists of the nucleus of a universal human pattern, which is called an archetype of the collective unconscious. ... [W]e must strive toward a transformation of the potentially disturbing or disruptive complexes by reaching their archetypal cores. ... When we confront the myth—the mythical (archetypal) core of our complexes—we confront the ultimate border line of our place in transcendental meaningfulness. (Whitmont, 1969, pp. 67, 68, 73, 84)

Many of our dreams reveal personal complexes and their mythic faces. The next example shows how we can transform a disruptive complex by touching its archetypal core.

## The Dream of the Snake Woman and the Sheriff

A woman named Andrea was grappling with binge drinking and depression. She enjoyed drinking wine and partying with her friends, but she felt she was doing it too much. Both her father and her stepfather were alcoholics. She said, "Everybody in my family drinks. It's a family of charismatic people who destroy and deaden themselves through alcohol." Andrea periodically stopped drinking, and would feel better for a few weeks. Then she would start drinking and smoking cigarettes again. This cycle kept repeating. She called smoking and drinking "a layer between me and my life." Andrea dreamed:

> *A snake woman is standing, waving her body around, loose and out of control. She is belligerent and uncontainable. I was trying to get*

*hold of her and said, "You're supposed to be doing something. Get it together." A sheriff woman was sent to try to catch her. The sheriff had fetal alcohol syndrome with distorted features. She anxiously talked about herself, creating a cocoon of words, protecting her wound. I thought of the sheriff, "You're a useless authority, incompetent and self-consumed. You're sent here, but I'm going to have to deal with her myself. You couldn't hold her while she was belligerent and falling down."*

Andrea said, "This snake woman represents my pleasure drive. She has no structure. It's the part of me that drinks and smokes and is really into sex." The snake woman personified a complex centred around drinking and feeling out of control. Her belligerent qualities reminded Andrea of her own angry feelings and resentments. The snake woman had an uncontainable quality that almost begged to be reined in. That reminded Andrea of recent weeks of drinking and voracious sex with a man who repeatedly slept with other women, which made her feel humiliated and caused her to want to drink more. Andrea felt that she couldn't control herself, and realized that she couldn't control this man; he was out of control too.

The dream depicted a complex cantered around a pair of opposites: the elusive, uncontainable snake woman, symbol of Andrea's extraversion, her partying and active sex life; and the sheriff, which represented exercising greater self-control. In psychoanalytic terms, the snake woman represented the id, or the *libidinal ego*, the part of Andrea that sought pleasure and connectedness, while the sheriff signified the superego, the principle of self-restraint. The sheriff woman was a symbol of Andrea's effort to control her impulses and maintain sobriety. Her transformation was occurring within this tension of opposites.

The sheriff was also a symbol of the transference. I said, "Maybe you think this is how I'm supposed to be with you, to whip you into shape and get you to control yourself, like a policeman. But the dream tells you that's useless! You're going to have to deal with her yourself. You have to catch hold of her. You have to find the strength of will to catch hold of your drinking; no one else can do this for you. But that doesn't mean rejecting the snake woman. She's a part of you too. She's a symbol of your sexuality, your urge for love, laughter, and pleasure."

The fact that the sheriff woman had fetal alcohol syndrome implied that Andrea's parents didn't realize how she'd be emotionally damaged by their lifelong heavy drinking. Now her inner, self-regulating police officer was impaired and incompetent. It was also noteworthy that the sheriff woman was protecting her wound; the dream suggested that Andrea's drinking might be a way of protecting her own wound, her depressed feelings. Telling the sheriff woman she was useless reminded Andrea of her intense self-criticism. "It reminds me of how useless I felt my mother was, and also how I feel about myself." The inadequate sheriff also represented her fear that therapy couldn't help her stop drinking, and that I (her therapist) would be incompetent. Andrea was longing for a competent holding environment that would help her take hold of herself.

This dream mandala outlines the core themes of Andrea's dream:

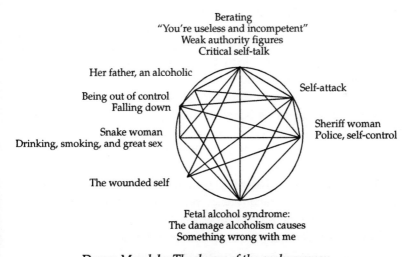

*Dream Mandala: The dream of the snake woman*

The archetypal core of the dream was the snake or serpent, primordial symbol of instinctual energy, pleasure-seeking, transformation, and renewal. The serpent in the Garden of Eden was a symbol of desire, sexuality, and temptation. That reminded Andrea of her attraction to the forbidden—to charismatic men who, like her father, were emotionally unavailable and incapable of commitment. The fact that she couldn't heal her father, or wounded men like him, made her feel inadequate. The feeling that there must be something wrong with *her* was an experience she shared in common with many children of alcoholics. The snake woman dream initiated a process of healing these feelings of self-blame, and it affirmed Andrea's dynamic energy and capacity for connection. She said the snake represented, "freedom, pleasure, power outside of convention, an energy that's not civilized, that cannot be ruled and corralled."

I added, "It's a symbol of regeneration and the full liberation of libido, your awakened life force."

The Dream of the Snake Woman and the Sheriff also portrayed an inner urge toward containment and self-control. Andrea stopped seeing the man who was hurting her and transitioned into a different relationship. She also realized that her sense of aliveness was enhanced by reducing her smoking and alcohol intake. The dream conveys a message that's relevant to anyone grappling with substance abuse. We have to try to catch hold of it.

This example shows that when we identify a complex we touch something that's painful to us. But the image becomes a character that we can relate to, that we can think about. The dream gives us an image that allows us to look at our problems, so we can feel certain things that are difficult. "The unpleasant experiences can be held in the mind in a way that might render it meaningful, so it can be thought. This modifies frustration giving some containment of the painful experience, making it more bearable" (Symington & Symington, 1996, p. 70).

A year later, I heard from Andrea, who told me that she'd stopped drinking. Her relationship was positive and passionate. She'd digested this message from the unconscious, unfolding the snake woman, but no longer possessed by her in the same way. This is an example of what it means to resolve a complex. Something that has gripped us unconsciously now becomes conscious, and the energy transforms.

## Personifying and Pathologizing in Complexes

The snake woman and the sheriff woman are examples of what James Hillman (1978) calls personified complexes. *Personifying* refers to "the basic psychological activity—the spontaneous experiencing, envisioning, and speaking of the configurations of existence as psychic presences .... To personify carries us into myth" (Hillman, 1978, pp. 12, 16). Psychoanalysis personified in its figures of the censor, superego, primal horde, primal scene, the polymorphously perverse child, Eros, Thanatos, Oedipus, Id. The mythical basis of psychoanalysis is evident in its theories of castration anxiety, penis envy, repetition compulsion. All are myths, Hilllman notes, as are Jung's shadow, wise old man, great mother, anima, animus. All are *persons*. Complexes are independent entities, "partial personalities .... Dream persons are complexes walking around" (pp. 20, 22).

In Hillman's (1978) view, we're "constituted of multiple parts" (p. 24). Recognizing that the ego is not the whole psyche, we can

> save the diversity and autonomy of the psyche from domination by any single power .... [The dream is] a critique of the ego-complex .... [T]he psyche presents its own imaginal dimensions, operates freely without words, and is constituted of multiple personalities .... Personifying means polycentricity, implicating us in a revolution of consciousness, from monotheism to polytheism. It will feel like breakdowns and regression. (Hillman, 1978, pp. 32–33, 35)

Our understanding of complexes is deepened through considering Hillman's use of the term *pathologizing*, which refers to:

> the psyche's autonomous ability to create illness, morbidity, disorder, abnormality, and suffering in any aspect of its behaviour and to experience and imagine life through this deformed and afflicted perspective .... [T]o envision pathologizing psychologically is to find a place for it .... We want to know what it might be saying about the soul, and what the soul might be saying by means of it. (Hillman, 1978, p. 57)

We saw pathologizing in the Dream of the Pig (Chapter Two) and the Dream of the Homeless Wanderer (Chapter Four). The next example describes a dream that carried an intense feeling charge and revealed the presence of an autonomous personality with mythic overtones of the archetypal wounded healer. It illustrates how, in personifying our central characters and complexes, dreams portray our affliction, suffering, or vulnerability in a manner that is healing, strengthening, and integrative.

## The Dream of the Emasculated Batman

Roger, one of my clients, was very upset after his girlfriend, Gwen, slept with another man, and his trust had been violated. Their relationship continued for several more years, but Roger felt emotionally shut down, and felt he could no longer trust Gwen, remaining highly ambivalent about their relationship. He dreamed:

> *An emasculated Batman was sitting on my couch. He was shaking, his eyes were closed. He looked thin, effeminate. His eyes had been removed, and his eyelids were stitched together. He was naked, wearing only stockings and a black garter belt, and no underwear. He had no penis; instead he had a vagina. He was wearing tennis shoes with the tops removed and the lips folded up. Puss was coming out of the shoes.*

This dream figure mirrored Roger's depressed state. I asked Roger to comment on the details of the dream. For example, what did it mean that Batman was blind? He said, "It's like the way I'm afraid I'm being blind about continuing this relationship. I'm always wondering, will she hurt me again? His closed eyes made him seem like he was deep into his own world and out of touch with the world around him. That reminds me how withdrawn and moody I've been ever since Gwen cheated on me. Batman was pale and thin and shivered a lot. He looked emaciated, weak, and vulnerable."

"That describes the way you're feeling—vulnerable and emotionally undernourished."

"And I feel weak because I haven't left her or broken up with her."

I asked Roger about the way that Batman's eyes were stitched together. He said, "His eyes were closed tight. That reminds me of my closed-heartedness with Gwen. I don't feel open-hearted. I can't open up to her any more. I don't feel like making love with her." Puss coming out of Batman's shoes suggested a festering wound, something that had infected the relationship. He said, "I just can't get over what she did."

I asked Roger about dreaming of Batman, a superhero. He said, "A superhero reminds me of how my dad used to get pumped up and belligerent when he was drunk and would start going after all these women. He thought he could do whatever he wanted. He was totally grandiose."

I said, "So Batman also represents an idealized male self-image, perhaps a part of you that wants to feel sexy and to experience lots of women. Here the superhero is a wounded figure—like the archetypal wounded king or wounded healer."

The emasculated Batman reminded Roger of his father's vulnerability and depression, his debility and illness. "It reminds me of his drinking and womanizing, his male chauvinism and machismo, his narcissism and belittlement of others, but also his sadness after my mother left him and married somebody else. That also reminds me of how my sister Ruth's husband, Ike, was devastated by Ruth's infidelities."

"So the emasculated Batman reminds you of how men in your family are wounded by women and emotionally castrated by them."

Roger said, "My dad was devastated when mom left him, even though he brought it on himself through his own behaviour."

"And you feel devastated by Gwen's affair."

Roger said, "I do. I'm having a hard time forgiving her for hurting me. I also have a hard time forgiving my dad for how he treated my mother. This wounded Batman with a vagina makes me realize I feel like my mother felt when my dad was unfaithful. She was the victim, he was the persecutor who robbed her of her dignity. And that's what Gwen has done to me."

The dream depicted a conflict between the inflated, omnipotent hero, and the deflated, emasculated hero. The emasculated, castrated Batman was a symbol of wounded pride and male sexuality. The dream depicted a complex connecting the hurt, deflated feelings arising in his current relationship with his experience of the wounded father.

In the dream, Batman was androgynous, male and female, suggesting the possibility of an inner union of opposites. The powerful, masculine superhero was merged here with the feminine side of Roger that was receptive and emotionally vulnerable. The emasculated Batman was a symbol of wholeness to guide Roger's development.

This example illustrates how a personal symbol of a troubling impasse or complex also depicts broader archetypal themes. For example, the mythic hero always undergoes some initiatory wound, ordeal, or defeat that leads to maturity. In another sense, the dream portrays a complex rooted in the interplay of puer and senex archetypes. The heroic son-puer with his youthful, somewhat inflated sense of confidence and possibilities, transforms into the wounded father, the senex or wounded king—burdened by responsibilities to others and carrying the disappointment and sense of betrayal we meet in any long-term relationship, but also able to survive it, to endure, to bear his suffering gracefully. By experiencing and metabolizing these feelings, Roger had the potential to become a wise and mature man, a wounded healer, emotionally and psychically whole. In the year after working with this dream, Roger was able to let go of his moody depression and to let Gwen back into his heart. Eventually they moved in together and established a home. The dream of the emasculated Batman served as a numinous personal healing symbol.

This dream features themes noted throughout this book: father-son dynamics; archetypes of the hero, wounded king, and wounded healer; understanding feelings and relationships through dreamwork; meeting the shadow; and the appearance of androgynous, male-female, cross-gender dream imagery.

I portray some of the dream's central themes in this diagram:

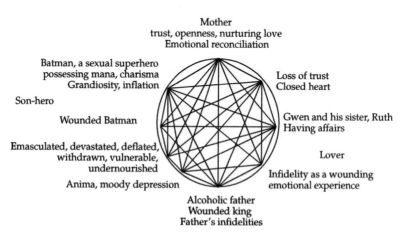

*Dream Mandala: The dream of the emasculated batman*

## The Dream of the Admiring Fan and the Guy with a Knife

The next example features several dreams depicting archetypal elements and complexes. Travis, a thirty-five-year-old musician, was grappling with discouragement after several years of solid artistic productivity had yielded numerous albums but little commercial success. He was feeling lost, wistful, as if he was losing the spark of light and hope and love. Were all his dreams coming to nothing? He was also experiencing conflict with his long-time girlfriend, Bella, and wondering whether to leave her or stay in the relationship. His deflated state was a reflection of high hopes that hadn't been fulfilled. Travis's dreams illustrate inflation and deflation, and the integration of grandiose symbols of personal potential into a more realistic sense of identity. This example also illustrates the evolution of archetypal symbolism within a series of dreams. Travis dreamed:

> I was at a keg party. One guy knew about me and my music. I was his star, his idol. It felt good, but I was just trying to hang out at the party. I felt it was time to go. I went to my car and there was a Mexican guy with a knife. He charged me, but I had a makeshift weapon, a taped-up piece of wood. We scuffled. His knife was pretty serious, so I yelled for help. Some guys came out from the party to help and the Mexican guy ran off. Then I drove to a shantytown on the outskirts of a city. It was like the Great Depression, in the 1930s. I met a beautiful woman with crooked teeth. I was very attracted to her. She said, "I have all the letters you sent me." She had a beautiful daughter.

The keg party reminded Travis of the party atmosphere in which much of his life as a working musician was conducted. The guy at the party who knew his music reminded Travis of "a big fan who idolized me. He conveys adulation, gratification, recognition that I did good work and affected people. This kind of feedback confirms that I'm a star. I have a public, an audience."

The man with a knife reminded Travis of having a weapon, a tool of attack. "I'm mad about not making it. I'm coming under attack from music distributors who say I owe them money. There are so many current battles." Instead of adoring fans, Travis was attracting adversaries. I asked Travis to have a brief dialogue with the man in the dream and ask him why he was upset, why he was attacking. Travis said (in the voice of the Mexican man), "I don't have anything. I'm hungry. So I have to take something." Travis continued: "He feels desperate and jealous. I think I'm angry about not being recognized. I see people succeed who don't have any talent. Maybe I'm jealous. I think I have a lot of talent, and I'm still unknown."

The taped-up piece of wood reminded Travis of "using whatever you've got to defend yourself," and he recalled defending himself against his older brothers, and having to justify to them what he was doing with his life. He said, "They treat me like their unsuccessful younger brother."

The setting of the dream in a shantytown during the Great Depression signified Travis's depressed state and concerns about financially lean times. It reminded him of poor, destitute people with no jobs and no opportunities, and his own feelings of struggle.

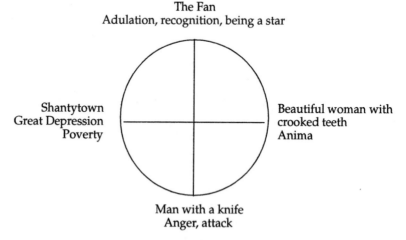

The Fan
Adulation, recognition, being a star

Shantytown
Great Depression
Poverty

Beautiful woman with
crooked teeth
Anima

Man with a knife
Anger, attack

*Dream Mandala: The dream of the admiring fan
and the guy with a knife*

## The Dream of the New Year's Eve Party, Rolondo, and the Lake in the Desert

Next Travis dreamed:

> *I'm at an art exhibit. There are crystal moulds with beautiful designs, microphone sculptures. There are DJs upstairs. One of them, Rolondo, corners me to talk to him, but he's totally a jerk. I'm cool and distant in response. I feel I should've been more belligerent. Then I'm travelling down a highway in three cars, and I have to keep going back and getting the other ones forward. I'm hopscotching the cars forward. Then I'm wandering around an enormous party. There are important people there. I feel like "I've made it." I'm with my friend Marvin now. It's a New Year's Eve party held at a town built over a lake in the desert. Then Marvin goes off to bed, and I'm hanging out with a beautiful blonde woman. We hold hands and are starting to get down.*

Crystal moulds reminded Travis of "the art I create, my recorded music. The enormous party reminds me of the world and how I see my music fitting in the world." The important people represent "how I'd feel if I made it and had status." This repeats the theme of fame and stardom from the previous dream.

The desire to "make it" and be a star reflects inflation, which is an archetypal experience. We form grandiose fantasies of doing something that lights the world on fire, and renews the collective. There's a spark of a "star" or "world saviour" in each of us as we unfurl the sails of our individuated personalities. There's a promise of redemption in our inflations and great strivings. Inflation means we get puffed up and full of hot air, delusions of grandeur, or fantasies of greatness. But eventually the air is let out of our tires; the wind is taken out of our sails. Inflation is inevitably followed by depression, alienation, and wounding of the personality. Edward Edinger (1992) wrote, "Inflation has, as its inevitable consequence, a fall …. Ultimately, inflation will be checked by reality" (pp. 27, 29). Nonetheless, inflation is a necessary phase of individuation. Edinger continued, "Psychic growth involves a series of inflated or heroic acts. These provoke rejection, and are followed by alienation, repentance, restitution and renewed inflation. This cyclic process repeats itself again and again" (p. 42). It takes a heroic gathering of our energies to rouse thunder. We imagine ourselves actualizing our inner sense of promise. Those who strive for greatness in any field or enterprise must allow themselves to fill with a sense of potential, and a belief in the urgency and importance of the work. Travis has engaged in a series of heroic creative acts in recording numerous albums, an effort requiring immense expenditures of time, energy, and money.

The stressful interaction with Rolondo brought up memories of interpersonal clashes with several musicians Travis used to work with, and of struggling musicians who were bitter and competitive. This was also an aspect of Travis's shadow. In contrast, Marvin was a musician Travis was currently playing with; he described Marvin as "a consistent person, hard-working, dedicated, and unassuming."

The dream portrayed a tension between two inner positions—the party with important people, signifying an inner striving for fame and stardom; and Rolondo, the bitter, competitive, struggling musician, symbol of a central complex. Marvin represented an intermediary viewpoint, reconciling the tension of opposites through an earnest, grounded attitude, and mature awareness of the hard work necessary to become a star musician.

Hopscotching the three cars reminded Travis of "trying to handle too many things at once. I'm trying to be producer and promoter, as well as an artist. I feel pulled in too many directions."

I commented, "Hopscotch suggests hopping around, being agile and light on your feet. It suggests engaging in multiple enterprises, for example the way you're making music while also learning about money and business."

The blonde woman reminded Travis of "somebody I'm always searching for."

I said, "She's the face of your anima, the elusive woman who captivates you, and also the beauty of your own soul. In the dream you're holding hands, linked to the enlivening anima." This image was similar to the woman in the first dream. It was an idealized image of the perfect lover, in contrast to Travis's ambivalent feelings about Bella. I asked Travis about the woman with the crooked teeth from the previous dream. He said, "Nobody's perfect. She has this flaw, but I'm attracted to her; I can see that she's really beautiful. I guess that's how I feel about Bella too." The dream helped resolve the tension between the image of the perfect anima woman and his real-life relationship with Bella. In the dream, the woman tells Travis she has kept all of his letters. The archetype of the lovers was evoked with all of its tense urgency and longing for completion through love. The crooked-toothed woman's beautiful daughter represented the divine child, symbol of potentiality.

The new year's eve party implied rebirth, a new beginning, the start of something new. A lake in the desert reminded Travis of "the desert of our culture right now, our moment of history."

I said, "The lake in the desert is like water that appears in the desert, an oasis, the water of life. And your music is the water that preserves life in the cultural desert, the wasteland. The lake in the desert also reminds me of Salt Lake, in Utah, and that reminds me that salt symbolizes bitterness." Edward Edinger wrote:

> The symbolism of salt has been discussed comprehensively by Jung. Basically salt symbolizes Eros and appears in one of two aspects, either as bitterness or as wisdom. Jung writes: "Tears, sorrow, and disappointment are bitter, but wisdom is the comforter in all psychic suffering. Indeed, bitterness and wisdom form a pair of alternatives: where there is bitterness wisdom is lacking, and where wisdom is there can be no bitterness." (Edinger, 1985, p. 42; Jung, (1963)[1955–1956], par. 330)

I said, "Perhaps the dream is asking you to let go of your bitterness about your struggle to make it as a musician. In the dream, you end up at a celebration of new beginnings held at a place of redemption and spiritual rebirth, the lake in the desert, a beautiful healing image."

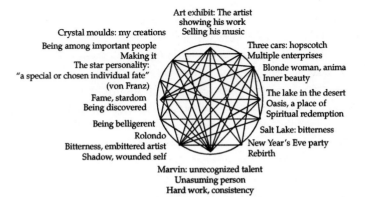

Art exhibit: The artist showing his work
Selling his music

Crystal moulds: my creations
Being among important people
Making it
The star personality:
"a special or chosen individual fate"
(von Franz)
Fame, stardom
Being discovered

Being belligerent
Rolondo
Bitterness, embittered artist
Shadow, wounded self

Three cars: hopscotch
Multiple enterprises
Blonde woman, anima
Inner beauty

The lake in the desert
Oasis, a place of
Spiritual redemption

Salt Lake: bitterness
New Year's Eve party
Rebirth

Marvin: unrecognized talent
Unassuming person
Hard work, consistency

*Dream Mandala: The dream of the new year's eve party, Rolondo, and the lake in the desert*

## The Dream of the Speakeasy and the Knife Fight with Desmond

Travis's next dream featured similar themes, beginning with a party and an altercation:

> I'm in a knife fight at a party with this DJ named Desmond. We got in to the party through knowing the doorman. It's a futuristic 1920s-style speakeasy in a vaudevillian style with curtains. We go to a place behind a second hand store. I notice a cool old Bake-a-lite plastic radio. But the store wants too much money for it. There's a basketball game going on but nobody is very good. I know that I'll do well in the game. Then I start fighting again with Desmond. It's a serious fight that lasts for a while. I end up blinding him and leaving him there to die. Then I go out and start wrestling with one of my brothers. I'm aware that the party is ending.

Knowing somebody reminded Travis of having connections. The doorman was like a gatekeeper, a psychopomp who assists a transition or passage. In the dream, doors opened for him. To dream it is to imagine it being so, and to invoke that outcome.

The 1920s speakeasy reminded Travis of being subterranean, part of an underground culture, a saloon, a place of taboo, forbidden illegal activities. "It was subversive but celebratory. The 1920s in America was Prohibition era, repression, a time of cultural shutdown, similar in some ways to where we are now collectively. A speakeasy is a clandestine party. It reminds me of sneaking into someplace lavish, wearing a deluxe suit." It suggested having a polished image, a celebrity persona.

Vaudeville suggested comedy, spoofs, skits, comedy and dance routines, laughter, finding humour in dark times. I told Travis that the second-hand store reminded me of a Goodwill store, a place for discarded items.

He said, "That reminds me of how unwanted I feel." Travis paused to allow a wave of sadness to pass through his body.

I asked about the Bake-a-lite plastic radio. He said, "That kind of plastic is valuable material. I heard that one family owns the patent, but apparently they're a tragic family."

"It's something of precious value that's also tragic. I think that's how you see yourself. You're the suffering artist. I call this the Van Gogh complex."

Travis said, "I don't want to be a starving artist. I want to make it. But in the dream the store wants too much money for the plastic radio. It's out of reach, it's not for me, just like buying advertising and getting radio airplay are too expensive for me."

I asked about the basketball game, and Travis said, "I'm in the game, but nobody is very good. It's my fear of mediocrity. There are lots of mediocre bands around."

"But it's still hopeful that you know you'll do well in the game. You can compete."

Travis described Desmond, his dream adversary, as "a contentious dude, a seriously embittered person."

I said, "That reminds me of the salt of bitterness from the previous dream, and the bitterness you're trying to overcome. The fact that you blind him suggests that you've been blind to your angry shadow." The impending death of Desmond, the embittered artist, symbolized the death of Travis's identification with this tragic, wounded figure. He was ready to free up the energy bound in the embittered artist complex.

The knife fight reminded Travis of times he was in fistfights. "That reminds me of my friend Jason, who was always in fights. He died in an accident. He lived wildly and was killed. He was magnetic, and women were totally drawn to him because of it. Jason was like our local James Dean, a tragic young man who made love with many beautiful women."

The name Jason reminded me of the Greek solar hero, seeker of the golden fleece. Travis's friend Jason was radiant, a magnet. But here the solar, charismatic, creative personality was a tragic figure, like a suffering messiah, and he was destroyed. The dream constellated the myth of the tragic hero, and the tragic artist. The artist is the modern messiah, the one who reveals himself or herself and is sometimes viewed as a fool or eviscerated by critics. But the artist is also the saviour or redeemer, bringing inspiration, new vision, and hope to humanity. Travis was transforming within the archetypal patterns of the artist-saviour, and the death-rebirth of the hero.

The conflict with Desmond reminded Travis of "strife in bands, and the bitterness you feel on the road to success because you have to sacrifice so much trying to make it." Stardom and band strife reminded Travis of Fleetwood Mac, "the ultimate band contentiousness."

I said, "Fleetwood Mac also represents ultimate band success—complete artistic, commercial, and financial success. Fleetwood Mac symbolizes your inflated fantasy of being a rock star on tour with lots of money, drugs, fame, beautiful women, tumultuous relationships, wild parties. You want sunbursts of love and sundowns of heartbreak. It's an ideal, and it's an inflated fantasy. Fleetwood Mac signifies your feelings about fame, stardom, and success. Anything less than this feels like a letdown to you."

Celebrities often symbolize the Self and recognition of its radiant internal wholeness pattern. The appearance of celebrities is analogous to a timeless theme of myths and fairytales, the appearance of a star, which, according to von Franz (1977), represents a "sign of the hero," the sense of having a "special or chosen individual fate." It symbolizes "outstanding personalities," and "the conscious individuality of a person" (pp. 13–14). It represents our potential to individuate, to express our uniqueness and successfully unfold our individuality.

The scene of wrestling with his brother stirred the memory of how, years earlier, Travis's father died the week before Travis competed in a big, state-wide high school wrestling tournament. Travis said, "That contest marked the low point of my wrestling career. It was my biggest failure. My school, family, and friends invested a lot of hope in me, but I was defeated in a big match. It was a huge letdown. Everything went to hell in a two-week period. I was stunned by my dad's unexpected death and the sudden end of my wrestling career." Here the dream provided a quick rewind to a pivotal and formative moment in his development.

I said, "The theme of letdown connects your wrestling career, your father's death, your lack of artistic recognition, and your relationship with Bella. You're afraid of being a big disappointment to yourself and everybody else. The knife fight in the dream and your wrestling memories evoke the mythology of the hero-gladiator. Being defeated in battle is part of the archetypal experience of the hero. So was the experience of losing your father. Your defeats in athletics and in trying to sell your CDs—these are all part of your path of heroic initiation. In the dream, you leave the bitter artist to die and you test your strength again in competition, which suggests renewal of your natural warrior energy. I hope that one day all of your efforts lead you to the plaza of triumph. I truly hope you will succeed. The dream suggests the need to heal your embittered artist by accepting the competitive nature of music and the entertainment business. That's just the way it is. You have to get in the game and keep going with your music and creativity. You're still a player." I'll come back to Travis in Chapter Nine.

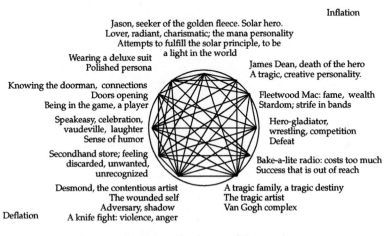

Inflation

Jason, seeker of the golden fleece. Solar hero.
Lover, radiant, charismatic; the mana personality
Attempts to fulfill the solar principle, to be
a light in the world

Wearing a deluxe suit
Polished persona

James Dean, death of the hero
A tragic, creative personality.

Knowing the doorman, connections
Doors opening
Being in the game, a player

Fleetwood Mac: fame, wealth
Stardom; strife in bands

Speakeasy, celebration,
vaudeville, laughter
Sense of humor

Hero-gladiator,
wrestling, competition
Defeat

Secondhand store; feeling
discarded, unwanted,
unrecognized

Bake-a-lite radio: costs too much
Success that is out of reach

Desmond, the contentious artist
The wounded self
Adversary, shadow
A knife fight: violence, anger

A tragic family, a tragic destiny
The tragic artist
Van Gogh complex

Deflation

*Dream Mandala: The dream of the speakeasy
and the knife fight with Desmond*

Each dream aids us in unfolding the universal evolutionary drives. Through dreamwork, we experience the timeless archetypes, which lend mythic depth to our personal struggles and tasks of development, and which form the core of our most fascinating complexes. Now let's explore four archetypal patterns of transformation that frequently appear in dreams: persona, shadow, anima/animus, and the Self.

*CHAPTER SEVEN*

# Persona and Shadow in Dreamwork

Dreams perform three functions that are essential to our growth in consciousness. They help us evolve our social adaptation and self-presentation in the world, which Jung called the *persona*. They illuminate unconscious beliefs, behaviours, and feelings, which Jung termed the *shadow*. And they reveal the central tasks and challenges of our personal *individuation*, the process of actualizing our unique potentials and identities.

In the course of personality development, certain aspects of the personality are banished from awareness as we attempt to conform to social conventions. We adopt the norms and values of our families and social group, and develop a socially acceptable presentation of self to the world—a persona, a social mask. It's important to develop an appropriate persona so that we can adapt to our environment; otherwise, we may feel rejected or ostracized. Edward Whitmont (1969) calls the persona "the adaptation archetype," and he notes that the persona often appears in the images of "clothes, uniforms, and masks" (p. 156). The common dream images of being naked or unclothed, or wearing dirty or inappropriate clothing, suggest "the refusal of the collective"—not enough persona adaptation (p. 158). Ted, a man whose

141

new job in business management involved increased responsibilities and required that he dress up a bit, had this dream:

> *I see John, a former colleague of mine who was always neatly dressed in a shirt and tie. He looks like a man you can trust. I run outside on the street. My shirt is unbuttoned and not tucked in, and I step on my tie and tear it in half.*

Ted was uncomfortable with his new responsibilities and whether he was up to the task of "acting the part." He was afraid his newly formed image would come apart at the seams, leaving him exposed. In the dream, John represented the kind of new persona Ted was trying to form, one that would instil in others a sense of trust in his capacity to do a difficult job.

A well-developed persona is necessary for social adaptation. We need to act sufficiently in congruence with our roles in the world, in a manner that enables us to be easily identified as a doctor, a parent, a teacher, a police officer, an artist, a judge, or a therapist. Otherwise, we will not be adept at giving and receiving the social cues that govern daily life. Nonetheless, the persona by itself is not genuine individuality; it lacks the psychological depth necessary for true selfhood. We can become too attached to our social mask, or feel that our persona role is empty and meaningless, suffocating, or too superficial. We long to live, and be known by others, as we really are, free of pretence. Daniel Levinson (1978) says that we must strive to create an identity and a place in the world that are both socially viable and suitable for the self. A persona that is socially viable but not suitable or congruent with who we are can cause much inner conflict. A central task of personal transformation is to evolve a persona that is true to who we are, so that we feel whole and authentic.

At some stages of life, our persona image is challenged by the emergence of dreams containing images of the *shadow*, representing qualities that are foreign or forbidden to our conscious sense of self. The persona may be especially threatened by our urge to express anger or sexual drives that we believe are unacceptable and need to be suppressed. For example, Dawn, a soft-spoken, devout Christian, dreamed that a woman with a loaded gun was chasing after her. Discussing this dream allowed Dawn to recognize that she was carrying a lot of anger inside her.

## Meeting the Shadow in Dreams

Shadow figures in dreams signify qualities, feelings, attitudes, or behaviours we're unable to acknowledge in ourselves. An encounter with the shadow makes it possible to integrate these qualities or feelings. To do this, we must meet the shadow, not run from it. Marie-Louise von Franz wrote:

> If one focuses attention on the unconscious ... it often breaks through in a flow of helpful symbolic images. But not always. Sometimes it first offers a series of painful realizations of what is wrong with oneself and one's conscious attitudes. Then one must begin the process by swallowing all sorts of bitter truths .... The need usually arises to re-adapt the conscious attitude in a better way to the unconscious factors—therefore to accept what seems to be 'criticism' from the unconscious. Through dreams one becomes acquainted with aspects of one's personality that for various reasons one has preferred not to look at too closely. This is what Jung called 'the realization of the shadow' ... . When an individual makes an attempt to see his [or her] shadow, [s/]he becomes aware of (and often ashamed of) those qualities and impulses he denies in himself but can plainly see in other people—such things as egotism, mental laziness, and sloppiness; unreal fantasies, schemes, and plots; carelessness and cowardice; inordinate love of money and possessions ... . The shadow usually contains values that are needed by consciousness, but that exist in a form that makes it difficult to integrate them into one's life .... Whether the shadow becomes our friend or enemy depends largely upon ourselves ... . The shadow is not necessarily always an opponent. In fact, he is exactly like any human being with whom one has to get along, sometimes by giving in, sometimes by resisting, sometimes by giving love—whatever the situation requires. The shadow becomes hostile only when he is ignored or misunderstood. (von Franz, 1964, pp. 170–171, 173–174, 178, 182)

Dreams help us integrate shadow material into awareness. A shy and devoutly religious young woman who was conflicted about her sexuality had a dream set in a warehouse. When I asked for her associations, she said, "It's a wide open space. Warehouse reminds me of whorehouse." The dream brought up fears that exploring her desires would mean she'd become promiscuous, too wide open. Her path to wholeness asked her to reconsider this attitude and to accept sexuality as an aspect of her full human experience.

The shadow embodies qualities that are threatening to our conscious attitude, persona, or sense of self. Barbara, a woman who often saw herself as a victim of other people's aggression but who was, in fact, quite aggressive herself, dreamed of a male assailant brandishing a large dagger. She called this figure "the slasher." He symbolized her unacknowledged aggression and hostility, her tendency to make acerbic, cutting remarks. Barbara began to see that she'd been overly identified with being a victim—innocent, unprotected, vulnerable, and frightened. Integrating the slasher helped Barbara develop a clearer and more accurate sense of self.

## The Dream of the Paisley Suitcase

Here's another example of a woman encountering her shadow. Deborah, a high-ranking law enforcement officer, dreamed:

> I'm preparing for a trip but am not prepared or packed. I'm rushing around frantically. I don't have on any underwear, and I'm naked underneath my uniform. Suddenly Dave, a man I went to school with, hands me a suitcase that is already packed. It's rectangular with a paisley pattern and earth tones. Then Dave is waiting downstairs in a car to drive me away.

Being naked under her uniform suggested Deborah was connecting to her authentic instincts, not tied to her persona. She said, "I feel stifled by the fact that I'm always in uniform, always in my role. Hardly anybody knows the real me." I asked Deborah about the suitcase with paisley and earth tones. She said, "It reminds me of being a hippie earth mama." In describing her association to Dave, she said, "The last time I smoked grass, it was with him. We had so much fun." A shadow issue was revealed: The high-ranking cop (persona) is also a pot-smoking hippie earth mother (shadow). The dream facilitated a union of opposites within the personality. At this stage of her life, Deborah wasn't interested in smoking marijuana, but she realized that she missed having relaxed time for enjoyment, music, and conversation with friends. This would provide a welcome respite from the demands of her public role.

The major themes of Deborah's dream are illustrated below:

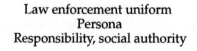

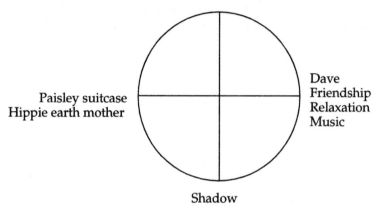

*Dream Mandala: The dream of the paisley suitcase*

## The Dream of the White Rabbit, the Black Cat, and the Black Snake

Doris was a twenty-six-year-old woman from a Muslim family in which women were expected to be subservient and docile. She was a strong, fiery, assertive woman with intense sexual drives, but was conflicted because these traits went against her social and religious conditioning. Doris also had problems at work, where her bluntness and directness with clients had ruffled some feathers. Doris told me this dream:

> *I'm walking alone in a city. I see a white pet rabbit inside a caged area in front of an apartment complex. The rabbit is scared, running toward me. Behind it is a black cat chasing the rabbit. Suddenly I saw a black snake on the ground. I froze. The snake jumped up at me and bit me on both of my hands. Then the snake slithered away. I could feel venom sinking into my veins and deeper into my body. My hands*

*were swollen. I saw a Middle Eastern man, a pure-hearted doctor with gentle features and nice skin. He had an ointment and took it out. He put a few drops on my hands. He said, "You're fine." My wounds were healing. The venom didn't hurt me.*

The doctor reminded Doris of a surgeon all scrubbed up and ready to operate, and that reminded her of her father, who was a surgeon. The appearance later in the dream of the gentle, pure-hearted doctor implied healing of a wound regarding her father, as well as healing by accepting her own masculine energy. He was an attentive, reassuring, healing animus figure. Surgery also reminded Doris of "trying to see through people, to psychologically cut people open. The black snake reminds me of my aggression and bitchiness, my impatience with clients." The dream helped her recognize how her assertive side was being expressed as unconscious hostility toward others. The apartment complex reminded Doris of "a depressing housing project in a city, where it's cold, people are on welfare or poverty stricken, and depressed. It reminds me of my depression."

When I asked Doris about rabbits, she said, "Rabbits are defenceless and innocent; they're prey. That reminds me of how I'm susceptible to my moods." The white rabbit also represented a *persona* image of the kind of gentle, submissive woman other people wanted her to be. Then Doris said, "It probably wouldn't hurt me to learn to be gentler and softer with people, like a rabbit—and like the gentle doctor with nice skin."

Doris said of the black cat, "Cats are selfish; they only come to you when they want food. They're manipulative." That reminded her of the men in her life. But the cat also reminded her of intuition, of acting on her instincts and desires. She said, "The black snake and the white rabbit remind me of how I can be a predator when I see vulnerability in people. Sometimes I go for the jugular. The black snake is a predator with a poisonous bite, like me with my Scorpio personality." In the dream, Doris received the bite of the snake, suggesting that something of its venom is in her too. The black snake represented her outspokenness, her anger, and her personal power. When the snake bit her in the dream, at first Doris panicked, but then she realized that the snake's venom wasn't dangerous to her. In fact, it seemed to make her stronger. Working with these animal symbols helped Doris express her true nature.

## The Dream of Wild Children, the Silent Insurgent, and the Seductress

Emily, a young married woman who was having problems with her husband and had just started couple's therapy, dreamed:

> I was in a chaotic situation where there was an air of apocalyptic doom. Children were roaming around in gangs, like wild, unsupervised children who had to fend for themselves. They chased me and threw rocks at me. I fell off a ledge and didn't know how far I'd fall before I hit bottom. Then I hid in a secret base of insurgents. While I was there, the head of the insurgents, a man—slender, silent, foreign—took an interest in me. The only way I knew how to escape was to seduce him. He lay on the ground, and I climbed on top of him and blew softly in his ear. I ran my hand over his smooth shoulder and began to kiss him passionately. He began to fall in love with me. In the morning I left the secret base, which I now saw was a hotel. I wore a dark, hooded cape so I wouldn't be recognized.

The wild, unsupervised children reminded Emily of being young and free, and her feeling of being restricted and without much autonomy, because her parents, and now her husband, had dictated many of her life's choices. She longed to be free and unsupervised, not under somebody's control. Emily's association to the apocalyptic situation was the possible end of her marriage, which she felt would be catastrophic. Then she'd be like a child who had to fend for herself. The final section of the dream revealed the shadow of the faithful wife—the hot seductress, who uses her sexuality to get what she wants. This dream brought Emily awareness of her seductive power, a topic of recent fantasies. The secret base of insurgents symbolized her sexual secrets and fantasies of rising up against the confines of her marriage. The dream allowed her to acknowledge these feelings while wearing the dark, hooded cape of invisibility. Acknowledging this shadow material was an important step in growing self-awareness.

Jung wrote:

> The self is a union of opposites *par excellence* ... . Once the exploration of the unconscious has led the conscious mind to

an experience of the archetype, the individual is confronted with the abysmal contradictions of human nature, and this confrontation in turn leads to the possibility of a direct experience of light and darkness, of Christ and the devil ... . Without the experience of the opposites there is no experience of wholeness and hence no inner approach to the sacred figures ... . Although insight into the problem of opposites is imperative, there are very few people who can stand it in practice ... . [I]n the self good and evil are indeed closer than identical twins! The reality of evil and its incompatibility with good cleave the opposites asunder and lead inexorably to the crucifixion and suspension of everything that lives. (Jung, 1968 [1944], pars. 22–24)

## The Dream of Catacombs, Bugs, and the Steady Firemen

The next example portrays an intense encounter with the shadow stemming from a man's childhood experiences with his father. Owen, thirty-three years old, came to his first session and told me a long, anguished story about a betrayal by his ex-girlfriend, and made brief reference to the fact that his father was mentally ill. During his second session, he told me that the night after our first meeting he had this dream:

> *I turn on my car and a thick cloud of black smoke pours out of the exhaust pipe, like a big belch of smoke.*

This dream was a signal from the unconscious that, in beginning therapy, Owen was about to clear his emotional exhaust pipe of much backed-up pain, negativity, and black smoke.

Then Owen told me an even more significant dream, one filled with both disturbing and healing symbolism, including some psychotic imagery. Working with the unconscious is a path for the courageous, not for the timid.

> *I was at a resort with lots of trees and interesting stone masonry and woodwork. I went into an underground catacombs under the resort. I'm holding a book,* Night *by Elie Wiesel. I got a feeling that Jews had been incarcerated or tortured there at some time. I felt a horror of being in a place where such things had happened. But I kept exploring.*

*Lots of sunlight found its way into these halls. At one point I stopped again. Something horrible had happened there, really bad torture, inhuman things. I made a choice to go on. I walked on a steep incline spiraling upward toward a room. I no longer had the book in my hand. Now I was in the driveway of an old firehouse. A meeting was taking place of solid, vibrant, steady, stern firemen. They were young and old, and of various races. They wore firemen dress but also unusual medallions and symbols adorning their clothes. I was easily accepted and taken in by them. I looked down and found crushed insects on my left foot. Bugs had burrowed under the skin and had to be dug out. They were still alive and moving. I leaped out toward the street on one foot. My foot was packed with these insects. Then my foot came apart, and all these slimy insects came pouring out into the gutter. It was frightening to watch. I didn't realize all this was in my foot. I dipped my foot into water in the gutter to clean it out and get the bugs out. I had a wonderful feeling of release. An old man with a hose sprayed me down, cooled me off, and revitalized me. He knew exactly what was needed, without my asking him to do it. I looked down and saw that I had grown a brand new foot. It had the white goop of a newborn all over it. The skin was fresh and raw as the hose rinsed the goop off. I tried walking and the new foot worked perfectly.*

I asked Owen about the stone masonry. He said, "Someone had to do a lot of work to make this." This implied that Owen had much work to do, and that a process of constructing the self was underway, a masonry of the soul. The catacombs reminded Owen of how in ancient Rome people went underground to go into hiding. Some catacombs were lined with skulls; some contained huge burial crypts. People also lived down there if they were being persecuted. I wondered how Owen felt persecuted, and he'd soon tell me.

The place of torture in the dream implied that something had been torturing Owen. The dream stated, "Something horrible had happened there." I said, "I want to know if something horrible has happened to you."

Sometimes in dreamwork, we ask a question that strikes an emotional chord or touches a sensitive spot. This occurred when I asked Owen for his associations to "a place where atrocities had been committed." This reminded Owen of his father, whom he described as "completely mad, schizophrenic, an extremely violent and unstable person." His father was institutionalized when Owen was six, although he'd unexpectedly show up at home from time to time, often leading to violent confrontations. On several occasions, Owen had been forced to call the police to restrain his father and return him to the hospital. "He had delusions and heard voices. Once he slammed me into a car so hard I cut my face and was knocked unconscious. Paramedics took me to the hospital. My dad was arrested. Then I was taken out of our home and placed in a home for abused kids, which was like a jail. I had to stay there for a week. Dad never changed his clothes. Sometimes he lived homeless on the streets. He wouldn't take his meds. I tried to help him but he would go into my room and steal stuff from me." Our discussion of a place of past atrocities in the dream elicited a flood of relevant personal history.

The firemen in the dream represented Owen's desire for stability, and for steady, consistent male energy. This also referred to Owen's longing for his therapist to be a reliable man capable of rescuing someone in an emergency. The firemen were a guild of solid, competent, responsible men. They represented a positive father *imago*, an image of the kind of father Owen had never had, but which now greeted and blessed him from within. The fact that the firemen welcomed and accepted Owen as one of them reminded him of "the feeling that I'm steady and competent. I'm not like my dad. I'm trustworthy and dependable."

I said, "The fireman is a vibrant, potent man who is established, respected, and in community with other men. And a fireman possesses inner fire, strength, vitality, and creativity. The fireman reminds me of the ancient figure of the blacksmith, who works with fire to refashion metals. The fireman is a shamanic and alchemical figure representing dynamic inner transformation."

The firemen were in striking contrast to the image of the bugs, which reminded Owen of decomposition, madness, and delusions. He said, "The bugs symbolize my fear that I'll be crazy like my father." The belief that bugs are crawling under their skin is a delusion often reported by people in the grips of psychosis. Owen had to get the bugs out of his body, to wash off the madness. "The bugs represent my fear of all this toxic material taking over, my fear of falling apart." The image of bugs inside his foot suggested that Owen had to integrate the madman within his unconscious, as well as the steady firemen. Thus the dream depicted a union of opposites—a state of fragmentation and madness (bugs) and a state of fiery metamorphosis (firemen).

The new foot covered with baby goop was a symbol of rebirth and renewal, constellating the archetype of the divine child. The dream's image of death, rot, and decomposition was followed by an image of rebirth, suggesting a hopeful outcome. In the dream, Owen dipped his foot in water, evoking the mythic theme of healing through the sacred pool or stream.

The older man with a hose represented someone who knows what to do, and showed an archetypal transference that constellated his therapist as a wise healer. Owen needed someone to guide him, and help him contain and digest this material about his father's madness. The man with a hose also signified phallic potency. He was a symbol of the wise old man, the mentor and guide, who appeared in this helpful form to aid Owen.

The firemen who were both old and young suggested that Owen was integrating the young and old parts of himself, the vulnerable child and the competent adult. This theme was also stated in the contrast between the old man and the baby goop. At age thirty-four, Owen was starting to feel like he was fully an adult, while still feeling his youthful possibilities. The medallions and symbols, worn by the firemen, represented individuation, finding his own identity. This powerful dream helped Owen come to grips with his father's mental illness and the fact that he himself was a healthy person. Owen went on to become successful in his career, his friendships, and eventually a loving relationship. A mandala diagram of this dream appears in Chapter Ten.

## Two Dreams during a Divorce

Liz, a woman going through a divorce, dreamed:

> I'm walking over snowy mountains. I thought to myself, "Now that I'm single I can try skiing again."

The snowy mountains reminded Liz of a period of childhood when her family was very poor and couldn't pay the utility bills, and the house was cold during the winter months. That reminded her of fear she wouldn't be able to pay the bills and properly raise her child now that she was living on her own. Anxiety from childhood was re-emerging in her present transition. I said, "I think the dream is saying that you're feeling out in the cold emotionally, with no one to love you and hold you during this difficult time." Liz burst into tears when I said that. Discussing the phrase "out in the cold" evoked strong feelings of abandonment.

The skis reminded Liz of "the way I'm trying to be strong and appear independent and happy to be single. I tell myself now I can do all these things I couldn't do when I was married, like skiing. But I'm not happy about it. I feel lonely and scared." This dream helped Liz recognize a part of her that felt needy and dependent.

One week later, Liz dreamed:

*A crazy woman is chasing after me.*

Dreams of being chased often indicate the presence of shadow material. The crazy woman reminded Liz of her mother during her (Liz's) childhood, a period when her mother couldn't manage her life and came unglued emotionally. It represented Liz's fear that she herself would go crazy from the pressures of paying bills and raising a child alone. In reality, Liz was a brave, strong, and capable woman, but she also needed to face the shadow, a part of her that was afraid, vulnerable, and emotionally unstable.

Encounters with the shadow often occur in dreams that are especially scary or disturbing. Shadow characters appearing in our dreams symbolize, and exaggerate, the most regressive, underdeveloped parts of ourselves, the qualities or behaviours we fear or dislike the most. For example, Joe, a man who was having trouble supporting himself financially, dreamed about a man in a wheelchair. Symbolically, Joe had no legs under him; he couldn't support his own weight. The dream revealed the truth of his debilitated outlook.

## The Dream of the Rat

A woman named Sarah had a dream about a rat. Her first reaction was that she was disgusted by this image, and afraid that it represented a sickness or bitterness growing inside her. I asked what a rat reminded her of, and she said that reminded her of lawyers, and that she was currently dealing with several lawyers in a dispute regarding copyright infringement and needed to hire her own attorney to represent her. The rat reminded her of how tired she was of fighting these people. Sarah said the other side's lawyers had been trying to make her feel guilty for standing up for herself. She felt that she must be a rat because she was defending her rights, as if it was a sign of terrible egotism and bad character. As Sarah reflected further on the image of the rat, she suddenly remembered being nine years old and biting her brother when he tried to molest her. She said, "He never bothered me again after that." The rat was a positive symbol of her capacity to protect herself, to use her teeth when necessary. It was a spirit totem, an ally. The dream of the rat uncovered something deeply buried from the past, but also provided guidance for Sarah's present and her future. She fought tenaciously and prevailed in this dispute.

## A Gory Dream of Violence and Blood

By grappling with scary, upsetting dreams, we access highly charged emotional material. Here's an example of an intense, disturbing dream of a woman named Wendy who had a history of severe physical abuse in childhood. Wendy was a quiet person who found it difficult to express anger and maintain personal boundaries, and she grappled with feelings of victimization and persecution. She dreamed:

> My ex-fiancé ties up my feet and hands so I'm unable to resist or fight back. I eventually fight back and attack him violently, viciously mangling his body until blood spurts everywhere.

Wendy's associations to this dream were of childhood memories of being bound by her father and unable to resist. The dream reflected feelings of being weak and helpless, and also depicted violent impulses, murderous rage, a desire for revenge. Wendy said, "This reminds me of a part of me that's like a dog and will fight to the death. It's a part of me that would like to act fiercely in my self-defence. Getting angry in the dream reminds me of how violent my father was."

I said, "The dream seems to express a fear that if you get angry at someone, you'll do it in a vicious, destructive way." Clearly she felt violent rage toward those who hurt her in childhood. This dream helped Wendy see why it was so hard to express anger or defend herself. The dream depicted two ends of a continuum: a state of complete helplessness, and violent, murderous impulses. By becoming conscious of her rageful shadow, Wendy was able to learn to assert herself and express anger when necessary, without becoming violent. In discussing this dream with Wendy, I used the metaphor of "showing your claws" as a way of describing the capacity for self-protection. A week later Wendy reported the Dream of the Wildcat (discussed in Chapter One) in which she went to an animal rescue shelter where a big cat jumped on her and put her claws into Wendy's leg. It's interesting how Wendy's unconscious responded to my remark about the claws.

## A Dream of a War Veteran

Todd, a young man who had served in the military during Desert Storm, the first Gulf War, had serious physical and psychological problems, including major depression, violent outbursts, substance abuse, delusional thinking, chronic unemployment, and lack of friends; he was a complete loner. I saw him on a short-term basis. In his second session, he told me this dream:

> I go to an AA meeting, and I'm totally naked. I told them, "I don't think I belong here. I live in a different world." Then a wolf with red eyes appears with an army helmet on. I keep it at bay with a palm knife.

When I asked Todd for his associations to the wolf, he said, "The wolf is wild. He represents my own violence and bad temper, the destructive force of my anger. I was trained by the army to be a wild dog, a killer. The wolf is a noble creature that lives in the hills by itself. It reminds me of somebody who has been kicked too many times and has become mean and ferocious. It's an outsider to civilization; it's hated by farmers and hunted."

I said, "That reminds me of how you feel and live—like an outsider, with no place you call home, living on the margins of society."

"I can't tell if my perceptions are real or not. I get depressed a lot, or I feel really angry. Mostly I'm a hermit and hole up in my apartment."

"The wolf represents the pain of what you're really feeling, the loneliness, the feeling that nobody understands you."

The dream portrayed the shadow of anger and violence that was so troubling to Todd as he attempted to readjust to civilian life.

Soon after having this dream, Todd was hospitalized with severe symptoms of the mysterious Gulf War Syndrome that has afflicted so many Desert Storm veterans. His dream offered a personal symbol that seemed to encapsulate the pain and fury this young warrior experienced.

## The Dream of the Black Transvestite

A man named Jim had been sexually assaulted (by a man) during his childhood. As an adult, Jim was acutely homophobic and uncomfortable around other men, especially gay men, suspicious that men were attracted to him, but also occasionally panicking that he himself might be gay. He shared two dreams with me that illustrate the encounter with the shadow. In the first dream:

> I met a woman at a party, and went home with her. When we got to the door of her apartment, she turned around and I realized that she was actually a black transvestite, a flaming fairy with jewellery, thick makeup, and false boobs. Then I couldn't tell if it was a man or a woman. He or she seemed to be both. I woke up screaming.

The dream initially frightened Jim, but he found the image of the black transvestite so outrageous that it also seemed comical, as if the dream were mocking his fear of metamorphosizing into a feminized gay man, even though he'd always been heterosexual. The image of the black transvestite suggested that Jim was encountering an aspect of his shadow, embodying forbidden, repressed, or underdeveloped personal characteristics. This androgynous figure symbolized an internal union of opposites and indicated the value of integrating both male and female qualities into his self-image and self-experience. Exploring this dream helped Jim to feel comfortable expressing the feminine, emotional, sensitive aspects of his personality without feeling diminished as a man.

## The Dream of the Frenchman

Jim soon reported a second dream:

> I'm on a train. A French man comes into my compartment and says that his wallet is in my suitcase. I deny this vehemently. Nevertheless,

*he insists on searching my luggage and finds his wallet in my suitcase.*
*I'm shocked and embarrassed and say that I really didn't know it was*
*in there.*

This dream reminded Jim of how he'd once been propositioned by a Frenchman. He remarked, "My next thought is that all Frenchmen are gay or have at least experienced gay sex." He feared that discovering the Frenchman's wallet in his suitcase might symbolize discovering himself to be gay.

I mused that uncovering a wallet suggested finding something of value to him. I suggested that Jim ask the Frenchman, "Who are you? Why are you in my dream? What are you trying to communicate to me?"

Jim, speaking in the voice of the Frenchman, said, "I am your sexual wisdom. To know one side is to know all sides." This comment suggested to Jim that once we become more awake as sexual beings, then all possible permutations and expressions of sexuality become more evident. As he put it, "When I think of France, I think of a culture that's very open and very knowing about sex. The sexual wisdom of the Frenchman means that I don't necessarily have to do any of these wild, kinky things, but I do have to know about them. The dream is saying that to be sexually mature means to be wise about the full range of sexuality, and also to respect other people's choices." After working with this dream, Jim became more comfortable and trusting in his interactions with other men, which greatly benefited his capacity to enjoy friendships—which he'd previously avoided.

## The Dream of the Bunker and the Psychotic Killer

The next example demonstrates the integration of shadow material and difficult memories and emotions. A fifty-five-year-old woman named Laura had recently returned to work after a long illness and was regaining her strength and creative energy. She had the following dream:

*I'm with a mate at a beach. We see a weird, angry man who is mad at us,*
*but I don't know why. There's a communal event where he's the recipi-*
*ent of awards and attention. The people there have no idea that the man*
*harbours this other angry side. To them, he's the most fantastic man.*

*There have been some murders in the area. One person is missing this night. My mate and I are getting ready to leave when we discover a wooden structure on the beach with a door. We go inside and down a ladder. It's a bunker in the sand. There are vials and bottles filled with substances, some of which are toxic. On a shelf there's an array of Number Eight hypodermic needles. Number Eight needles go easy in and easy out, and so they're perfect for humans. We get out of there fast. This guy is a dangerous nut. We know that it's his bunker. He sees us. Everyone is all upset about the disappeared person. We tell them about the toxins and the needles and why that's so important. They all agree the man couldn't do anything so dreadful, but they call the authorities just in case. The guy is psychotic now. We can see it, so we split fast. We drive along the coast. He's in hot pursuit. I'm scared but also clear that I don't trust him. We're ahead and have some time on him. Suddenly we turn a bend and find that we're in the middle of a battleship parking lot. There are lots of battleships, huge grey ships sitting in vivid green water.*

The setting at a beach suggested being at the edge of the ocean of the unconscious. It reminded Laura of walking, enjoying picnics, fantasy, and sand castles. This suggested to me that the dream might reveal insights about unconscious fantasy material.

Going down a ladder into a bunker reminded Laura of going to a deeper level, and being a missing person like the mythic Persephone, who was abducted and held in the underworld by Hades. Being in the underworld reminded Laura of being at home with her illness for many years. This also symbolized the possibility of resurfacing, as Persephone periodically re-emerged—coming back into life, going back to work.

The dream presented two faces of the masculine. The presence of a mate in the dream implied union with a supportive male figure, a positive animus-lover. For Laura, who was single, this was a healing image of having a boyfriend or partner. But she was also encountering the presence of the negative animus, a violent, dangerous, destructive male. "This guy reminds me of my fear that any man I try to love will be hostile and destructive." Laura continued, "The weird angry man reminds me of my daughter's ex-boyfriend. This man was tricky, suave, and dishonest, a real con man. The man in the dream has conned all these people into seeing him in a positive light, hiding his shadow. I often fall prey to people like him. I trust people, I put up blinders. Then I feel deceived. Being deceived also reminds me of my mother. She was inconsistent and dishonest. She was often mad at me for reasons I wasn't clear about, just like the man in the dream. It also reminds me of my feelings of being below standards in my work skills. I sometimes think I've deceived myself that I can make it at my new job."

"I think the angry, psychotic killer signifies your feelings of inadequacy and self-attacking thoughts, which undermine your confidence and attack you from inside."

"I think that has affected my health too."

The man receiving awards reminded me of Laura's effort to achieve, to be seen, to advance in her new job, as opposed to feeling invisible, weak, defeated. Receiving awards implied hope and healthy striving, trying to realize her potentials and become more accomplished in the world. This was in contrast to the image of the dangerous, angry man, symbol of self-attack, an inner critic or persecutor who negated her ambitions and striving for connection.

The image of the bunker with toxic substances reminded Laura of a bomb shelter, and of being under siege. Laura said, "The bunker reminds me of a place to ride out an attack." The vials and bottles reminded me of a laboratory, like an alchemist's laboratory. Toxins reminded Laura of the many medications she'd been taking, but also toxic emotions. I said. "The bunker-laboratory filled with toxins suggests to me that you're engaging in a process of alchemically transforming toxic emotions such as anger and bitterness."

That led us to the hypodermic needles, which Laura associated with lashing out, stingers, and snakes injecting venom. I said, "The dream reminds you of experiences that have stung you emotionally."

Laura said, "Snake venom reminds me of my mother's poisonous way of turning against me." Snakes also reminded Laura of "speaking with a forked tongue," which brought us back to the theme of duplicity and deceit.

I asked, "What does it mean that in the dream the needles work perfectly?"

"The injections don't hurt."

"Perhaps the dream is saying you can tolerate re-experiencing these difficult feelings. They won't hurt you. It reminds me of being inoculated with a pathogen to make you immune to it."

The number eight in the dream reminded Laura of "infinity, eternity, regeneration, the unending cycle of life."

I said. "That's paradoxical. The hypodermic needles used to inject poisons also symbolize rebirth. Perhaps by being injected with the anger you feel about family deceit, by revisiting these toxic memories and feelings from the past, you may be reborn and regenerated, like a snake shedding its old skin."

Battleships reminded Laura of "a pod of whales," which reminded her of "family, connection, community, protection."

I said, "This suggests that, for you, family is a battleground, a place of anger, deceit, and lies. The battleships evoke memories of abuse of parental authority, and all the anger you feel about that. All of this is connected to your mistrust of men, and your fear that they'll deceive you. It's important to understand these feelings so you can have healthier relationships." Examining this dream allowed Laura to face her shadow and to integrate a range of feelings and memories.

## The Metaphor of the Sea Serpent

Therapeutic dreamwork performs a different role in the evolution of consciousness than spiritual practices such as meditation. Dreamwork is a path of increasing consciousness by integrating memories, feelings, and emergent qualities from the unconscious. Some contemplative disciplines, such as Hindu and Buddhist yoga, emphasize silent meditation to quiet the fluctuations of the mind and emotions in order to experience a thought-free state of pure awareness. The first *Yoga Sutra* of the sage Patanjali reads, "Yoga is the cessation of the fluctuations of the mind." By bringing the mind to one-pointed focus in meditation, we reach a place where the mind is silent and calm like a clear, glassy lake, without a ripple. When the mind is clear and its surface ripples subside, we can see through to the bottom, into the vastness of spirit, the Self, the silent witness consciousness.

But the waters of the psyche can be turbulent and difficult to quell. Meditators still have powerful upsurges of undigested feelings, memories, and traumas. From the perspective of depth psychology, the reason we can't bring the ocean of the mind to silence is that there's a sea serpent swimming around under the water—the sea serpent of the unconscious, of libido. We need to grapple with the sea serpent before the waves of the mind will become calm. We need to let the unconscious breathe and ventilate a wide range of feelings, including some that are difficult or painful. The path of dreamwork requires a willingness to look at ourselves with radical honesty. Dreams enable us to explore both the shadows and the light that dwell within us. We need both the stillness of deep meditation and the direct engagement with our drives, feelings, and relationships through the practice of dreamwork.

## The Dream of the Amphitheatre

As counselors psychologists, analysts, and spiritual guides, we do well to pay special attention to our own emotional states and shadow material. Attention to our own dreams helps us to be fully present in our work with others. The next four examples describe some shadow work that occupied me during a stressful period. At that time, I was feeling impatient and grouchy toward one of my clients, who was angry at me. Around the same time, several students were complaining about my highly structured teaching style. I dreamed:

> *I'm walking around an amphitheatre in the shape of a horseshoe crab.*

The amphitheatre reminded me of a classroom and giving a performance. The crab is a symbol of the astrological sign of Cancer, representing emotions and the feeling function. I was reminded of crabs nipping, which made me think about how these students and this client were complaining, nipping at me. This, I realized, was evoking crabby feelings in me. I was sad and hurt. The dream was also a message to let myself be guided more by my emotions in my work, rather than relying so much on intellect.

## The Dream of God Pissing

Some time later, after a difficult professional setback, I dreamed:

> *I was in my backyard and felt a mist falling on me. I thought at first that an airplane was dropping moisture and debris from the sky, dumping garbage. Was God pissing on me? Or was I receiving the rain of grace?*

According to Edward Edinger (1994a), dew signifies a gift from heaven down to earth. It represents divine intervention, fate, synchronicity, purification. The setback in my career might have seemed like a bad turn of fate, but actually it led to needed changes. It was grace. Working with this dream helped me move through a period of self-pity and resentment that was affecting my work with others.

## The Dream of the Dejected Bird

A few months later I dreamed:

> *I was sitting in my front yard when a large, furry bird landed and stood with his head down in a way that looked dejected. Then the bird was transformed into a horse, and I rode on its back as it climbed a steep sand dune.*

The dejected bird reminded me of my own dejection and discouragement at the time. I was hanging my head. Even therapists get into an emotional funk sometimes. But the bird's transformation in the dream into a horse climbing up a steep dune renewed my sense that I could advance myself through vigorous effort. This dream released creative energy inside me, and I began to throw myself wholeheartedly into my work as a therapist, teacher, and writer for the first time in months. These dreams helped me look at the part of my shadow that was burdened by hopelessness and surly resentfulness. Because we often work with clients who are depressed, anxious, angry, or afraid, it's essential for psychotherapists and counselors to become conscious of their own comparable feelings, to pursue the constant inner work we need to do to be effective healers.

## The Dream of the Salamander

Sometimes encounter with the shadow involves feelings that are quite outside our typical emotional range. I had this dream at a time when I was feeling angry and misunderstood and harboured fantasies of revenge against someone I felt had unjustly attacked me:

> *I'm swimming in the ocean. Someone asks me what fish or animals come around. I say, "I'm washing a salamander with ocean water,"*

*but the guy checks my kitchen water faucet and finds it's ordinary tap*
*water, so my claim (that it's ocean water) is proven to be false. We go*
*in the water, and there are visitations of birds, fish, dolphins. A big*
*wave comes along, and we dive under.*

In the dream I make a false claim about the water, which is common tap water rather than ocean water. Making a "false claim" reminded me of an erroneous astrological prediction I made about John Kerry winning the 2004 U.S. presidential election, which left me concerned about losing face or credibility. The birds, fish, and dolphins reminded me of how I'm often guided by intuition, but also of how the shadow of my work as an astrologer can be intuition that's misguided and ungrounded—expressing the negative aspects of the archetypal medium (described in Chapter Five). On another level, my dream commented on the circumstances by which George W. Bush assumed office in the first place, seizing power in the bloodless coup of the 2000 election, aided by the U.S. Supreme Court—another "false claim."

The dream contrasted tap water, which seems mundane and ordinary, with ocean water, the timeless, vast unconscious. This signified union of sacred and profane. The ocean water of infinite spirit was now ordinary water coming out of a faucet, a tiny spigot. It raised the question of how spirit can be manifest in secular life, with its fiery conflicts and challenges. And somehow this involved washing a salamander.

Jung referred to the salamander as "the Hermetic vessel, ... the full Moon and the rising sun" (Jung, 1968 [1944], par. 391). He wrote, "the prima materia in alchemy was symbolized by the salamander in the fire" (Jung, 1950a, par. 705). The fire baptism of the salamander was a theme in alchemy.

> The monster frolicking in the flames is the magical salamander ... . It dwells in the 'hellish fire' as the mercurial animal the fire does not consume. Since the spotted and blood-filled salamander feeds on the fire, he is not consumed by the dragon's mouth. On the contrary he represents the fiery principle which conquers the fire. (Fabricius, 1994, p. 76)

John Conger, an analyst whose work combines the approaches of Jung and Melanie Klein, interpreted the dream for me thus:

In alchemy, the Salamander is what can be in the fire without being consumed. It's a model for the Stone, the enduring Self, the Soul—what will not be consumed by fire. In Kleinian terms, the ego can form because it's able to internalize the good object and deal with the bad internal objects that persecute us. The ego exists in a vicious and dangerous inner landscape. We face hostile, persecuting internal figures that feel like they're destroying us from within. Fire refers to surviving internal attacks from these primitive superego elements. There's an internal battle between good and evil. Can our capacity to love and trust survive the sadistic, attacking elements that evoke feelings of rage and futility? Sometimes we want to inflict pain and punishment on others, trying to gain mastery over the hostile internal objects by getting revenge or turning our anger on them. That's one way of dealing with the internal forces that attack us. In Jungian, alchemical language, the Salamander represents the conflict with these terrifying, destructive, persecutory elements. This process burns off egotism and presumption. All that isn't part of an enduring Self (the Sun) is burned away in the fire. We become at home in the fire, grateful to the fire because it is purifying us. The Salamander represents enduring the fires of the Sun. Our ego investment in being important and thinking things should be easy leads to attacking ourselves mercilessly because we don't want to let go of the false ideal—that success should come easily and everyone should love us. These idealizations take us away from reality. The Salamander represents burning off the false ideal that things should be easy, so the enduring Self can emerge. Who you really are is what can survive the fire. (John Conger, personal communication)

Working with this dream helped me metabolize my angry, persecuted feelings, which were binding energy I was soon able to direct more constructively. The salamander in the fire represented my own fires of passion and creativity, as well as the process of testing and purification—an apt image for encountering the shadow. The liquid running through my kitchen faucet could also be viewed as waters of purification, healing waters.

Washing the salamander with ocean water reminded me of being cleansed in the alchemical water of life, the *aqua permanens*.

According to von Franz (1977), "Mercurius, the mysterious figure of the *prima materia*, is generally a mysterious liquid, the elixir of life, the eternal water which usually generates silver and gold." The water of life often appears as a spring. It represents "the feeling that life is flowing in a meaningful way." Silvery or gold water represents vitality and "the feeling of being alive" (pp. 33–34). This dream is similar to the Dream of the Pig (Chapter Two) in its depiction of a watery process of emotional healing and reconciliation.

The salamander dream combines volatile elements. Jung wrote, "Sometimes the water is associated with fire, or even combined with it as fire-water (wine, alcohol)" (Jung, 1959, par. 353). The mix of emotion and passion generates a revitalizing liquor—the elixir of consciousness embracing its polarities.

Reclaiming and transforming the shadow magnetically draws us to a deep internal centre, a place where fire and water mix. Dreams show us previously unconscious traits, attitudes, and feelings, which often challenge the public face of our persona. Meetings with the shadow reveal that we're composed of multiple, competing inner forces seeking amalgamation into a complex whole. Jung wrote:

> The problem of opposites called up by the shadow ... leads in the ultimate phase of the work to the union of opposites in the archetypal form of the *hieros gamos* or "chymical marriage." Here the supreme opposites, male and female ... are melted into a unity purified of all opposition and therefore incorruptible. (Jung, 1968 [1944], par. 43)

In the next chapter we'll delve further into the union of male and female represented by the archetypes of the animus and anima.

# CHAPTER EIGHT

# Anima and Animus in Dreams

T he approach to dreamwork I'm presenting in this book could be summarized as the practice of creating consciousness by recognizing the coexistence of opposites within the personality. This process includes the urge to unite the gendered poles of our experience represented by the anima and animus, archetypes that have varied and elusive meanings. First, they signify our realization of the maleness and femaleness within all of us, the fact that both men and women possess, to some degree, characteristics of both genders. The classical Jungian formulation depicted anima as the carrier of a man's unconscious *Eros*, his capacity for feeling and relatedness. The animus was portrayed as a woman's unconscious *logos*, her capacity for logic and intellectual certitude.

> [A]nima/us is a psychic structure that is complementary to the persona and links the ego to the deepest layer of the psyche, namely to the image and experience of the self … . [T]he persona is the habitual attitude that an ego adopts to meet the world. It is a public personality and facilitates adaptation to the demands of physical and … social reality … . The anima/us is … concerned with adaptation to the inner world … . [T]he

anima/us allows the ego to enter into and to experience the depths of the psyche. (Stein, 1998, pp. 128, 130)

The anima is an unconscious feminine complex, apparent when a man (or woman) is emotionally reactive, whiny, and oversensitive, full of touchy, hurt feelings. The animus is an unconscious masculine complex that is apparent when a woman (or man) becomes overbearing, domineering, self-righteous, and stridently opinionated. She becomes bossy, pushy, domineering. According to Murray Stein, a man's anima is evident when he is moody, intensely emotional, and overreactive to slights.

> His relationships typically are fraught with conflict because he has emotional reactions that are too powerful for him to manage … . Similarly, a woman with an "animus problem" is also overcome by her unconscious, typically by emotionally charged thoughts and opinions which control her more than she controls them. This is not very different from the anima-possessed man, only the accent tends to be more intellectual on the woman's side. These autonomous thoughts and opinions end up disturbing her adaptation to the world because they are delivered with the emotional energy of a bully. Often they wreak havoc on her relationships, because the people near her must build self-protective shields around themselves when they are with her. They feel on the defensive and uncomfortable in her presence … . [S]he is abrasive and gripped by unconscious strivings for power and control … . Men in the grips of the anima tend to withdraw into hurt feelings; women in the grips of the animus tend to attack … . [T]here is also the problem of too little development in the anima/us structure. This lack of development is like an undeveloped muscle … . Men will then typically look for a woman to help them manage their emotions, and women will typically find a man who can receive their inspired thoughts and do something with them. Thus other people enter the game of ego-anima/us relations. (Stein, 1998, pp. 131–132)

The anima or animus activates the unconscious, especially when we're stirred by our attractions to others. Whereas the shadow is generally seen in dream figures and waking life persons who are scary, threatening, or repellent, the anima and animus announce themselves through people or dream characters who attract, captivate, and fascinate us. Stein wrote:

> If the image of the shadow instils fear and dread, the image of the anima/us usually brings excitement and stimulates desire for union. It engenders attraction ... . We want to be part of it, we want to join it. (Stein, 1998, p. 142)

When we fall in love, we project the archetype onto someone who carries it for us. We find a person who embodies qualities of the anima or animus, which we project onto our beloved. The anima/ animus often manifests as a feeling of attraction to an enticing, attractive person who we hope will complete us. The anima and animus are carriers of tempestuous storms that inspire our souls and ignite our passions. The encounter with this person (or dream figure) moves us and stirs us to change in our feelings, our thinking, and our motivations.

## The Dream of the Handsome Prima Donna

A woman named Frieda dreamed:

> I was with a tour group in a country akin to Tangiers or perhaps somewhere in Mexico. There was a man on the tour who was a bit of a prima donna, very handsome but also a bit of a jerk. I didn't want to be near him, but I was also a little intrigued with him. We ended up in a group ritual with each of us paired up man/woman. He was my partner. I was disappointed, anxious, and excited too. There was some sort of Tantric exercise to explore with each other. I lay down. He said, "Sit up and meet me."

The dark, mysterious man was the animus, seeking her out for union. Frieda said, "I saw him as foreign and a jerk. Yet I was also attracted to him because intuitively I knew he would bring me healing."

"What about him was attractive to you?"

"His power and good looks. He was very outgoing and confident."

"I think these are qualities you're developing."

"But I didn't want to be associated with his arrogance. He was unable to see he was a jerk; it was something unconscious. I feared being taken over by him, consumed by him."

I asked Frieda about his being a prima donna. That reminded her of being "a show-off, like how I was as a youngster."

"So the prima donna is a symbol of healthy narcissism, self-esteem, inner radiance. That's what your animus possesses: healthy self-esteem."

"That's what I keep looking for in a partner. I project this out onto men."

"He projects himself outward, without inhibition. Perhaps that's what you need to learn to do."

"Bingo," she replied.

The animus has a captivating quality that evokes admiration. Emma Jung said the animus is characterized by *logos*, which encompasses four masculine principles: will, word, deed, and meaning. Will refers to drive and ambition. Word refers to a gift with words. Deed means that one becomes a person of action. Meaning is the orientation toward philosophy and spiritual practice (Jung, 1981 [1957], p. 3). The handsome prima donna embodied a capacity for will and deed that Frieda admired.

## Anima, Projection, and Animation

The anima and animus describe the dance of attraction, projection, and illusion making that are such an integral part of the experience of love. Jung wrote:

> The projection-making factor is the anima ... . Not all the contents of the anima and animus are projected, however. Many of them appear spontaneously in dreams ... . In this way we find that thoughts, feelings, and affects are alive in us which we would never have believed possible ... . The autonomy of the collective unconscious expresses itself in the figures of anima and animus. They personify those of its contents which, when withdrawn from projection, can be integrated into consciousness ... . [B]oth figures represent functions which filter the contents of the collective unconscious through to the conscious mind ... . [T]he anima and animus are felt to be fascinating and numinous.

Often they are surrounded by an atmosphere of sensitivity, touchy reserve, secretiveness, painful intimacy, and even absoluteness … . Anyone who wants to achieve the difficult feat of realizing something not only intellectually, but also according to its feeling value, must for better or worse come to grips with the anima/animus problem in order to open the way for a higher union, a *coniunctio oppositorum*. This is an indispensable prerequisite for wholeness. (Jung, 1959, pars. 26, 39, 40, 53, 58)

Stein says that engagement of the ego with the anima or animus

is the work of raising consciousness, of becoming aware of projections … . The anima/animus is captured in projection by a person who bears its traits and features … . The anima/animus is eternally active in psychological life, and its absence defines the nature of depression … . The ability to differentiate between projection and projection-carrier, between fantasy and reality, is rare indeed … . [T]he anima/animus is Maya, the creator of illusions, the mystifier, the ever-receding mirage of the eternal beloved. (Stein, 1998, pp. 143–145, 148)

Stein's statement here that absence of anima "defines the nature of depression" implies that the anima/animus appears as a person or dream figure who enlivens and inspires us, quickening our feelings, longings, and aspirations. The anima/animus is what animates us. It's the archetype of life and love, and the struggles we endure to sustain love beyond projections and expectations. Once we take back the projection-making factor and find our own inner feeling of aliveness, the anima/animus anticipates our wholeness, and internally incites us to attain it.

## Anima Aliveness

In his essay *The Anima in Film*, John Beebe (2001) wrote that anima is "a confusing, deceptive presence with the capacity to engender inner transformation" (p. 208). Some of the signs the anima is present—in a film character, a dream figure, or a person in waking life—include:

unusual radiance, … mind-blowing presence, … a star personality … [and] a desire to make emotional connection as

the main concern of the character ... . [T]he anima figure wants
to be loved, or occasionally to be hated, in either case living
for connection. [Her role is] representation of the status of the
man's unconscious eros and particularly his relationship to
himself ... . The loss of this figure is associated with the loss of
purposeful aliveness itself ... . In life, we know her as moods,
impulses, symptoms, and as a shape-shifting fleeting personage in our dreams. (Beebe, 2001, pp. 208–212)

Beebe notes that a man may come alive if he responds to the anima's need for emotional connection. The anima possesses unconscious energy and magnetism, but she overdramatizes everything.
She may offer advice or a rebuke. A man often becomes victim of
the anima's seduction, giving rise to situations of "hopeless love,"
"ideal romantic love" and romantic illusions and disillusion-
ments. In this way, the anima sometimes plays a role in a man's
psychological demise. The anima catalyses for a man in midlife
"the discovery of the value of his aliveness to him." According to
Beebe, "When the anima is irretrievably lost," a vulnerable man
may be initiated into "psychological senescence" (Beebe, 2001,
pp. 217–219). In other words, when a man has lost touch with a
sense of "purposeful aliveness," he begins to grow old, stagnant,
and lifeless. The connection with both inner and outer anima
figures—both dream goddesses and real women who embody
vital emotional and erotic energy—feels like it could be our ultimate salvation. The anima is also the inspiration that we can access
from within, in our joyous spirit and infectious creativity. We find
our own axis of Eros, enhancing our relationships and pleasurable
enjoyment in daily life.

The secret to resolving the moody depression, sensitivity, and
unhappiness of the male anima is to find what inspires us, bringing
beauty and soul to daily living. We men tend to get moody when
we feel our beloved is not sufficiently nurturing, affirming, responsive, or exciting—just as women get angry when they feel their
intelligence and leadership are not validated. We look for a spouse
or lover to carry the positive, enlivening anima. We can unfold the
anima archetype by finding something that *animates* us, that brings
us alive, a source of pleasurable fulfilment. The anima is an energy
that is spirited and filled with life. In my own life, I live the anima

through music, guitar, composing songs, playing in jazz bands. Men can integrate the anima through exploring the spontaneity and creativity of the dynamic feminine, becoming one with the youthful, vibrant, revitalizing energy that we long for and often expect women to provide.

## Revisioning the Gender Basis of Anima/Animus

I believe that Jung was ahead of his time in stating that men have an inner femininity that needs to be developed, and women have an inner masculinity that needs to be cultivated. But Jung's formulation of the anima/animus has been criticized for its implicit assumption that men and women are weak in their feeling and thinking functions, respectively. Jung's formulation reflected the biases of an era, where gender roles and divisions were more strictly demarcated, so that men were socialized to be strong, powerful, and unemotional, and thus were less apt to express their feelings. Women of previous generations had fewer educational opportunities and were correspondingly less likely to develop intellectually, but this was due to social conditions more than any constitutional reality. Thus, it's worth considering the possibility that anima and animus complexes really exist but aren't strictly tied to gender stereotypes. Both men and women express unconscious moodiness and angry dogmatism. The appearance of these complexes would also vary according to sexual orientation.

I formulate this as follows: For a heterosexual man, the anima embodies the characteristics of an attractive, desirable woman who stirs our feelings. For a heterosexual woman, the animus represents the inner image of an attractive, desirable man who impresses us with his power, logic, and confidence. For a gay man, the anima may be a male figure (see the Dream of Uriah Heap, the Cathedral, and the Kung Fu Fighter in Chapter Two; and the Dream of the Blind Date and the Shy Weightlifter in Chapter Thirteen); or it may become a feature of his own persona. For a lesbian, the animus may appear in a female form, or it may become a feature of her own persona. In short, the anima and animus aren't strictly limited in their manifestations to a particular gender. They are archetypes that operate in men and women's psyches regardless of their gender or sexual orientation.

Jung believed the anima or animus could only be realized through relationship with a partner of the opposite gender. But anima or animus energies can also be carried by members of the same sex (Stein, 1998, p. 144). Lionel Corbett and Cathy Rives explained:

> [In] Jung's description of the anima-possessed man and the animus-possessed woman ... [t]he former is said to possess traits such as irritability, moodiness, jealousy, vanity, and bitchiness, while the latter is described as obstinate, dogmatic, argumentative, and opinionated .... The classical concepts have attracted confusion and controversy among feminists and Jungian writers alike, because Jung ascribed particular characteristics to only one gender .... [M]any people take exception to the typical cliché that masculinity is necessarily and essentially assertive, while receptivity is a feminine trait. Such bias is the unfortunate result of a patriarchy that dictated such norms. Furthermore, certain of Jung's opinions suggest that women are less capable of independent action and objectivity than men .... In spite of these difficulties, we believe that the terms anima and animus do, in fact, describe essential intrapsychic functions whose nature can be clarified in a manner that will free them from both culturally contaminated gender issues and a tendency to devalue women. This requires that these concepts be completely freed from both their rigid, historical associations with contrasexuality and instead examined in terms of fundamental intrapsychic processes .... The terms anima and animus refer to the intrapsychic contrasexual, the bridge to the unconscious, the unconscious itself, eros and logos, feeling and thinking, the inferior function, or soul and spirit. Anima has also been used to mean the archetype of life itself .... Same-sex figures may guide us to the unconscious, such as the appearance of the chthonic masculine in the dream of a modern man who has lost touch with it. Such a figure is a soul figure whatever its gender, while spirit or organizing figures may also be of either gender and are not limited to male figures in women's dreams—the spirit may perfectly well take a feminine form .... We believe that Jung overgeneralized when he described the bridging factor as necessarily contrasexual. For him personally, it was always personified as feminine .... But such is not universally the case ....

[B]oth men and women experience intrapsychic soul figures which bridge to the unconscious and spirit figures which order and provide discrimination and meaning … . [T]he function of relation to the unconscious is a genderless, archetypal potential, but the way we experience it is shaped by our contact with gendered beings. (Corbett & Rives, 1991, pp. 251–252, 254)

## Four Anima Dreams

The anima, like all archetypal patterns, evolves over time as we change and grow. Here I'll recount four dreams reflecting my own work to integrate this archetype and develop my inner aliveness. During my early twenties, I dreamed:

*I saw an elusive, beautiful woman who was very seductive and then disappeared out of reach. I couldn't connect with her because she was so flighty and aloof. I had the feeling that I wasn't good enough for her.*

This dream accurately described a type of unavailable woman I was attracted to in waking life. But when I looked at this figure as a reflection of my own feminine side, things began to change. I realized that I myself was cool, aloof, distancing, always treating women who were interested in me as if *they* weren't good enough. This dream was a spot-on image of my own insecure-avoidant attachment style (Holmes, 1993). Once I recognized this attitude, I started to have better relationships, and the anima was no longer so elusive.

Some years later, another anima figure appeared in a dream:

*A woman I knew as a neighbour but had never really spoken to sought me out and wanted to talk to me. She was a very thin, frail, flat-chested Asian woman. She was quite shy, introverted, and not at all sexy.*

This inner figure who wanted to talk to me was asking to be integrated. She reminded me of being shy and socially awkward, bookish and withdrawn. I had this dream after attending a conference where I felt painfully shy and had difficulty connecting with others. As I worked with this dream figure, I came to appreciate the Asian woman's humility, her unassuming, comfortable attitude about being behind the scenes. She wasn't interested in the spotlight or getting attention. This was a soulful contrast to the part of me that craved attention and validation. She, too, was part of my inner femininity.

At another time, I dreamed of a woman named Jennifer. My first association was that "Jennifer is a tall woman who exudes a kind of snotty superiority." I recognized how this was related to an unconscious touch of arrogance of my own. With further reflection, I felt that the dream Jennifer was also a bridging figure to my own unconscious potential, signifying the expression of healthy and stable self-esteem.

## The Dream of the Lace Curtain, an Open Book, and the Refined Woman's Painting

Another anima image appeared in this dream:

> I climbed a staircase to a room in a tower or turret. I walked past a delicate white lace curtain in the doorway into a room where a very refined, beautiful woman with long hair had left an open book and one of her watercolour paintings sitting on a table. She wasn't in the room, but I was hoping to see her. I noticed there was a stain or smudge on the painting.

This dream reminded me of several artistic women I'd loved in the past, and my feeling of inner emotional union with them. The delicate white lace curtain, the refined woman, and the watercolour painting all evoked feeling, purity, sensitivity, and artistic and spiritual inspiration—qualities suggesting the presence of anima. The white lace was like gossamer, a shimmering, delicate, see-through fabric, representing the ultimate in feminine beauty and refinement. The refined woman reminded me of Sophia, gnostic goddess of wisdom. In India, the same archetype appears as Saraswati, goddess of art, music, philosophy, culture, and education. The stain on the painting represented sadness about relationships that had ended, beautiful love that had been stained, but also a streak of self-doubt and self-denigration that stained my soul's purity. The smudged painting reminded me of making something beautiful and then ruining it. When this dream occurred, I was in a loving relationship but was afraid I'd do something to spoil it. The stained painting made me aware that loving somebody means learning to accept that person's imperfections, and also to express the ways that he or she is beautiful and precious to you. The open book in the dream was also significant. To be an open book means to let people see in, rather than remaining hidden. It shows a desire for relatedness; it suggests becoming visible to others, making oneself accessible, not hiding. Climbing the stairs to the room in the tower reminded me of entering my own private space of solitary, introspective study and self-reflection. The dream conveyed the insight that I myself was the beloved anima I longed for.

## The Dream of the Italian Man

A woman named Liz dreamed:

> *I'm with an Italian man, a little older with a moustache. I'm receiving an award or medal of some kind.*

Liz said, "He was my hero, charming, dashing, exotic, but he was also cunning and sneaky. He is 'here to save the day.' He was like my Prince Charming, the perfect man—even though he wasn't that good-looking." The dream of the Italian man stirred Liz to greater self-confidence. Receiving the award suggested acknowledging the valuable, worldly wise, socially confident animus qualities of her personality. The Italian man's cunning was a gift too. She said, "I'm not just an innocent, naïve little girl. He reminds me that I know how the world works."

As Corbett and Rives (1991) explained, "Spirit, or animus, is … the principle that provides meaning, discrimination, value, and order … . It may become manifest in either masculine or feminine form" (p. 255).

## The Dream of the Bed, Princess Fergie, and the Child

The next dream not only explores the animus but also contains the fourfold symbolism of maiden, mother, amazon, and wise woman. In addition, the dream features archetypal symbolism of the child, the shadow, and the *hierosgamos*, the royal marriage.

A woman named Alice dreamed:

> *I'm in bed with Greg [my therapist] at his house, which is in a place that reminds me of New Orleans. There was a balcony that looked*

*down on the streets. Greg and I were sitting on top of a bed, fully clothed. Books were spread out all over the bed, which was covered with red and gold bedding. I felt close to him, but I wasn't sharing everything I wanted to share with him about my dreams. I held back. I left the house and went to a woman friend's house, where I was going to baby-sit. The woman looked like the British Princess Sarah Ferguson, "Fergie." She was crying on the side of a partition, near the kitchen table. She was drying her eyes with a broken-down Cheerios box. I don't know what she was upset about, but I thought it was because she was in an unhappy marriage. She received a phone call from an aunt who said she was sending a present. This made Fergie smile and say, "I'm getting a present!" Then I was walking around with Fergie's son, Simon. We got helium balloons. Simon held onto one while we flew up into the air. I tried to keep Simon entertained. We ended up in a music room, with rich colours like red and gold.*

The setting of the dream in a place like New Orleans reminded Alice of partying and being around lots of people in high school and college; it signified her extraverted personality, youth and freedom, being full of possibilities. Alice and I called this part of her the party girl, a variant of the *puella aeterna* and the maiden. She described it as "the superficial, extraverted, bitchy side of me."

Reading books on the bed signified introversion, self-study through therapy and dreamwork, developing her positive animus, her spirit and intellect. Alice said, "You represent safety; you respect me. You're the part of me that's intellectual and spiritual, and into meditation, camping, and going on vision quests. You represent the part of me that wants to practice yoga and be a shaman." Alice had read a book I wrote in which I described camping out in the woods doing a vision quest (Bogart, 1995). The dream portrayed a male figure representing Alice's urge to develop as a wise woman. It showed her evolving the qualities of Artemis, goddess of the forest who is wild and free in nature. In another sense, it represented her development within the archetypal pattern of the introspective mystic or medium.

Being on the bed with Greg, her therapist, suggested erotic energy in the transference. It reminded Alice of safety, comfort, lots of blankets, warmth, and trust. This marked a change in her relationship to the masculine principle. I commented that there seemed to be something positive about meeting a man fully clothed—within the roles and boundaries of a therapeutic relationship. The scene suggested that, within the container of therapy, we could meet, reflect, and grow together. The image of Greg was a symbol of the animus, and of delving deeply into her emotional, intellectual, and spiritual growth. The dream portrayed an inner marriage, a *coniunctio*, through union with this inner male figure.

Holding back from her therapist suggested issues of trust, some transference issues. But Alice confirmed my own sense that we were steadily building trust. That moment in our conversation felt like the scene depicted in the second Rosarium image, which shows a King and Queen, fully robed, meeting and exchanging flowers (Figure 3). The therapeutic relationship was becoming charged with feeling and intensity. "Holding back" also reminded Alice of her relationship with a man named Richard, who wanted to marry her. She was holding back, delaying decision about their future. The dream brought into focus conflict between her current relationship with Richard, and her fantasy of going to the woods to become a shaman. She was torn between a strongly intellectual and spiritual, introverted orientation and the pressure she felt to commit to Richard and their life together. There was also a connection between meeting a trustworthy male figure in the dream, and her inner feeling that she could trust Richard.

It's interesting to note that the colours red and gold appeared twice in the dream. Red signifies passion, while gold suggests royalty, dignity, self-respect, and intrapsychic wholeness. The royal quality of the red and gold bedding suggested that the scene on the bed was a symbol of the alchemical royal marriage.

Fergie, the princess, also introduced the principle of royalty, symbol of the Self, wholeness, and radiant individuation. Fergie also carried additional meanings for Alice. Fergie didn't accept her role as princess and was uncomfortable as a member of the British royal family. Similarly, Alice felt unsure she could accept being a wife and mother, a domesticated woman. The princess reminded Alice of living a fairytale life. A fairytale reminded Alice of fantasies about how things are supposed to be. Alice said, "I'm outgrowing my illusions, especially the illusion that things will just happen without becoming more committed to my work and my relationship." Fergie also represented taking a personal stand even if it causes embarrassment or humiliation. Alice was fiercely independent and felt that she had to be true to herself, even if it disappointed other people. In this sense, Fergie could be seen as a symbol of the archetypal amazon. Alice said, "She represents walking on my own path." Sarah Ferguson's admission of her problems with alcohol and overeating made her a symbol of honesty, a willingness to show her woundedness and problems without pretense. That reminded Alice of unmasking with me in therapy and becoming more emotionally honest with herself. The downfall of the princess was a mythic collective event comparable to death of the king, and signified death of the puella, the youthful, carefree side of Alice that always remained uncommitted. Fergie also signified overcoming fear, insecurity, and lack of self-confidence to become a poised, unaffected beauty. As an archetypal personality, Fergie combined royal pride, human vulnerability, and graceful recovery from setbacks.

The woman crying reminded Alice of unhappiness, sadness, hiding her feelings, and her fear of being trapped in a boring, bland, dull life. Alice said, "She didn't want anyone to see she was in an unhappy marriage. This reminds me of my fear of commitment to Richard. I don't want to become a depressed, unhappy woman. In my mind, marriage equals confinement. I want to run away." Alice was examining her fear of the commitments and routines of having children and becoming a mother.

The box of Cheerios cereal reminded Alice of something kids like, but also something with no sugar, and therefore boring, not gratifying and delicious. Her next association was to the bland life of the unhappy woman trapped in the kitchen. Drying her eyes with the broken-down cereal box reminded her of feeling broken down and depressed. It was an image of her depressed shadow. Cheerios also reminded me of pretending to be cheerful, maintaining a *persona*, putting on a good face.

Receiving a present reminded Alice of "someone consoling me, placating me, like my ex-husband, who bought me presents to make up for being a jerk, who treated me more as a trophy than as a person. I wasn't taken seriously." This is something that infuriates many women and, understandably, moves them into the experience of a dissatisfied animus.

The dream figure of Simon was a symbol of the divine child. The male child suggested birth of the dynamic masculine principle and its fiery initiative (Hill, 1992). von Franz (1970) wrote, "Interpreted one way, a child dream figure could mean renewed vitality, spontaneity, and a new possibility suddenly appearing within or without and changing the whole life situation in a positive way" (pp. 34–35). The emergent possibility represented by the child was marriage, having her own children, and her own birth as a developing professional and spiritual practitioner. My association to holding the helium balloon was that it represented the alchemical process of *sublimatio*, which implies flying, spirituality, transcendence. This theme was also stated by the image of the balcony, which permitted Alice to achieve a vantage point of elevated consciousness.

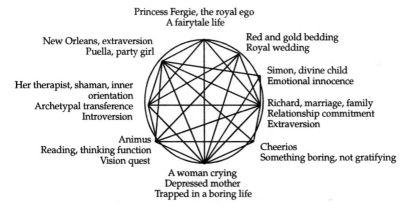

*Dream Mandala: The dream of the bed, princess Fergie,*
*the child, and the helium balloon*

The dream symbolism of the royal marriage emerged at the same moment as Alice was at the threshold of emotional commitment with Richard, and it imbued this relationship with archetypal meaning as a healing, sacred union. Integrating the animus validated her strivings for intellectual and professional growth, which need not be thwarted by moving forward into marriage. The dream highlighted the union of the extraverted maiden with infinite possibilities, the mother with responsibilities, and the introverted shaman/mystic/wise woman. It contained the symbolism of the royal marriage as a symbol of individuation.

In the next chapter, we explore further the process of individuation that unfolds as we unify the polarities of the personality into a complex, cohesive whole.

*CHAPTER NINE*

# Dreamwork and Individuation

reamwork aids us in the process of integrating the shadow, our core traumas and suppressed emotions, our sexuality and anger, so that we gradually become more unified individuals. We experience ourselves as a totality comprising many parts, many complexes and mythic personalities. The symbols of dreams aid us in individuation, the process of realizing our individuality and uniqueness, and fully living the truth of who we are. Aniella Jaffe wrote:

> Like the alchemical opus, individuation is a wearisome procedure to be accomplished in stages: by consciously collaborating with the unconscious, the individuant performs a work of self-redemption that makes him a whole and undivided personality, an "individual" (Jaffe, 1984, p. 65)

To understand individuation, consider the principle of the seed: Each of us is born like an acorn with particular traits and potentialities that are apparent from early in our lives. We unfold the kind of tree that we are. We sink deep roots and draw nourishment from the past, our history and ancestors. We grow slowly, reaching upward,

181

aspiring, flowering, and releasing the fruits that grow within our bodies. Like a tree, we pass through seasons of falling leaves, winter dormancy, and fresh new beginnings. Marie-Louise von Franz (1964) noted that the goal of individuation is the realization of the uniqueness of the individual man or woman, so that our "inborn possibility" becomes conscious and we act to bring this into reality (p. 163). It's like a pine cone, which "contains the whole future tree in a latent form," finding its way to the soil in a particular place and climate. "Thus the individual pine tree comes into existence, constituting the fulfilment of its totality, its emergence into the realm of reality" (p. 163).

## The Dream of the Baseball Team and the Hotel

Individuation implies discovering our own identity, rather than remaining caught in our conditioning by family and cultural expectations. Eya, a Japanese woman, dreamed:

> I'm with a baseball team, but not because I want to play baseball. I take care of the baseball players. They fly to a game in Oakland. I clean up the room after the players leave. Then I fly somewhere and arrive at a train station. I go to a hotel to relax.

When I asked for her associations to this dream, Eya commented, "My friend's boyfriend is into baseball. Most Japanese men like baseball. I find it boring."

I said, "The dream suggests to me a collective attitude, a herd mentality where everyone is the same."

Eya replied, "No uniqueness." Thus, the dream reflected on a condition in which there's a lack of individuality. Eya described this as characteristic of Japanese culture, which emphasizes conformity and dedication to tradition, the family, the company, the team. Cleaning up after the men reminded Eya of her father. "He socialized me to believe that a woman's place and role is to take care of men." From this perspective, a proper woman is dutiful, Eya said; "she supplicates herself to take care of others, especially men and children." In the dream, Eya played this role, enacting a socially acceptable persona. But then she went off to a hotel, which implied pursuing her own interests and pleasure, and movement toward individuation.

## Two Dreams of a Promethean Artist

Sometimes individuation requires choices that challenge old beliefs and conditioning received from our families or culture. Amy, a thirty-year-old artist struggling to make it in a large city, was pulled between desire to conform to her family's expectations that she work, earn money, and settle down, and a deep commitment to her stormy creative process, a commitment that entailed unconventional lifestyle and relationships. She dreamed:

> I'm in New York. I'm meeting my father for lunch downtown in a diner by the bridge. I go to the one he suggests. It's a long, crowded, old chrome diner. It's noisy and wet. I go next door to another restaurant and get a table there. My father comes and joins me there.

The dream symbolized Amy's conflict about staying bound to the lifestyle and activities that would be acceptable to her parents (going to the diner her father recommends) versus pursuing a path of creativity and freedom, where she could find a different menu of life choices.

Next Amy dreamed:

> There's a hole where my liver is. Something or someone cut out half my liver. Is it possible to live without a liver? Then I got a lung transplant, replacing it with a plastic bag.

Amy commented, "I feel as if my spirit is dying. All my joy is dead right now. Things are dissolving around me—my relationship with my boyfriend, the art group I've been a part of. The lung transplant reminds me of the fact that I've taken up cigarette smoking again as a way of comforting myself."

"The dream raises the question of whether this is healthy for you."

"Transplanting reminds me of my recent move to a new apartment."

"The hole in your liver reminds me of Prometheus, who stole fire from the gods and gave it to humanity. He brought the gifts of civilization to humanity. His liver gets eaten away, and then it grows back."

Prometheus bringing fire to humanity reminded Amy of her artistic path, the process of unleashing powers into the world through her creativity. It also reminded her of "my overly grandiose artistic strivings. My dream is to make a contribution that will lead to progress in culture, new consciousness. That feels kind of grandiose and inflated."

I said, "The life of an artist necessarily involves grandiose strivings. To create, you inflate. In the creative act there's a euphoric feeling of being tapped into something greater, a spiritual and creative intelligence, and you experience yourself as its instrument. Perhaps that might look a little inflated. But that's your path as an artist. It's a promethean path. You explore and experiment with materials. You unleash fire and radiance. You get filled up with excitement about what you're creating. That's natural. And it's also natural to want your work to have some impact on others. The hope that you'll make a really big splash and become the next big sensation in the culture—that's the inflated part. This is balanced by the depressed part of you that feels it's impossible to be an artist and that your efforts are futile."

Amy said, "I feel I'm not entitled to my feelings because my family has money and I'm economically privileged. My parents kept telling me this when I was a kid. Mom carefully avoided spoiling me and denied me affection. It's not fair. Prometheus is punished. And I'm being punished for being who I am. I punish myself too. I tell myself I'm not worth it, I can't be an artist."

Exploring the mythic symbolism of Prometheus was deeply healing for Amy. Prometheus embodied agonizing ordeals and luminous revelation, the eternal cycle of creativity. Conscious participation in this creative process was the essence of Amy's individuation.

## The Dream of the House, the Spider's Web, and the Old Man's Daughters

Sandy, a young woman in her mid-twenties grappling with individuation and independence from her parents, had this dream:

> I see a big house on a slanted hill. In front there's a tree and a spider web. I keep walking back and forth in front of the spider web. I can't believe how thick it is. I'm house sitting for an old man who has many daughters. The oldest daughter lives at the airport, but the rest live at home. I go inside. It reminds me of the hotel from the movie The Shining, with lots of big, empty rooms. The house is full of beds. There's

*one room for sick people. Beds are everywhere, even in hallways, all with floral bedspreads. Despite all the beds, the kids sleep in a hallway, in cabinet cubbies, near the old man's room. These are sleeping shelves, up on a wall, on foam pads. It looks uncomfortable to sleep on these shelves, yet the daughters claim it's very comfortable. The old man tells me and my sister that we can sleep in whatever beds we want. We want to be on a different floor from the kids so we'll have peace and quiet. We go stay downstairs.*

The dream began with a tree, symbol of growth and individuation. The big house reminded Sandy of her family's house, and of having big potentials, with lots of room to grow. She said, "*The Shining* reminds me of an old, empty, antiquated feeling. The character Jerry from that movie reminds me of living in the past. The house on a slanted hill reminds me of people not being on the level with me. As I figure out who I really am, I feel like I'm not on the same level as my old friends and people in my family. I'm on a different wavelength." In the dream, Sandy wanted to be on a different floor from the children, reflecting awareness that she's not a kid anymore.

The spider web reminded Sandy of weaving something silvery and unique. "A spider spins its own web out of its own centre. It's sturdy, resilient; it's not going to break. There's a part of me that's strong and knows I'm weaving the web of my own life." The spider's web was thus a symbol of individuation. The dream's image that she could sleep in whatever bed she wants also validated Sandy's capacity to make her own choices.

The young daughters are symbols of the maiden, the youthful part of Sandy that was full of potential. The daughters living at home reminded Sandy of staying within the close orbital influence of her family. But the daughter who left home and was living at the airport represented someone going on a journey, going places, someone who makes her own choices. She was a symbol of Sandy's individuation.

I asked Sandy about the empty rooms, saying, "How do you feel empty in your life?"

She replied, "It reminds me of loneliness." The beds on wheels and sleeping shelves reminded her of an empty, cold place, and of loneliness and depression. We sat and let those feelings come into the room for a few moments. Sandy said, "I've been letting go of past relationships and my ex-boyfriend, but I haven't met anyone new yet. The empty room reminds me of facing the future on my own." Empty rooms symbolized the existential aloneness each of us confronts as we learn that we're responsible for our lives and choices.

In the dream, there were rooms for sick people, people who are helpless and need to be taken care of—dependents. Sandy felt discomfort about her continuing financial dependency on her parents. The room for sick people was a shadow image, reflecting Sandy's fear of being helpless, weak, and needing to be cared for. The white room brought to mind an orphanage, which reminded her of leaving home and being without parental support as she became an independent adult.

The image of the floral bedspreads was pivotal. Sandy said, "These bedspreads remind me of my mother, not me. I used to want to decorate my room all in black and wear punked-out, black, Goth-style clothing. But Mom kept buying me these dainty, girly, flowery, pastel-coloured things like these bedspreads, and floral dresses—things that were totally not me. Mom wouldn't allow me to be cynical and depressed. I could practically hear her say, 'Don't feel that; don't be depressed.' She wouldn't let me have my feelings."

I said, "The floral bedspreads imply that she wanted you to put on a happy face, to assume a persona."

The dream contained several pairs of opposites: mother and daughter; father and daughter; the lonely, depressed, empty self, the daughters at home, representing childhood and dependency, and the individuating daughter at the airport, symbol of going places, having an empowered sense of self, aliveness, and excitement. I'll return to Sandy's dream in Chapter Ten.

## Individuation, the Self, and Symbols of Wholeness

In Jungian psychology, individuation refers to realization of the Self, unfolding the archetypal potentials, unique talents, and chosen life path that express our totality. The Self is the inner intelligence that guides the individuation process and aids us in achieving a balance of opposites within the personality. It's the principle of wholeness within the psyche, revealed in symbols of our totality and potential. von Franz has called the Self an inner guiding factor, ... the regulating center that brings about a constant extension and maturing of the personality ... . Its subjective experience conveys the feeling that some supra-personal force is actively intervening in a creative way. One sometimes feels that the unconscious is leading the way in accordance with a secret design. It is as if something is looking at me, something that I do not see but that sees me. (von Franz, 1964, pp. 163–164)

The Self is the mysterious inner consciousness that scripts our dream images, depicts the opposing forces within us, and helps us to contain and unify them. The Self is the archetype of our totality, encompassing those features of character and personality that define our uniqueness. Each of us realizes and embodies the Self in our own unique way. We don't become a copy of some hero, celebrity, or divine being. Yet a hero, celebrity, or divine being may appear in dreams as a symbol of the Self as we can uniquely express it. Jung wrote:

[T]he term "self" refers neither to Christ nor to the Buddha but to the totality of figures that are its equivalent, and each of these figures is a symbol of the self ... . Not only is the self indefinite but ... it also includes the quality of definiteness and even that of uniqueness. (Jung, 1968 [1944], pars. 20, 22)

A variety of figures can represent our emergent wholeness. Jung said that the Self manifests through dreams featuring the symbolic form of "a God or a Godlike human being, a prince, a priest, a great man, an historical personality, a dearly loved father, an admired example, the successful older brother—in short, a figure that transcends the ego personality of the dreamer" (Jung, 1959, par. 354). In dreams, the Self appears as a king, leader, hero, or saviour, or represents itself in symbols of wholeness and totality such as a circle, a cross, or a square—the quaternity, which symbolizes "conscious realization" (Jung, 1950b, par. 583). Women may symbolize the Self as a queen, princess, priestess, great mother, and other forms of the divine feminine. The Self may also appear in the form of abstract images such as mandalas, valuable or sacred objects such as stones, jewels, and rings, as a tree or flower, or as a spiritual teacher, wise elder, or a royal or famous personality.

I once dreamed of meeting Jack Nicholson, the actor, who, for me, symbolized positive extraversion, popularity, the successful externalization of personality. Celebrities often represent the solar principle of radiance, confident expression, and unfolding our potentials. But individuation doesn't require becoming a famous celebrity. It's the path of completing tasks and works that bring us intrinsic fulfilment.

## The Dream of the Old Aztec Sage

The next example illustrates the appearance of the Self and intrapsychic wholeness in the form of a great, godlike personage. Antonio, an ex-Roman Catholic priest from a Central American country, had this dream:

> I learn of an old man, a kind of national treasure, who is living in a small Mexican village. His ancestry is Aztec, and he is one of the last remaining native speakers of Nahuatl (the Aztec language). He's a well-known and revered figure. I go to the village and ask about him. I'm directed to his home, where I meet him, and introduce myself, and he invites me in. We sit and chat. He shares his knowledge and his views with me. Then I see a group of five or six priests dressed in black, with roman collars, including some that I used to work with. They're at some distance from me. I stop and don't approach them. I don't care to. I don't want to get involved in whatever they're doing. One of the priests notices me. He says, "Una de nuestras perlas fuertes"— literally, "one of our valuable pearls"—referring to me. He was calling me "one of our leading lights or valuable resources."

The old Aztec sage was a symbol of the wise old man, embodying the wisdom of Antonio's pre-European, pre-Christian ancestors. This dream kindled new interest in exploring his spiritual and cultural history. From within, a figure embodying the shaman-healer-guru archetype validated and blessed Antonio's decision to leave the priesthood. He experienced inner connection with spiritual guidance, and enrichment of his faith through exploring pre-Christian, indigenous spirituality. Antonio told me, "The fact that the old man spends time with me suggests that I'm worth it. It represents my value."

Avoiding the priests indicated differentiation: Antonio is no longer one of them. He has integrated his inner priest, but he has left that life path behind. He's also acknowledged by the priests as a pearl, a leading light, a national treasure—a symbol of individuation. Distancing from the priests and meeting the old Aztec sage, Antonio found that he himself was "the pearl beyond price." The pearl was a gnostic symbol of the divine soul that becomes trapped in the imprisonment of matter and the body, and that must be retrieved by the initiate, aided by his spiritual messenger (Jonas, 1958, p. 112).

## The Dream of the Oval Stone

Alchemy's central symbol of wholeness is the *lapis*, the *philosopher's stone*—goal of the transformative opus. I found the philosopher's stone in a dream at age twenty-four. After graduating from college, I worked at several jobs, saved some money, and then entered an introspective period of reading, dreamwork, hatha yoga practice, and mandala drawing. During this period I was passing through a lengthy transit of the planet Neptune, symbol of dreams and mysticism. All I wanted to do was to stay home and study books, and do my own journal writing, mandala drawing, and meditation. I had enough money saved that I didn't need to work for a year. At one point I took a job in a bookstore because I thought I *ought* to be working. But what I really wanted was to be at home reading, because that was where I felt my most important work was unfolding. Then I had this dream:

> I left the bookstore and walked on a little cobblestone path to a little cabin. Inside the cabin all of my papers and books were strewn about all over the floor. As I looked through the papers, I found a perfectly symmetrical, smooth, oval stone, half white and half black.

The symmetrical black and white stone was a symbol of integration and wholeness, the Self, the goal of individuation. The dream implied that I would find the philosopher's stone by leaving the bookstore job and returning to my own place. I would find the stone amidst my own work, my books and papers. Soon after this dream, I quit my job and returned to my studies. That was an important moment in my life. I had to follow my own path.

Individuation can be viewed as a process of carrying out specific tasks that enable us to shape and define our identities. von Franz wrote:

> [I]n order to bring the individuation process into reality, one must surrender consciously to the power of the unconscious ... . One must simply listen, in order to learn what the inner totality—the Self—wants one to do here and now in a particular situation ... . [T]his is a process in which one must repeatedly seek out and find something that is not yet known to anyone ... . The fact is that each person has to do something different, something that is uniquely his own. (von Franz, 1964, pp. 165–167)

Individuation is a lifelong work in progress, a Herculean labour, an opus of self-creation. Each step we take to express our inner truth is impelled by internal streams of necessity, by urgent drives and longings. Tasks arise from within us that must be completed. Like a sculptor, we chisel one small piece of the granite at a time, polishing each facet of the jewel of personality. Along the way, synchronicities confirm our feeling of transpersonal intervention and spiritual intelligence—the sense that we're unfolding according to "a secret design." I'll return to this topic in Chapter Eleven.

## First Dreams

The Self, our essence, the totality of what we can become, is present from the very beginnings of our lives, and may reveal itself through our first remembered dreams. These dreams can foreshadow themes that become central to our unfolding life and individuation process (Maguire, 1987, p. 61).

The first dream I remember occurred when I was four years old:

> *Square-shaped docks appear in the middle of the ocean. Suddenly there's a flash of light as a missile or rocketship shoots up from the depths of the ocean into the sky.*

The ocean reminds me of infinite being and consciousness, the realm of spirit, source. The docks are like a life raft. They float on water; they're a place of safety and refuge in the middle of the water, a lookout point. The square dock suggests stability, structure, integrity of form, organization, construction. A square is four-sided, like the four seasons or the four directions. Order and stability are found floating on top of the water: the ocean of the unconscious and of infinite Spirit.

This first dream seemed to portend my lifelong path as a meditator, yoga practitioner, and student of mysticism and depth psychology. Through these practices I experience a sense of order and meaning that emanates from infinite being and the structures of the archetypal domain. The dream is what philosopher Mircea Eliade (1959) calls a *hierophany*, a manifestation of spirit. The rocket or missile emerging from water and shooting into the sky depicts the *kundalini shakti*—evolutionary power—unfolding along the *axis mundi* of the spine, a streaming of energy from the deep ocean to the heavens, showing dynamic interplay between unconscious and superconscious realms. This is the intersection of time and eternity. This dream portrayed my life path in seed form.

## Jung's Individuation

There are many aspects of Jung's individuation that are worth noting. Jung's individuation from conventional Christianity was a central task because his father and grandfather were ministers. As a child, Jung couldn't find satisfying answers in theology, and he wrote that Church was "a place of torment to me" (Jung, 1961, p. 45). Jung sought new sources of meaning in his studies of philosophy; Freud's psychoanalysis; Indian, Chinese, and African worldviews; gnosticism, and alchemy. His separation from Freudian psychoanalysis led to the establishment of a new vision of psychology. A paradigmatic moment of individuation was Jung's process of self-discovery after his break from Freud. During the period he called his "confrontation with the collective unconscious," Jung was flooded with confusing visions and dreams, several featuring archetypal imagery of the hero's death and rebirth. This corresponded to Jung's loss of identity as a Freudian psychoanalyst and his eventual re-emergence as the founder of analytical psychology (Goldwert, 1992). After a period of internal chaos and the integration of immense amounts of unconscious material, Jung assumed a new identity as "psychotherapist and critic of Freud, moralist and social critic of modernity, and prophet or re-interpreter of Christianity" (Homans, 1979, p. 79).

In *Memories, Dreams, Reflections,* Jung (1961) described his childhood fascination with the architecture and construction of medieval castles. Later in life it became an inner necessity to build his own castle, the Tower at Bollingen. This was an important individuation task. Each of us has tasks that are essential to our sense of wholeness and completeness. At one point during his childhood, Jung fantasized about what it would be like to be a hermit, or to have a wife and family but to live separately in a hut with a pile of books, a table, and an open fire. He imagined himself in his castle where he had a sort of alchemical laboratory (Jung, 1961, pp. 78–82). These were foreshadowings of the life that he'd create as an adult, in which he divided his time between his home with his wife and children, and his retreat at Bollingen. There was an inner feeling of necessity; this was something he had to do. These tasks of individuation were clear from his childhood. I draw from this the lesson that individuation is a process of imagining the life and the person we want to create, and it's a process of working tirelessly to actualize the life and the self that we envision. It's the work of a lifetime.

One of the most radical aspects of Jung's individuation was his relationship with his lover, Toni Wolff. He sustained this relationship for many years, openly, with the full awareness of his wife, Emma. Some people may judge him disapprovingly, but this controversial arrangement was part of Jung's path to wholeness. His individuation required it. In his astrological birth chart, Jung had the planet Uranus, archetypal symbol of freedom and rebellion, in the seventh house, the zone of love and relationship. This relationship was right for him. It was part of his destiny. Toni inspired and aided him. She paid her own price of sadness for her love of a married man, but she, too, individuated, choosing her life path freely. Individuation means we unfold the uniqueness and truth of our personality. In Jung's life, freedom was achieved through a triangular relationship that lasted for decades. My point is not that everyone should have polygamous relationships, but that sometimes individuation requires facing social disapproval in the pursuit of personal freedom. This may be due to our involvement with socially unconventional pursuits or lifestyles, political or artistic movements, or pursuing any personal path that others consider unusual or controversial.

## Christ: A Symbol of the Self and the Union of Opposites

One of Jung's great innovations was to reinterpret religious symbolism not in theological terms but as archetypes, representations of universal human experiences. Some of his pivotal insights about individuation and the Self came from his reflections on the central symbol of the dominant world religion, the archetypal figure of Christ, described by Jung as

> the still living myth of our culture. He is our culture hero, who regardless of his historical existence, embodies the myth of the divine Primordial Man, the mystic Adam. It is he who occupies the centre of the Christian mandala ... . He is in us and we in him. His kingdom is the pearl of great price, the treasure buried in the field, the grain of mustard seed which will become a great tree ... . [T]he dogmatic figure of Christ is so sublime and spotless that everything else turns dark beside it. It is, in fact, so one-sidedly perfect that it demands a psychic complement to restore the balance. This inevitable opposition led very early to the doctrine of the two sons of God ... . The coming of the Antichrist was not just a prophetic prediction—it is an inexorable psychological law ... . No tree, it is said, can grow to heaven unless its roots reach down to hell ... . [A]lthough the attributes of Christ ... undoubtedly mark him out as an embodiment of the self, looked at from the psychological angle he corresponds to only half of the archetype. The other half appears in the Antichrist. The latter is just as much a manifestation of the self, except that he consists of its dark aspect ... . [T]he progressive development and differentiation of consciousness leads to an ever more menacing awareness of the conflict and involves nothing less than a crucifixion of the ego, its agonizing suspension between irreconcilable opposites. (Jung, 1959, pars. 69, 77–79)

This last statement clarifies the phenomenology of the Self, which we experience as a growth in consciousness through holding the tension of charged polarities within us.

> [T]here is a considerable difference between *perfection* and *completeness*. The Christ-image is as good as perfect ... while the archetype ... denotes completeness but is far from

being perfect ... . [T]he realization of the self, which would logically follow from a recognition of its supremacy, leads to a fundamental conflict, to a real suspension between opposites (reminiscent of the crucified Christ hanging between two thieves), and to an approximate state of wholeness that lacks perfection ... . Natural as it is to seek perfection in one way or another, the archetype fulfills itself in completeness ... . Where the archetype predominates, completeness is *forced* upon us against all our conscious strivings ... . The individual may strive after perfection ... but must suffer from the opposite of his intentions for the sake of his completeness. (Jung, 1959, par. 123)

To realize the Self is to embrace our inner conflicts, divisions, and contradictions. Individuation involves the interplay of what appear to be irreconcilable conflicts within us. Jung's view of the Self is not the same as the impersonal Self of Hinduism. In Indian yoga psychology, the Self is the silent, formless field of pure being-consciousness-bliss, reached through deep meditation. Jung's concept of the Self refers to the consciousness that is born from the tension of paired opposites and their conscious coexistence. To individuate means to live the complexities and contradictions of the personality. The Self is an individuated expression of the divine, lived through the tension of paired opposites, which appear in symbols of wholeness, or what Jung called a personal "God-image" (Jung, 1959, par. 73, and Jung, 1968 [1944], par. 11).

## The Dream of the Girl with a Penis

The next example illustrates the embrace of tensely paired opposites in the service of completeness, as well as the way that individuation is often marked (and sparked) by symbols of wholeness in dreams. Eric, an actor and cross-dresser, told me this dream:

> *Somebody said to me "There's somebody here you haven't seen for a really long time." It was Beth, a girl from my hometown. She stripped off her clothes, and I noticed she had a penis. In fact, it was rather large. How could this be? We used to be on the swimming team together, and surely I would have noticed a bulge in her crotch.*

Eric told me, "Beth's family came from a higher social class than my family. Their kids took dance classes and orchestra. Beth was a dancer and musician. She reminds me of being given opportunities to develop artistically, of being advantaged."

"She reminds me of your dynamic feminine side that's expressed in your work as a performing artist. Stripping off her clothes suggests achieving greater psychological honesty, getting down to the naked truth. A girl with a penis is a union of opposites. It's an appearance of the androgyne or hermaphrodite. It suggests that you're transforming within this archetype."

"I refuse to be just a man. I wear pink clothes, earrings, makeup. I shave my legs, arms, chest. When I cross-dress and act like a woman, I feel freed up from the macho need to be all-powerful. My power is in grace and beauty."

"In the dream, Beth's youthful creativity is merged with phallic potency. Your creative, youthful anima has a man's equipment, which is large and powerful. You don't have to be solely masculine or feminine. You can live the tension of the opposites. You have the soul of a girl, but also phallic potency. It doesn't diminish your manhood to embrace the feminine."

I asked Eric to draw a picture of the girl. He drew two pictures. One was an angelic image of a young girl with wings. She was the enlivening, inspiring, artistic anima. The other picture depicted an older, larger girl with larger hips, with her ribs showing. She seemed like an adolescent, and reminded Eric of Liz, a high school schoolmate, an anorexic cheerleader. He said, "Liz was emaciated. That reminds me of how I obsess about my body image and what I eat. I feel I'm not attractive unless I'm in perfect shape. There's nothing worse than a fat guy in a dress."

I said, "Your feminine experience involves this kind of heightened concern about appearance, and the tension of anorexia. I think the dream is asking you to heal your relationship to the female part of you by learning to accept your body. The dream affirms your path of androgynous embodiment."

Several days after discussing this dream with Eric, I experienced a synchronistic event. I was cleaning my office when a book fell on the floor. It was Jung's *Psychology of the Transference*. I opened the book at random. The page I chose discussed the tenth picture of the Rosarium series, which depicts a winged Rebis, a hermaphroditic, crowned, male-female being holding three snakes in a chalice with the right hand, and a fourth snake wrapped around the left arm (see Figure 5).

Jung commented:

> The Self is the total, timeless man and as such corresponds to the original, spherical, bisexual being who stands for the mutual integration of conscious and unconscious ... . Human wholeness can only be described in antinomies, which is always the case when dealing with a transcendental idea ... . The symbol of the hermaphrodite ... is one of the many synonyms for the goal of the art. (Jung, 1966 [1946], pars. 531–533)

Eric's dream affirmed that cross-dressing was an expression of his "original, spherical, bisexual being," and a facet of his path to wholeness.

Individuation is achieved through a union of opposites. Throughout this book I refer to this principle because I believe it's the key to dreamwork as a path of emotional, relational, and spiritual healing. Anthony Stevens wrote:

> Jung was convinced that the psyche, like the body, was a self-regulating system. It strives perpetually to maintain a balance between opposing propensities, while at the same time, actively seeking its own individuation. A dynamic polarity exists between the ego and the Self, between the persona and the shadow, between masculine consciousness and the anima, between feminine consciousness and the animus, between extraverted and introverted attitudes, between thinking and feeling functions, between sensation and intuition and between the forces of Good and Evil ... . A vital expression of this propensity is the way in which the unconscious gives rise to symbols capable of reuniting conflicting tendencies which seem irreconcilable at the conscious level. This phenomenal capacity never ceased to fascinate and move Jung, and he called it the *transcendent function*. (Stevens, 1990, p. 51)

Eric's dream expressed the transcendent function by reuniting the masculine and feminine poles of his personality.

## The Dream of the Rundown Shack and the Cosy Cottage

In the next example a house serves as a symbol of individuation. Nicole, a woman in her sixties, was starting a new life after ending a thirty-year career and relocating. She was living frugally on a tight budget. She had this dream:

> *I see a rundown shack. It looks like it could fall down at any moment. Suddenly the earth splits and then part of the house falls into the ocean. Waves are crashing on a cliff. I notice the sky is colourful like in a Van Gogh painting. Then the earth becomes solid again. There's an open crevice. I have to jump to get to the other side. I felt resolute. There's no alternative but to cross over. I walk hand-over-hand across a railing. There's no way around the shack. I find that the door of the shack is unlocked. I enter and am flooded with warmth. I go inside and find it's a cosy cottage with a roaring fire in the fireplace. A fresh pot of tea is waiting for me, along with a soft chair, and a deck of Tarot cards sitting on the table. The whole place is soft and beautiful. Outside there's an amazing garden with flowers, vegetables, fruit, vines. Everything is in full bloom. A huge grey cat is sleeping on the gate.*

The rundown shack reminded Nicole of poverty, neglect, and abandoned houses. This in turn reminded her of abandoned family life, the fact that she never spoke to her grown children anymore. She said, "I used to live in a nice house and have money. Now I'm living on the edge in a small rented room." In the dream, there was no way around the shack. Nicole had to face her loss and depression; it couldn't be avoided.

Waves crashing on the cliff suggested that the ocean was agitated; there was turbulence in the unconscious. In the dream the earth split, which reminded Nicole of an apocalypse, feeling as if she was on a precipice in her life, a fear that she might fall through the cracks. Nicole noted that the ocean was a dark, deep forest green. Forest reminded her of rich brown earth, composted soil, mulchy woods, a fecund place where anything would grow. That reminded her of "forest before there were people, the original untouched state of the earth." The garden in full bloom, where everything thrived, reminded Nicole of self-sufficiency. "You could grow anything here. It's my potential to accomplish anything."

I said, "I think the garden in full bloom and the original, untouched state of the earth symbolize Eden, your original, innate wholeness."

The Van Gogh sky reminded her of someone who goes mad, a tortured artist. She said, "My son lives on the streets. He's a tortured person." Talking about this brought up a lot of sadness and grief for Nicole. She needed to feel this. "The tortured artist represents my conflicts about creativity, and my difficulty with survival, like Van Gogh. My homeless son reminds me of my own tenuous existence. I feel homeless and impoverished." The rundown cottage and the tortured-artist-Van-Gogh-sky represented the part of Nicole that felt alone and depressed, her sadness about loss of family life and feeling neglected by her children.

In the dream, Nicole had to cross an open crevice, implying a test, crossing a threshold, an initiation. It suggested liminality, being in transition. I told Nicole, "In the dream you are resolute about crossing the crevice. That suggests your determination to reach your new goals. Crossing over requires heroism, an act of courage to reach your potential. You're taking a big leap." The image of a fire burning in the fireplace also evoked determination and inner fire and drive.

Going hand-over-hand reminded Nicole of playing on the monkey bars as a child. This reminded Nicole of a childhood memory. "I remember that when I was a child my first conscious goal was to be able to walk on the monkey bars. I worked hard at it and learned to do it." This event represented positive will and goal-directedness. The dream suggested that she could meet her current challenges by drawing on this childhood strength. Walking hand-over-hand was a symbol of resilience, courage, achievement, and taking things one step at a time.

Arriving at the cosy cottage reminded Nicole of "coming home." The unlocked door suggested that her way forward in life was unimpeded, not obstructed. The Tarot deck reminded her of wisdom, of becoming a wise woman, and of being in touch with spiritual mystery. Nicole's individuation task was to embody the archetype of the wise elder, the crone.

The dream depicted a transition from an abandoned shack to a cosy cottage, a symbol of home, safety, family. The big grey cat sleeping on a gate signified that Nicole was crossing a threshold; she was at a turning point. The cat represented instinct, ease, and a relaxed attitude as she went through this transition. Soon after this dream,

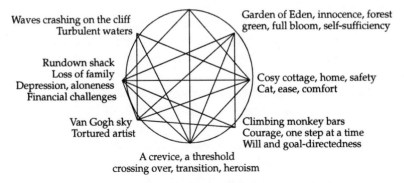

*Dream Mandala: The dream of the rundown shack, the crevice, and the cosy cottage*

Nicole moved into a house with new friends and found a part-time job. These were exactly the next steps needed for her survival and individuation.

## The Dream of the Desert and the House by the Water

The next example illustrates individuation through resolving a father complex and encountering a famous celebrity who represented emergent potentials. We'll note how dreamwork helped a man undergo a rather dramatic change in a short period of time. This case also illustrates consciousness being born out of the tension of opposites.

During a brief course of counseling (three sessions), I worked with a twenty-nine-year-old man named Ray, who was struggling to find permanent full-time employment and working part-time as a waiter. He was also examining his habit of spending his spare time drinking in bars. He told me this dream:

> *I'm climbing on the frame of a house by the shore, with my friend, David. We spoke about Robert DeNiro and his role as a producer of the movie* Smoke Signals, *a movie about Native Americans, but DeNiro had not yet seen* Powwow Highway *[another movie about Native American life]. Then I went to a Nautilus Club to work out—a really nice club. I had trouble getting in because my membership card didn't*

*work. Then I was on a long boardwalk in Egypt. There was a town on*
*one side, desert on the other. Then I saw an old house. On the posts on*
*the staircase there were caps that had come unscrewed. I went into the*
*basement to get a screwdriver and tried to screw the caps back in, but*
*it was no use because the wood was worn and rotten.*

The house by the shore reminded Ray of childhood visits to his friend David's family home by a lake. He said, "I always wanted something like that. His family has a lot of money. I always felt envious." In the dream, Ray had trouble getting admitted to the Nautilus Club. This reminded him of "getting into the club. I always feel like an outsider, because I'm not from a privileged social class."

The main character in the movie *Smoke Signals* was a young Native American man in conflict with his father. Ray said, "There are lots of father-son issues in that movie. The main character had issues with his dad, like I do." Ray's father was irresponsible, alcoholic, depressed, absent, uninterested in his children. "He abandoned our family when I was twelve." *Smoke Signals* reminded Ray of the stereotype of the drunken Native American man, and of his alcoholic father; this reminded Ray of his own alcohol abuse. The absent, alcoholic father is contrasted with Robert DeNiro, who was a patron of the young filmmakers who made *Smoke Signals,* and thus signified the good father providing support to his son.

Robert DeNiro is an actor Ray idolized, a man with a huge persona. He was the symbol of an ego ideal. In archetypal terms, DeNiro, the celebrity, represented the solar king, and thus was a symbol of the Self and of Ray's potentials. DeNiro symbolized an inner ideal of greatness, specialness, and notoriety, in contrast to Ray's humble job in a restaurant.

The movie *Powwow Highway* followed the journey of a Native American man who is innocent, simple, and pure, and seeks deeper knowledge of Native American traditions and spirituality. Ray said, "He was on a quest to be a warrior." Thus, he signified the archetypal hero, and Ray's own quest for meaning, roots, and identity.

Trying to attach screws to rotten wood reminded Ray of futility. "Why am I doing this? What's the point? What can I do that's unique? I feel a sense of futility about my career search. I feel like what's the use? What does it take to break in, to be unique? It's all been done before. What can I do that's original, that will make me stand out like DeNiro?" These questions brought up sadness and anger that he'd never received his father's praise and encouragement during his adolescence and early adulthood. There was an inner void where the positive father should have been supporting his ambitions.

The boardwalk in Egypt reminded Ray of sand and desert, lack of water, dryness, a vast, empty feeling. I said, "It reminds me of walking through the desert, like someone on a vision quest, like the man in *Powwow Highway*, in the same way that you're on a quest."

The dream contrasted the desert and the house by the water, which Ray said symbolized "success and prosperity, the feeling that you've got it made." This was the mythic destination of the dream and of Ray's individuation. He noted that in the boardwalk scene the desert had a warm yellow-amber hue, and said, "I can enjoy walking through the desert; it's not unpleasant."

Egypt reminded Ray of a place of ancient mystery. "When I was a kid, I was fascinated by Moses and biblical characters and legends."

I said, "That reminds me of the mythic quality of your search for meaning and purpose. You're not just looking for a job. You're on a quest for meaning, to know who you are, to find the Promised Land, the house by the water."

There were several pairs of opposites in the dream: a young man on a quest, and a famous, accomplished man who represented attainment and fully unfolded potentials. The dream also contrasted a desert—a place of testing, questing, and spiritual revelation—and a house by the water—symbol of family, social class, and material prosperity. Ray's path involved achieving a union of these opposites.

A few weeks later, Ray called to say he had found a better job, in the computer industry. Also, his girlfriend was pregnant, and they'd decided to get married. He was excited about becoming a father. He'd been attending Alcoholics Anonymous meetings. He thanked me and said goodbye. That was the last I heard from him. Exploring this dream allowed Ray to do some work that prepared him to find a new inner centre—to make commitments and advance his life. Here's a diagram of his dream:

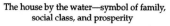

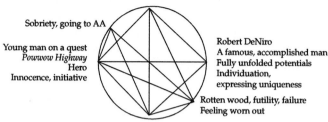

The house by the water—symbol of family,
social class, and prosperity

Sobriety, going to AA

Young man on a quest
*Powwow Highway*
Hero
Innocence, initiative

Robert DeNiro
A famous, accomplished man
Fully unfolded potentials
Individuation,
expressing uniqueness

Rotten wood, futility, failure
Feeling worn out

Egypt: a desert, a place of testing, questing, and
spiritual revelation
Absent father, the emotional desert of their
father-son relationship
Alcoholism, depression

*Dream Mandala: The dream of the house by the water*

## Three Dreams of Midlife Individuation

Certain transitional periods of life offer special challenges and opportunities of individuation, for example, adolescence and early adulthood, midlife, and later life. In this section I discuss three of my own dreams that occurred during the turbulence of my early forties—a period when I was grappling with a business failure, obstacles in my professional life, and depression. I had self-published *The Nine Stages of Spiritual Apprenticeship*, a book I poured my heart and soul into (Bogart, 1997). I had hopes the book was going to do very well, but unfortunately it didn't sell many copies, and in the end I lost a tidy sum of money. Writing this book about the spiritual teacher-student relationship was an important individuation task for me. It was something I needed to do for myself. I loved the experience of writing and producing the book, but I felt let down by the outcome. Also, I was encountering obstacles in my search for a teaching job that I hoped would provide a steady income to supplement my work as a psychotherapist. I was experiencing defeats of the ego on several fronts. Edward Edinger (1994a) once wrote, "It is definitely not good psychologically always to be a winner, because then one is deprived of the full experience of the opposites. It keeps one superficial. Defeat is the gateway to the unconscious" (p. 16). It was in this context that I had these dreams.

## The Dream of Immersion and Spiritual Cleansing

The first dream was this:

> I'm at a local bookstore on a Sunday afternoon. People have gathered
> and are standing in rows waist deep in water. A few of those present
> are experiencing a ritual immersion in the water. I'm one of those
> undergoing this spiritual cleansing and baptism. I lower myself into
> the water, and it's clear and soft. I'm renewed through this immersion
> in the restorative waters. I'm whole again.

This dream depicted the alchemical *solutio*, the cleansing, purifying
bath that is symbolized by dreams of baths, showers, sprinkling,
swimming, immersion in water, and baptism—"which signifies a
cleansing, rejuvenating immersion in an energy and viewpoint transcending the ego" (Edinger, 1985, p. 58). The dream signified spiritual renewal through conscious immersion in the unconscious. It
also expressed the theme of "the watery initiations, the 'night sea
journeys,' or 'dark nights of the soul' that move a person toward an
inner orientation and a more fully realized sense of self, a state of
renewed union with one's own wholeness" (Hill, 1992, pp. 25–26).
We return to source and feel ourselves affirmed, free of the need
to prove ourselves in the world through our accomplishments.
The watery initiation is a return to a place of deep self-acceptance
and reconciliation with ourselves. After this dream, I felt an inner
spiritual blessing and a feeling of emotional renewal.

## The Dream of the University, Timothy Leary,
## Mickey Mantle, and John Mclaughlin

A second dream occurred after I taught a class at a school for several
years, but wasn't rehired after receiving some tepid evaluations
from students. I felt a deep sense of failure. I dreamed:

> I'm trying to get onto a university campus, but all access roads are
> being blocked off. There has been an outbreak of a deadly virus like
> Ebola on campus, and people are dropping like flies and being car-
> ried off in ambulances. I go to a restaurant to eat and pick up the
> newspaper and see the news that Timothy Leary has died. Later I'm
> going to perform in a nightclub. Out in the lobby I spot guitarist

*John McLaughlin. I go over and say hello and play his beautiful guitar. In the final scene, Mickey Mantle is receiving an award at a large banquet. His achievements are recognized and lauded and celebrated. It's a climax or high point of his career.*

Timothy Leary represented the renegade professor banished from campus and academic life, and my own feelings of exclusion and exile. The dream symbolized the death of my ambition of finding a teaching job. In the dream, I can't find the campus entrance. Indeed, the campus is toxic, in a state of crisis; it's a place of death. The alchemical *mortificatio* symbolizes death and transformation of an attitude, a feeling, a complex. According to Edinger, "*Mortificatio* ... has to do with darkness, defeat, torture, mutiliation, death, or rotting," but it often leads to growth, resurrection, birth (Edinger, 1985, p. 148). "[A] frequent subject for *mortificatio* is the 'king' .... [Or] it may be *sol*, the Sun, who is to be killed." Or the lion:

> King, Sun, and lion refer to the ruling principle of the conscious ego and to the power instinct. At a certain point these must be mortified in order for a new center to emerge .... [T]he mortificatio of the king or the Sun will refer to the death and transformation of a collective dominant or ruling principle. (Edinger, 1985, pp. 150–151)

Timothy Leary, in his brief glory days, was a charismatic, solar figure who captivated the attention of the world. Here Leary has died, signifying death of the part of me that felt like an outsider, an academic pariah; it was also the death of false hopes, and the part of me that hoped to captivate the world with my *Spiritual Apprenticeship* book. My dream depicted the *mortificatio* of the exiled professor. Identification with this viewpoint was not a functional basis for my further development. But a new centre was beginning to form within me.

The dream represented the possibility of rebirth, and showed an image of my potential as a musician, waiting in the wings, about to go on stage. Mickey Mantle, the legendary star of the New York Yankees, symbolizes the champion, the hero, the triumphant ego. John McLaughlin was a hero of my adolescence, a radiant, spiritual musician who embodied qualities of artistry and mastery. The dream's concluding image of recognition, awards, apotheosis or zenith in career indicated the possibility of a positive outcome to my situation. After this dream I became less concerned about teaching and got increased enjoyment in being a dedicated amateur musician. Paradoxically, about one year later I found an excellent teaching job.

The dream contained a union of several pairs of opposites: Timothy Leary, pariah and man of infamy, and Mickey Mantle, the celebrated solar hero, being awarded and celebrated. There was a deathly situation, a deadly Ebola epidemic, and the life-giving joy of playing John McLaughlin's guitar. The dream heralded an inner union of the musician and the scholar-professor. This union has been gradually realized in my life.

## The Dream of Isidor, the Heart Attack, and the Competent Woman

Here's the third dream:

> I'm travelling in a foreign country and don't know where I am or what my destination is. I get off a bus somewhere and walk around the streets. I see an old man—it's the old man named Isidor from the movie Gadjo Dilo—and I gesture to him. He's able to understand that I'm lost, and he brings me to his house and indicates that I can stay there. There are a number of people in the house. We stay up late into the night while Isidor, who is a musician, leads us in singing songs, softly and beautifully. In the morning I'm walking around the city and see a group of the people from the house, except that now the old man is a young man with dark, olive-coloured skin. He's waving his hands at airplanes that are hovering overhead—a futile gesture. The planes are either waiting to land or waiting to take off. They're stuck in a stagnant holding pattern. Suddenly as this young man tries to cross the street he's nearly struck by a car, narrowly avoiding being killed. Then he's stricken with what appears to be a heart attack and collapses to the ground. A girl screams, "Somebody help him!" A woman lifts him up and drags his body down the street to a telephone. She's very competent and knows what to do in an emergency. She calls for help, then tries to resuscitate the man. But he's too far gone. I walk over to where he's lying on the ground. He's clearly fading; his eyes are glassy. I put my hands in the namasté gesture, then hold my hands palms up in a gesture of surrender, acceptance, and letting go. The man sees

*this and at that moment he dies. I'm filled with the conviction that the*
*reason I was brought to this place was to be present for, and to witness,*
*the man's death.*

There were several archetypal elements of this dream, which began
with the theme of the journey. Isidor represented the Wise Old Man,
the soul guide. In the movie *Gadjo Dilo* (Crazy Foreigner), Isidor is
an old Romanian gypsy musician who mentors a young man from
France and initiates him into the life of the gypsies. At the funeral of
a friend, Isidor throws himself onto the man's grave, pours wine on
it, and cries out in anguish that all his friends miss him, and why did
he have to leave them now? After the drunken funeral, Isidor and
his musician friends are scheduled to play at a wedding where they
must muster joyous songs of celebration from their tearful sorrow.
In the film, Isidor is a man who expresses a full range of feelings.
For me, he symbolized fully lived emotional experience, and the
ability to transform depression through song, transmuting sadness
into joy. Over the next several years I found great fulfilment in my
song writing and deepening involvement in jazz studies and performance. Developing as a musician became a central task of midlife
individuation.

The young man represented the puer, the archetype of youth,
and my creative aspirations in teaching, counseling, and publishing
books. The man waving his hands at the airplanes in a futile gesture
suggested a sense of futility, depression, and helplessness, and my
personal struggle for success in these ventures. It was the symbol of a
complex I had about success and failure in the world. It was unclear
in the dream whether the planes hovering overhead were waiting
to land, or if they were waiting to take off. This suggested my questions and doubts about whether I would ever land, get grounded
in my life, and if my work would ever "take off." The young man's
death symbolized the end of this struggle. I realized that I had done
everything I could to market my book and to find a teaching job,
but now it was out of my hands; all that struggle needed to die. The
puer's grandiose dreams of success as a writer and teacher had to
die. Dream images often exaggerate to portray our inner condition,
and to cast our situation in an archetypal light. Here the psyche's
symbol-forming function accurately portrayed my feeling that I
was dying inwardly, as well as my discouragement—a loss of heart,

a "heart attack." The dream conveyed a clear image, and visceral *experience*, of the death of the ego. My sense of struggle, helplessness, and failure needed to die.

The little girl suggested an immature attitude of wanting somebody to help or rescue me. The woman who takes charge was an anima symbol, an image of woman as saviour and heroine, and represented my desire to be rescued by women. At that time I was extremely grouchy toward my spouse for not making me happy and pulling me out of my sullen mood. This reflected an unconscious expectation that a woman will bring excitement into my life and rescue me.

Jung noted that fourfold dream symbolism is a representation of wholeness and balance within the psyche. This dream contained a quaternity of images: the young man or puer (inflated hopes, helpless feeling, deflation); Isidor, the wise old man, the senex, a musician and tender soul, symbolizing the healing power of music in my life; the anima-saviour figure who is competent in an emergency; and the experience of death, and its implicit rebirth.

The dream evoked the spiritual quality of surrender. Responding to the final image of the dream, I let go and tried to accept my situation. I immersed myself in the spiritual practices of dreamwork, yoga, meditation, astrology, and music. I tried to cultivate contentment with a simple life. And when I bottomed out and surrendered, a miraculous thing happened: I found a great teaching job, at a local university. My book still didn't sell many copies, but some things in life just don't work out. It isn't destined. But other doors open.

The dream's archetypal core is the Job story. The man waving his arms symbolizes Job-like suffering, the feeling of being persecuted by God and wondering, "Why me?" This is similar to my earlier dream that God was pissing on me (Chapter Seven). The final image of the dream—the hands extended in a gesture of acceptance and surrender—is reminiscent of the William Blake painting of Job's illumination. Job is depicted with his arms raised to the sunlike light of the deity.

Edward Edinger said:

> Blake has captured the essential feature of the individuated ego in his picture of the repentant and rejuvenated Job. What is pictured is the *sacrificial attitude*. Having experienced the transpersonal center of the psyche, the ego recognizes its subordinate position and is prepared to serve the totality and its ends rather

*Figure 4. William Blake, Job's illumination.*

than make personal demands. Job has become an individuated ego. (Edinger, 1992, p. 96)

My dream portrayed a central symbol of individuation—the death and rebirth of the hero. This archetypal theme is also symbolized frequently as the death and rebirth of the king.

## Death and Transformation of the King: A Symbol of Individuation

The fate of the king was a recurring theme of alchemical texts, which are a useful source of wisdom about individuation. Jung's research showed that alchemical procedures for transforming physical substances were analogous to stages of psychological transformation. In this section I sketch out some speculative ideas about alchemical transformations of the king and the psychology of individuation. According to Edinger (1985), the king symbolizes "the ruling attitude of consciousness," which must die to make way for a new attitude or perspective to emerge (p. 19). The death of the old king is a central symbol of alchemy and personal transformation. The king represents the royal ego, which is defeated, slain, and is eventually succeeded by his son, the young king, the reborn, rejuvenated self.

In the next example, a dream states the imperative of individuation rather forcefully. Kim, a woman who had always conformed to her father's expectations, dreamed:

*I'm fucking the corpse of a dead president.*

This dream coincided with a crucial decision to change careers. The old career was the one her father had always validated, but it no longer felt right for Kim. She was changing her relationship to the static masculine principle as she consciously chose new commitments. The dream depicted Kim overcoming the rigid or lifeless attitude of the dead president, a symbol of the old king. Only then could Kim begin to follow her own authentic life path.

The king symbolizes a cohesive personal identity. Heinz Kohut's theory of self psychology is a useful framework for understanding the archetypal king (Kohut & Wolf, 1978). According to Kohut, we develop a cohesive sense of self by receiving *mirroring* from our *selfobjects*—our caregivers and attachment figures (mother, father, friend, lover)—which makes us feel seen, validated, special, and wonderful. A parent affirms a child by acknowledging the child's thoughts, feelings, and personhood. Mirroring affirms us, builds self-esteem, and gives us confidence to express our talents and emanate solar radiance. It enables us to develop healthy narcissism, a sunny feeling of being lovable and special, a bright star. This is the origin of our experience of ourselves as a king or queen. Figuratively speaking, we assume our throne and emanate warmth, generosity, and confidence, projecting ourselves into the world effectively. In the alchemical Rosarium, a king and queen meet, embrace, and make love. We're mirrored and affirmed by our loved ones, experiencing pleasure, connectedness, and mutual responsiveness.

But the king (or queen) can be unseated, defeated, disempowered. If we're starved of mirroring and validation, we become depressed and deflated. This inner emptiness becomes the root cause of symptomatic behaviours such as addictions, binge drinking, compulsive gambling, stealing, overeating, or risk taking, all of which can be understood as attempts to energize a depleted, depressed sense of self. We'll see an example of this in Chapter Thirteen.

A person whose solar narcissism has been severely wounded may develop a sense of entitlement or a need for attention or to be seen as special. These are negative expressions of the king: self-importance, grandiosity, wounded pride. The king also signifies the healthy striving to be seen and to externalize our individuality, as well as self-validation, enjoying who we are. Individuation means that we find what lights us up; we find fulfilment in achieving our personal goals. But the king (or queen) also represents an attitude that rigidifies, becoming imperious and inflexible.

## Calcinatio, Solutio, Coagulatio

Some alchemical pictures depict the king in a sweatbox. At times we're transformed by sweating out toxins, and sweating out difficult situations that we can't escape from. In the alchemical *calcinatio*, a substance is heated until reduced to ashes. We burn up fiery emotions, desires, and drives for power.

At other times, the king is portrayed drowning, or bathing in a pool of water with a white dove hovering over his head. Drowning and bathing motifs in dreams refer to *solutio*, the alchemical bath. These dreams elicit an experience of watery initiation and purification, an immersion in the unconscious through dreams and fantasy, or illumination in a state of faith, openness, and receptivity. We experience confusing meltdowns, grandiose fantasies, receive spiritual blessings, or all of these at the same time. The Dream of Immersion and Spiritual Cleansing (earlier in this chapter) illustrated this.

After the bath, we need to find solid ground. In one image the drowning old king calls out for help to his son, the young king, who stands on land. Edinger wrote, "[T]he old ruling principle, which has undergone *solutio*, is calling out to be coagulated again in a new, regenerated form" (Edinger, 1985, p. 52). The *coagulatio* stage of alchemy refers to the solidification of liquids and vapours into material form, and represents coming into form in a specific place and time, becoming fully embodied, working, establishing self-discipline.

In Chapter Six, I told the story of Travis, the musician who worked through fantasies of stardom and feelings of angry disappointment while forming an inner commitment to continue performing and competing in the field of music. Travis was undergoing *coagulatio*, the process of manifesting the divine nature, transforming into earth, into something with definite form and location. His most pressing current individuation task was to form a viable life structure within which he could gradually accomplish his artistic goals. In his dream about the new year's eve party, Travis was aware that "the party is ending." At this time, Travis drastically reduced his pot smoking and got more grounded, coming to grips with his responsibilities. He worked to expand his business and get his finances in order while continuing to make great music. His productivity was constant and outstanding. According to Edinger, *coagulatio* is the process of solidifying the personality by encountering reality. It's the experience of actualizing our potential. We get fully involved in our lives, fully incarnated.

> The substance to be coagulated is elusive quicksilver. This is the Spirit Mercurius ..., the autonomous spirit of the archetypal psyche, the paradoxical manifestation of the transpersonal Self. To subject the Spirit Mercurius to coagulatio means nothing less than the connecting of the ego with the Self, the fulfillment of individuation. (Edinger, 1985, p. 85)

## Mortificatio and Redemption of the Wounded King

Another central alchemical theme is the king's illness or death, sometimes depicted as the son slaying the king. These images refer to *mortificatio*, the experience of death, endings, losses, or defeats of the ego. The king's death symbolizes death of a dominant attitude, or the death of our sense of specialness or greatness, through experiences of narcissistic wounds or injuries. In the Dream of the Speakeasy and the Knife Fight with Desmond (Chapter Six), Travis left Desmond to die. This reminded me of the son slaying the king; it depicted the death of a wounded, bitter attitude. Each of us must decide if we'll make this sacrifice. As the old saying goes: The king must die. von Franz described the theme of the wounded king as follows:

> Many myths and fairy tales symbolically describe this initial stage in the process of individuation by telling of a king who has fallen ill or grown old. Other familiar story patterns are that a royal couple is barren; or that a monster steals all the women, children, horses, and wealth of the kingdom; or that a demon keeps the king's army or his ship from proceeding on its course; or that darkness hangs over the lands, wells dry up, and flood, drought, and frost afflict the country. In myths ... the magic or talisman that can cure the misfortune of the king or his country always proves to be something very special ... [,] a white blackbird ... [,] a fish that carries a golden ring in its gills ... [, or] the king wants 'the waters of life' or 'three golden hairs from the head of the devil.' ... Whatever it is, the thing that can drive away the evil is always unique and hard to find. (von Franz, 1964, p. 170)

Individuation is a process of finding the magic or talisman that can cure our misfortune, our inner malaise, our depression. Recall Owen's dream (in Chapter Seven) of the medallions worn by the steady firemen. As we individuate, we experience ourselves as possessing something special and rare. We're like a white blackbird, full of divine contradictions. In Owen's dream, the firemen affirmed Owen as a competent, responsible young man now ready to take his place in the world, surpassing his father, the painfully wounded old king. We redeem the desolate state of the wounded king by plucking the fish with a golden ring from the healing waters of the unconscious, by unfolding dream symbolism.

In alchemy, the king always changes form. He dies, and he is reborn as a young king. Or he turns into a hermaphrodite. Recall how Karl dreamed of a transsexual (Chapter Two). Also recall the Dream of the Black Transvestite (Chapter Seven) and the Dream of the Emasculated Batman (Chapter Six). In the tenth Rosarium image, the king and queen merge into an androgynous being with four serpents, three on one arm, plus a fourth.

As Edinger (1994a) explains, three serpents are contained in the chalice, the fourth is uncontained. All are crowned, representing "the transformation of the reptilian psyche .... [T]he whole process

*Figure 5. Tenth Rosarium image. Crowned serpents and the winged androgynous body.*

of the coniunctio ... has brought the reptilian psyche into such a living connection with consciousness that it has undergone a transformation" (pp. 96–97). The number four is a reference to the quaternity, the Self's internal orderedness principle. The united hermaphroditic figure has wings, signifying that this united body is "a product of *sublimatio*, an upward movement from below." *Sublimatio* is a chemical event in which:

> if certain substances are heated—mercury is ... an outstanding example of this—they vaporize and then condense or crystallize on the cooler portions of the vessel .... I understand this image to refer to the creation of a non-temporal or eternal substance that has a nontemporal or eternal dimension to it, a kind of incorruptibility ... . [I]f one lives an alchemical life, one creates a product. And that product has a life and quality beyond

> temporal existence ... . [This image depicts] the creation of the
> eternal body. The life of the ego is translated into the archetypal
> dimension. (Edinger, 1994a, p. 97)

This passage describes the distillation of essences or vapours that
become incorruptible and enduring. This is analogous to the way
dream images emanate timeless messages, which form a lasting
basis for individuation over the course of life. We're permanently
changed by the alchemical extraction of essential meanings and
feelings through dreamwork.

## Coniunctio

The culmination of the alchemical opus is the *coniunctio*, the stage
where various procedures have induced a chemical change in the
base metals. In Jungian psychology, this is a metaphor for the transformation of personality through fusion of contrasting elements into a
more complex synthesis. Edinger (1994a) described *coniunctio* as "the
creation of consciousness, which is an enduring substance created by
the union of opposites" (p. 18). It's the union of masculine and feminine, young and old, king and queen, illness and health, thinking and
feeling, sensation and intuition, introversion and extraversion, spiritual detachment and emotional attachment. An example noted earlier
is Alice's dream in Chapter Eight, depicting a *coniunctio* of shaman-
scholar and wife-mother. In Jungian dreamwork, the *coniunctio* isn't
just an image of the goal; it's the path, the method of healing.

In alchemy a number of images represent this process, for example the marriage of the king and queen. A Hermetic saying states,
"Make of man and woman a circle. When you add the head to the tail,
you have the whole tincture"(Roob, 2001, p. 494). As this saying suggests, *coniunctio* is also portrayed in the symbol of the *ouroboros*, the
serpent or dragon eating its own tail, which signifies unifying the
mind and body, psyche and soma, intellect and instinct, and all
the pairs of opposites. In some images, two crowned snakes devour
one another, fusing into one. The fact that the serpents are crowned
is significant and relates the ouroboros to the king. Hermetic scholar
Alexander Roob (2001) wrote, "In the Coptic *Ouro* means king, and
in Hebrew *ob* means a snake" (p. 403). Thus, the ouroboros means
the "king snake" or "snake king."

*Figure 6. Ouroboros, illustration from Maier (1618).*

The transformation of the king into a dragon or an ouroboros suggests to me that the psychology of the ego-king is transcended and transformed. We bear our wounds, shed old skin, and morph into new individuated forms and expressions, becoming more unified. A related symbol is the caduceus with its two coiled snakes, symbolizing cosmic energy and its microcosmic expression in the human body, the *kundalini*. *Coniunctio* is the joining of the poles of the psyche—ego and divinity, conscious self and the deep unconscious, human and nature, king and dragon. The dragon's wings suggest his capacity for visionary flight; the sacred dragon travels in the upper spiritual realms. The ouroboros is also an earthly, embodied being whose coiled energy suggests the gathering of immense instinctual power—power that is sealed, as our internal energy circulates in a circular manner around the mandala of personality. The energy within the Self becomes organized and dynamic, individuated and intense.

The same week I was writing this section about the *ouroboros*, I had a therapy session with William, a brilliant, highly intellectual man who was shut down emotionally, hadn't dated anyone in years, and was unable to express and fulfil his sexual drives. William told me this dream:

> I'm in a room where I was surrounded by an enormous serpent, at least five feet in height and width. It was a cosmic snake. It coiled around the room and encircled me, but it didn't eat me.

Discussing the encircling cosmic snake dream brought William immediate feelings of satisfaction and wholeness. It foreshadowed the re-emergence of his instinctual intelligence.

A woman named Edith told me, "After my divorce, I dreamed that an enormous snake wrapped itself around my house. It was a very powerful dream. I felt like my home was protected."

In Chapter Thirteen, we'll discuss another appearance of the snake-ouroboros, in the Dream of the Swamp and the Snakes.

## The Dream of the Scruffy Old Guy, the Battle of the Giants, and the Ninja King

Travis, the musician discussed earlier, reported this dream:

> I'm in a fight with a scruffy old guy with a pickup truck. I go home to get my gun, but I don't want to shoot anybody. I let him drive away so he doesn't know where I live. Then I'm around a snow-covered castle. There's a fight between two giants, me and another giant. I find a small opening at the base of the castle, a secret passage. I crawl in and melt into the ground, which melts around me. I'm given some important information on how to defeat the opponent. I re-emerge and fly down from the top of the castle and fly right through the monster that was my opponent, and it dissolves. My friend is watching and is amazed at what just transpired. He's also happy to be released from the monster's oppression. He treats me like a ninja king. He opens the door of a Rolls Royce for me.

The scruffy old guy with a pickup truck reminded Travis of "a redneck guy who is ignorant, something I don't want to be. He's a man of the earth." He seemed like some aspect of Travis's shadow. I wondered why he took an aggressive stance toward Travis, so I asked him to enact a dialogue with the man, to ask him why he was in the dream and why he was bothering Travis. Travis said, in the voice of the man, "I'm the common working man. I'm after you because you live your life above other people, apart from connection to others, and you think you shouldn't have to work really hard. You need to get into the game, get going." He represented some pressing internal motivation, but also a corrective to Travis's sense of superiority. The man with a pickup truck was an earthy guy, and in the dream, Travis dissolved into the earth, becoming one with it.

Then the dream shifted to a snow-covered castle, image of the goal, a place of protection, a symbol of individuation and of the Self as an established edifice. The snow-covered castle suggested a mythic destination, like the kingdom of Shambhala or the Potala Palace in the mountains of Tibet, a sanctuary in the clouds, a dreamy, vision-ary place. This symbolized the part of Travis that was a dreamer and a visionary. The snow-covered castle reminded Travis of having a high mountaintop to reach in one's lifetime—a beautiful image of individuation. At this meeting place of earth and sky, Travis found an access point to another realm of existence. The hero's death-rebirth often occurs through an adventure in the underworld, a descent into the unconscious. In the dream, Travis descended from the base of the castle, and, like a shaman, he went down into the earth, taking a mythic journey to the underworld.

Encountering a giant reminded Travis of becoming a giant in the music business. The battle of the giants implied that he was resolv-ing an unrealistic, inflated attitude. Then, having received instructions (like an initiate) on how to defeat the giant, he flew right through him and the opponent dissolved. He was free of the monster's oppression. It occurred to me that perhaps the monster was the pressure he put on himself that he had to be one of the giants of music, and that he had to produce music that would be a monster—a huge commercial success.

The outcome of the dream was that Travis was honoured, treated like a ninja king, and a Rolls Royce arrived as his chariot. The ninja king and the Rolls Royce both represented the royal archetype, the king, and were symbols of self-respect, self-potentiality, and high self-esteem. A Rolls Royce suggested royalty, luxury, being a celeb-rity or a tycoon, having the best of everything. I told Travis, "It's time for you to enter the prosperous Rolls Royce of the imagina-tion." Regardless of whether he achieved significant notoriety, Travis felt pride in himself and energy to continue his passionate work. Inwardly, he'd already become a star personality.

This dream marked the *conuinctio* of the common working man and the royal ninja king. A Ninja King is a combination of a reptile and a human; it's a Dragon-King, a crowned serpent. This was a potent image of transformation (snake) and self-cohesion (king). The ninja king is a symbol of energy and power, as if the unconscious were granting Travis full internal permission to follow his instinctive creative drives. We may also view the Ninja king as an amphibious being, at home with both water and earth, feeling and practicality. Another meaning of this reptile-king symbol is that we need good reptilian survival instincts. To individuate, we need to be adaptable, keep a sense of humour about change, and remain responsive to the message of each moment. This is one of the primary ways that dreamwork aids us.

The ouroboros, the marriage of the king and queen, the celebrity, the discovery of a precious object, the stone, the ninja king—all are symbols of wholeness and individuation, the flowering of the tree of life. In the next chapter I describe a way of diagramming dream symbolism that enables us to experience each dream as an expression and emanation of our totality.

# CHAPTER TEN

# The Dream Mandala

In this chapter, I'll describe the technique I call the *Dream Mandala*, which can assist us in the process of achieving wholeness through dreamwork. You've already encountered dream mandalas in several chapters. This method is particularly helpful in integrating the complex imagery of our dreams.

C.G. Jung developed the method of drawing and painting mandalas during a personal crisis, the period of his confrontation with the collective unconscious. During this time of confusion and upheaval, Jung began painting circular mandalas, which he believed represented the current state of the psyche. He observed changes in symbolism over time, and how this reflected stages of individuation. Jung also used this method with his patients. In *Memories, Dreams, Reflections*, Jung wrote:

> Only gradually did I discover what the mandala really is: "Formation, Transformation, Eternal Mind's eternal recreation." And that is the self, the wholeness of the personality .... [T]he mandala is the center .... It is the path to the centre, to individuation .... There is no linear evolution; there is only a circumambulation of the self. (Jung, 1961, pp. 195–196)

The mandala is the path to the center in the midst of confusion. It is the path of wholeness. The psyche itself is a mandala, a union of opposites. I have found that the mandala principle of inner centering applies directly to the practice of dreamwork. Working with each detail of dream imagery is a circumambulation of the Self, the wholeness and totality of what we are. Exploring a dream in depth is an experience of walking around our center.

Jung called the mandala "the archetype of wholeness" (Jung, 1969 [1955], par. 714). Most mandalas are characterized by the circle and the quaternity, often divided into a light and a dark half.

> [T]hey appear spontaneously in dreams, in certain states of conflict, and in cases of schizophrenia. Very frequently they contain a quaternity or a multiple of four, in the form of a cross, a star, a square, an octagon, etcc. As a rule a mandala occurs in conditions of psychic dissociation or disorientation ... . [A] circular image of this kind compensates the disorder and confusion of the psychic state ... through the construction of a central point to which everything is related, or by a concentric arrangement of the disordered multiplicity and of contradictory and irreconcilable elements. This is evidently an *attempt at self-healing* on the part of Nature. (Jung, 1969 [1955], pars. 713–714)

Applying the mandala principle to dream interpretation helps us find order in the heart of our emotional and spiritual confusion, and powerfully facilitates our self-healing. In *Concerning Mandala Symbolism*, Jung wrote:

> Mandala means circle ... [T]heir basic motif is the premonition of a centre of personality, a kind of central point within the psyche, to which everything is related, by which everything is arranged, and which is itself a source of energy. The energy of the central point is manifested in the almost irresistible compulsion and urge to become what one is, just as every organism is driven to assume the form that is characteristic of its nature, no matter what the circumstances ... . Although the centre is represented by an innermost point, it is surrounded by a periphery containing everything that belongs to the self—the paired opposites that make up the total personality. (Jung, 1969 [1950a], par. 634)

Earlier, in Chapter Four, I described a dream in an underground cave where a mandala image was painted on the floor. However, I believe that dreams reflect the mandala principle even when they don't explicitly contain symbolism of the circle or the center point. Every dream can be depicted as a mandala, a totality consisting of images that portray the conflicts and divisions existing within the psyche.

Over the years, I evolved a technique called the dream mandala, a diagrammatic representation of the dream as a circular drawing. It allows us to map out opposing or contrasting figures and elements within a dream. We depict the different characters, scenes, or feelings within a dream along the periphery of a circle, depicting the paired opposites that constitute the conflict and tension of that moment. We draw out oppositions and crosses of paired opposites. We take note of how the dream contains images of paired opposites, such as male/female, light/dark, good/evil, saint/sinner, persona/shadow, young/old, careful/reckless, ascetic/hedonist, gay/straight, selfless/selfish, intellect/emotion, mystic/materialist, urban/rural, honest/devious, gentle/violent, sensation/intuition, Christ/devil, separateness/connectedness, love/hate, effort/fate, and so on. The result may take the form of quaternities (fourfold designs), which were emphasized by Jung, but also pentagons, hexagons, or septagons. The geometry of the dream mandala is infinite.

The process of creating a dream mandala is the essence of simplicity. Draw a circle and plot on the circle the different characters, places, actions, and situations appearing in the dream. Mapping the dream mandala gives rise to an experience of the Self, where we experience the center point within the psyche where we are poised between the opposing inner forces. The resulting tension can generate immense dynamism within us. The light of consciousness awakens. Like a mandala, the dream becomes a source of energy urging us to live the totality of what and who we are. Jung wrote:

> [H]uman wholeness [is] the goal to which the psychotherapeutic process ultimately leads … . The analysis of [the patient's] situation will therefore lead sooner or later to a clarification of his general spiritual background … . This phase of the process is marked by the production of the symbols of unity, the so-called mandalas … . often as the most obvious compensation for the contradictions and conflicts of the conscious situation … .

The way is not straight but appears to go round in circles ... .
[T]he whole process revolves around a central point or some
arrangement round a centre ... . [T]he process of development proves on closer inspection to be cyclic or spiral ... . The
development of these symbols is almost equivalent of a healing
process. The centre or goal thus signifies salvation. (Jung, 1968
[1944], pars. 32, 34–35)

We can initiate a powerful healing process by developing symbols of a
center within the personality, through the practice of the dream mandala.
To illustrate this, I'll use some examples of dreams already discussed in
this book. Let's begin with Sandy's Dream of the House, the Spider's
Web, and the Old Man's Daughters, discussed in Chapter Nine:

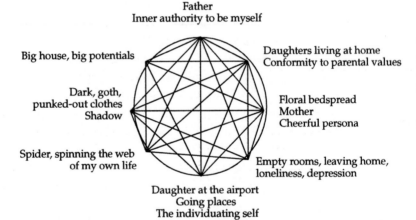

*Dream Mandala: The dream of the house,*
*the spider's web, and the old man's daughters*

Diagramming the dream in this way makes it possible to connect
elements that weren't apparent earlier. The diagram of the daughters at home in contrast to the individuating daughter at the airport highlights the pivotal transition in Sandy's current stage of life.
Behind it all is the supporting structure of the big house, Sandy's
big potentials. The floral bedspreads and cheerful persona are here
in vivid contrast to the Spider spinning its own web, including its
own dark fascinations. The characters of Sandy's family form a core
structure framing the mandala of the Self.

Here I've cast a dream mandala for Owen's powerful dream from Chapter Seven:

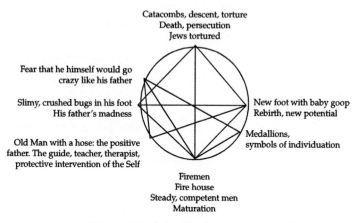

*Dream Mandala: The dream of catacombs,*
*bugs, and the steady firemen*

This dream mandala helps us sense how viscerally the dream is able to evoke the feeling of the inner forces persecuting Owen's father, the desperation of his descent into night. The dream image of the bugs conveys a visceral experience of what it feels like to be taken over by unconscious forces.

Here's a dream mandala of the Dream of the Prostitute-Mother-Transsexual from Chapter Two:

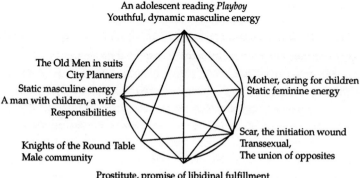

*Dream Mandala: The dream of the prostitute-mother-transsexual*

What's striking to me about this dream mandala is the oppositions of static masculine and feminine energy (the old men in suits and the mother) with two images of sexuality, the adolescent with *Playboy* and the prostitute, as symbols of revitalizing Eros. The figure of the transsexual with scars is a symbol of the initiatory wounds suffered in meeting the demands of social adaptation, career development in any field, joining our own Round Table of associates, not to mention the challenges of parenting and long-term spousal relationships.

Note that the Dream of the Prostitute-Mother-Transsexual (Chapter Two), the Dream of the Black Transvestite (Chapter Seven), the Dream of the Emasculated Batman (Chapter Six), and the Dream of the Girl with a Penis (Chapter Nine) are all expressions of the same androgynous archetype, portraying wholeness and individuation as the union of male and female. Interesting insights emerge when considering these four images together, forming a dream mandala. The image of the prostitute-mother-transsexual reflected Karl's acceptance of his wife's assertive animus. It represented his longing for erotic fulfillment (prostitute), and also symbolized Karl's own capacity to nurture and care for his family (mother). The girl with a penis was dreamed by Eric, a transvestite artist, and depicted the animus of his inner girl, portraying her with male anatomy as a symbol of potent creativity, and of his balanced, bigendered inner life. Jim's black transvestite dream portrayed Jim's anima and shockingly invited him to embrace feminine aspects of his experience. The emasculated Batman portrayed a man (Roger) in the grips of anima depression, the loss of a feeling of aliveness after a wounding experience, and reminded Roger of his father, a man obsessed with chasing women, love ever elusive. It also portrayed identification with his mother's vulnerability. These four cross-gender dream images are resonant with images of a bisexual creator or bisexual primordial being found in various cultures (Campbell, 1983). They express the same archetype portrayed in the tenth Rosarium image (see Figure 5), which depicts resurrection of what Edinger called "the united eternal body," which I call "the winged androgynous body." In India, Shiva is typically portrayed as both male and female, or in union with his consort; shiva-shakti are an inseparable unity, a symbol of indivisible consciousness and energy. The scars of the transsexual and the emasculated Batman are also noteworthy, reminding us that wholeness is achieved through wounding and reintegration.

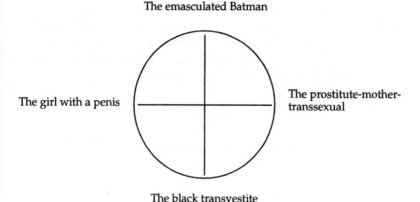

The emasculated Batman

The girl with a penis

The prostitute-mother-transsexual

The black transvestite

*Dream Mandala: Four dreams with androgynous imagery*

As a final example, here's a diagram of one of my dreams from Chapter Nine:

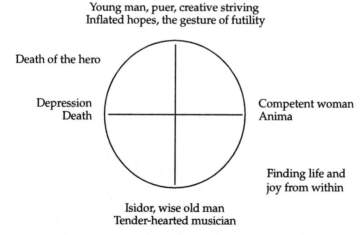

Young man, puer, creative striving
Inflated hopes, the gesture of futility

Death of the hero

Depression
Death

Competent woman
Anima

Finding life and
joy from within

Isidor, wise old man
Tender-hearted musician

*Dream Mandala: The dream of Isidor, the heart attack,
and the competent woman*

This diagram shows the tension of young and old, life and death. It clarifies how the dream depicts the archetypal death and rebirth of the hero, whose revitalization occurs here in midlife through integration of the supportive anima—the capacity for emotional expression and fulfilling aesthetic experience.

In *Psychology and Religion*, Jung wrote, "There is no deity in the mandala. The place of the deity seems to be taken by the wholeness of man" (Jung, 1970 [1938/1940], par. 139). We are the central deity of our own mandalas. We envision and perceive our totality; then we strive to embody it. This is individuation.

In *Aion*, Jung wrote:

> Individual mandalas are symbols of order ... . As magic circles they bind and subdue the lawless powers belonging to the world of darkness, and depict or create an order that transforms the chaos into a cosmos. (Jung, 1959, par. 60)

The dream mandala enables us to experience dreams as magic circles that bind, subdue, and organize the unruly, "lawless powers" within us.

Often I map out not only elements of a single dream along a circle, but also the symbolism of a series of dreams. In this way it becomes apparent how the content of our dreams is contiguous, connected. For example, I've mapped out the main characters from several of Ann's dreams, discussed in Chapter Two.

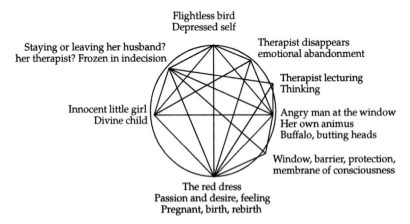

Flightless bird
Depressed self

Staying or leaving her husband?
her therapist? Frozen in indecision

Therapist disappears
emotional abandonment

Therapist lecturing
Thinking

Innocent little girl
Divine child

Angry man at the window
Her own animus
Buffalo, butting heads

Window, barrier, protection,
membrane of consciousness

The red dress
Passion and desire, feeling
Pregnant, birth, rebirth

*Dream Mandala: Six dreams of a depressed woman*

In this dream mandala we note that the angry man at the window, the butting buffalo, and the animus-therapist with his preachy intellect are in essence one figure, one energy within the psyche. There's also a connection between the angry man's demanding, assertive masculine energy, the passionate red dress, and the decisive will Ann needs to be able to choose whether to stay or leave her husband—as well as the resurgence of desire that represents rebirth of the divine child. Additional insights form: The window that serves as a barrier represents a defence, as does Ann's frozen state of sexual shutdown and pervasive relational ambivalence. This frozenness also evokes the theme of *petrification* found in many fairytales, to which I'll return in Chapter Eleven.

The dream mandala is a creative way to depict, and experience, the opposing and contrasting forces within the psyche. I utilize this method to seal the feelings and energies evoked by the dream so they're contained within consciousness and harnessed for intentional change. As we recognize the charge of the polarized opposites within us, we become more fully what we essentially are.

Arguelles and Arguelles (1995) emphasized the principles of centering, orientation, transmutation, and absorption in the practice of constructing a mandala.

> The universality of the mandala is in its one constant, *the principle of the center* … . The center is symbolic of the eternal potential … . It is the burning tip of awareness … . It symbolizes various levels of awareness within the individual as well as the energy that unifies and heals. Making a mandala is a universal activity, a self-integrating ritual … . [I]ts center is the center of the cosmos, the place where the person being healed may sit … . Orientation requires a central position, … a point of consciousness. From this point the other cardinal points are then defined—East, South, West, and North. This act consecrates. To consecrate is to make sacred … . The Mandala of the Transmutation of Demonic Powers requires the painful recognition and acceptance of the existence of negative or demonic forces at work within oneself … . Absorption involves intense concentration and meditation upon the completed Mandala so that the contents of the work are transferred to and identified with the

mind and body of the beholder .... Prior to the construction there was a relative state of chaos; after the absorption there is a new sense, or state of order. Consciousness has been articulated and expanded. (Arguelles & Arguelles, 1995, pp. 12–13, 15, 87, 92–92, 96)

Creating a dream mandala is a self-integrative ritual act that unifies and heals. It represents different feelings and levels of awareness and helps us to reside in our own center, the point of consciousness, and to consecrate everything revealed within the dream. We transmute "demonic powers" by working with our shadow material and difficult complexes. As we meditate upon the completed mandala, we identify all of its contents as parts of our interior reality and absorb it into ourselves. We become the wounded healer who is made whole through melding the fractured pieces of our souls into a multifaceted jewel. The dream mandala is a path to wholeness and our own unique patterns of integrity. I invite you to practice this technique to enhance your experience of dreams.

# CHAPTER ELEVEN

# Synchronicity and Dreams

The path of individuation is often marked by synchronicities, meaningful coincidences of events that occur in dreams or waking life. Synchronicities are those moments when waking life is most dreamlike. For example, a synchronicity occurred involving the unexpected reappearance of one of my teachers, a mystic from Venezuela named Andrés Takra. I apprenticed with Andrés in 1980, then never saw him again. I spoke to him once by phone in 1989. He never replied to my letters after that. I had no idea what had happened to him. One night in 2005 a friend was visiting me, and I showed him a book that Takra had written. My friend was looking at the book, and we were talking about Andrés. I said, "I don't know what happened to him." For a moment I casually checked my email, and my jaw dropped when at that exact moment a message from Andrés Takra appeared on my screen. It read, "Never too late to say hello to an old friend." This experience felt like a dream.

Soon thereafter, a synchronistic event occurred the same week I was teaching a book called *Synchronicity, Science, and Soul-Making*, by Victor Mansfield (1995). My friend Kaleo came to my house to hold a ladder for me while I did some outdoor painting.

Kaleo surprised me by bringing over a blueberry pie. Two days later, I was speaking on the phone with a second friend named Tem. We were discussing an astrological progression I was experiencing: progressed Venus was conjunct my midheaven. And Tem, purely in jest, said "Venus conjunct midheaven. I predict that within three days someone will bring you a blueberry pie." I couldn't believe it! I felt that Tem had contacted the timeless space of the universal mind where all events intersect.

One week later, another synchronicity occurred while I was driving my car. I was talking to someone, saying, "I have to decide whether I'm going to apply for psychoanalytic training, because if I want to do this I have to act right away to set things in motion. Or maybe I should just stay the course, keep doing the same things in my life, and not change anything." At that exact moment, somebody lurched into my lane and sideswiped me, smashing up the side of my car. Fortunately, we were unhurt. I remained poised. Ordinarily, I'd have been quite annoyed by this little scrape. But I tried to contain that reaction and just receive the experience, without a ripple in the mind. I remember thinking about what I was saying at the moment of impact about "staying the course," and I thought, "Apparently, that's not an option." I was also aware that at the moment of the accident there was a discordant astrological transit occurring; the Moon was conjunct Mars in a tense angle to Pluto. Aware that the collision was occurring in exact synchrony with this planetary alignment, I thought to myself, "Okay. I'll go with it." The other party appreciated my relaxed attitude, we exchanged information, and he ended up settling with me privately, paying the entire $2,600 bill. I felt that this jarring collision was a meaningful event, a moment of spiritual intervention indicating I couldn't just hold my current lane in traffic. I decided to pursue a course of in-depth clinical training. There was something in that moment that was bending to shape that decision. We could call it the wisdom of the Self, or the natural intelligence of individuation. We reach to meet, and craft, our destiny. Attunement to the lessons of synchronistic events guides our path.

Mansfield states that in synchronicity, outer events meaningfully relate to a subjective psychological state, such as a dream, fantasy, or feeling. "It's a guiding of the ego and not a production of the ego" (Mansfield, 1995, p. 24). The outer event and the subjective inner state aren't linked by a causal connection; rather, they are acausally related through meaning. The convergences of outer events and inner states aren't accidents of nature or chance coincidences. Jung understood acausal connection through meaning, or synchronicity, as complementary to causal explanations, and as an expression of the guidance of the Self. "The root meaning unfolding outwardly and inwardly is an expression of unconscious compensation and the individuation process—synchronicity is soul-making in action" (Mansfield, 1995, p. 27).

In synchronistic events, the fusion of related characters or events is truly dreamlike. In dreams, events and characters are weirdly juxtaposed against each other and yet, they're connected by inner threads of meaning, which tie everything together synchronistically. Marie-Louise von Franz wrote:

> The view of the world which Jung tried to bring into focus ... is that of synchronicity ... . [T]hrough the investigations of modern physics it has now been proved that on the microphysical level ... we can no longer think of causality as an absolute law, but only as a tendency or prevailing probability ... In Chinese philosophy such thinking has been developed and differentiated much more than in any other civilization; there the question is not why has this come about, or what factor caused this effect, but, what likes to happen together in a meaningful way in the same moment? ... Richard Wilhelm ... in his Introduction to the *I Ching* ... speaks of the complex of events which occur at a certain time moment ... . [T]he problem of time is much more central in the synchronistic way of thinking because there it is the key moment—a certain moment in time—which is the uniting fact, the focal point for the observation of this complex of events ... .
>
> The Chinese had two ideas or aspects of time: namely *timeless time* or eternity, unchanging eternity, with superimposed on it *cyclic time*. We live normally, with our consciousness, in cyclic time, ... but there is an eternal time ... underneath, which sometimes interferes with the other ... .
>
> [T]here is a tendency for things to happen together; it is not just fantasy, there is a noticeable tendency of events to cluster. So far as we can see, that has to do with the archetypes; namely, that if a certain archetype is constellated in the collective

unconscious then certain events tend to happen together. (von
Franz, 1980b, pp. 7–9, 14, 71)

In synchronicities and in dreams the unconscious is felt to be more
active, breaking through in creative ways that carry heightened
psychic energy and psychological intensity (von Franz, 1980b). Synchronicities and dreams are both experiences in which unconscious
forces alter our perception of something. The dream is a "uniting
fact," a focal point for a complex of inner and outer events occurring
at a meaningful time moment.

## The Dream of the Animal Skin

As von Franz noted, synchronicities are visible manifestations of
archetypal contents, apparent when events begin to cluster. A powerful archetype recently emerged in my unconscious. Here's how it
happened: An entirely different period of my life unfolded from the
period of struggle described earlier. I found a teaching job and held
it for some years. Eventually I applied for an academic promotion
at the university, and I was turned down, which was a great disappointment. At the same time I was also feeling discouraged about
my prospects for finding a publisher for this current work. Then
a powerful internal event occurred. I was reading Edward Edinger's
(1994b) book, *The Eternal Drama*, which described the tests and trials of Greek gods such as Heracles, Perseus, and Theseus. I learned
that most of the time the heroes experienced struggles and defeats in
battle. They got their butts kicked. Some were forced into the servi-
tude of women, or controlling father figures. Heracles had to capture
the Erymanthian boar, the creature that killed Adonis; it sounded like
a gnarly beast—a mammoth pig with huge tusks. Reading this was
consoling to me. Edinger described "the steps in every major increase
of consciousness. In each case, a suffering, deflating ordeal for the
ego must precede the epiphany of the Self" (Edinger, 1994b, p. 133).
Having experienced the deflation, I was curious how it might be a
catalyst to my growth in consciousness. That night I dreamed:

> *I'm standing outdoors at night wearing an animal skin.*

When I woke up and thought about the dream, it reminded me
of a brooding, wounded feeling, and of feeling tough, like a hero

who has been through battles and taken his share of blows. Then I picked up the Edinger book and opened to the next chapter, which was about Dionysus. The first page stated that Dionysus "is pictured as a beautiful young man draped in a fawn skin" (Edinger, 1994b, p. 143). That immediately got my attention. I was curious what other meanings might emerge if I looked at this dream as an appearance of Dionysus. Edinger wrote that, Dionysus was born "as a horned infant crowned with serpents" (p. 142). I take that to mean that Dionysus is a symbol of inborn potential (infant), decisive will (horns), and instinctual dynamism (serpents).

Dionysus was torn to pieces by the Titans; thus, he was known as Zagreus, which means dismembered. The Titans used his dust to fashion humanity. Therefore every human being contains a spark of Dionysus. I realized that I, too, possess this spark. Edinger also described the dismemberment imagery associated with Dionysus and the Dionysian ritual feast of the raw flesh, and he noted the connection between the symbolism of dismemberment and crucifixion.

> He was associated with the bull and with serpents, the imagery pointing to his wildness and his power, and to his place outside the bounds of civilized order ... . What Dionysus brings is wild, spontaneous, inspired behavior ... . He is connected to rapture, to the release of everything that has been locked up ... . He brings wisdom in a sudden flash, epiphany ... . Where he is, things change ... Creativity is an aspect of Dionysus ... . It is ... creativity in the inspired, almost intoxicated, sense, in which the unconscious wells up. It corresponds to the way Nietzsche said he wrote *Thus Spake Zarathustra*; while he tramped the mountains of the Engadine, Zarathustra shouted in his ear. That is Dionysus, that is Dionysian creativity, and Nietsche is probably the outstanding example of Dionysian possession. (Edinger, 1994b, pp. 143–144, 148)

Then Edinger cited this passage from Jung's *Zarathustra* seminar:

> Inasmuch as you say that these creative forces are in Nietzsche or in me or anywhere else, you cause an inflation, because man

does not possess creative powers, he is possessed by them. If he allows himself to be thoroughly possessed by them without questioning, without looking at them, there is no inflation, but the moment he splits off, when he thinks "I am the fellow" an inflation follows ... . Nietzsche of course could not help looking at the thing and then he was overwhelmed with resentments, because the creative powers steal your time, sap your strength, and what is the result? A book perhaps. But where is your personal life? All gone. Therefore, such people feel so terribly cheated; they mind it, and everybody ought to kneel down before them in order to make up for that which has been stolen by God ... . If you know you are creative and enjoy being creative, you will be crucified afterwards, because anybody identified with God will be dismembered. (Jung, 1988, pp. 57–58, cited in Edinger, 1994b, p. 148)

As I read this passage I felt myself become the scattered dust of Dionysus, whose creative spirit continually re-forms. Jung described Dionysus as a symbol of the creative process, possession by creative powers, and the surly moodiness and woundedness of the creative personality. This was fully relevant to my situation. I was huffy and resentful and felt I should have been recognized for my excellent teaching and original writing. At the time of this dream I was involved in the heroic labour of completing this book. I realized that I had to bear my wounds, my fatigue, and my discouragement. I had to keep going and find inspiration in my work. Dionysus's appearance signified that things were going to get stirred up, which they certainly were. Soon after this dream, I had the synchronistic car collision that coincided with an important decision. All of this emotional meaning and archetypal meaning was contained in condensed form in my dream of wearing an animal hide.

I worked with this material for several more months. Then another meaningful synchronistic event occurred: One of my clients dreamed that he was wearing an animal hide; it was fresh, and the blood of the animal was still on it. It was essentially the same dream as my own (see the Dream of the Buffalo Hide in Chapter Thirteen). The eternal archetypes constantly emerge within the fabric of the visible world.

## The Dream of the Black Skull

Dreams often arise synchronistically at the time of significant events. For example, the day after I learned that my father was gravely ill in the hospital, ten weeks before he passed away, I dreamed:

> I'm with my partner, Diana, digging next to our house. I unearthed a black skull, with prominent jaw and teeth. It could have been the skull of a wolf or wolverine.

The skull of death emerged within my unconscious. The skull reminded me of a mask, like the carved and painted masks that filled my father's study, and heightened my awareness that he would soon be joining the world of the beloved ancestors.

The skull's prominent jaw and teeth reminded me of biting aggression and anger, fierce oral hunger and craving, and the way Diana and I, like many couples, sometimes argue. It was unclear in the dream whether this was a fossilized skull, or whether it was carved in stone, a carved stone skull mask. It occurred to me that the skull was a philosopher's stone, comprising the union of opposites of love and hate. This dream image evoked the insight that a loving relationship with Diana also sometimes awakens fiery aggression.

The black skull also reminded me of having some teeth, some fierceness and aggression, the capacity for what the *I Ching* calls Biting Through, bringing things to completion. I realized that is what I needed to do with this present book.

The prominent teeth also reminded me of going to see B.B. King at the Apollo Theatre in Harlem when I was thirteen years old. I went with Ruth McGhee, my beloved black nanny. Ruth was the person who first suggested I learn to play the guitar. That night I was the only white kid in the audience, which mainly consisted of African Americans, and I remember how warmly welcomed I felt. I recall that while he played his solos, B.B.'s face lit up in a beautiful smile with the bright spotlight reflecting off his sparkling white teeth. Because Ruth was an old friend of B.B. King (she was the cousin of Brownie McGhee, another great blues musician), we got to go backstage where I saw Big Mama Thornton (author of "Ball and Chain" and other blues hits) stumbling around backstage with her bottle of whiskey. Frisky-looking women in tight dresses were fussing over their makeup. One of B.B.'s managers walked into the room and opened up an enormous briefcase stuffed with pornographic magazines. He made a point of showing them to me. The whole scene was dreamlike and surreal. Then I met the warm and gracious B.B. in the flesh, shook his hand, and he let me hold his guitar, Lucille. It was an amazing night!

I also remember that while I held B.B. King's guitar backstage at the Apollo Theatre in Harlem, I was wearing a cast on my arm, because I had broken a finger playing basketball. It was a Thursday night in February 1971, and my father took me to the Emergency Room of Roosevelt Hospital. I had been in the hospital before, but that was the first time I saw people with serious injuries and illnesses, gunshots and stab wounds. I saw the cuts and bruises of a man who'd been beaten up in a barroom brawl, as I sat waiting for the doctor to wind a plaster cast onto my hand. It was the night of a New Moon in Pisces, astrological sign of hospitals, disabilities,

*Figure 7. The author, age 13, with B.B. King.*

and the universality of suffering. My feeling of compassion for humanity was awakened. I felt the same concern when I walked around in Harlem among people who were visibly poorer than people in my neighbourhood. That was a time of awakening that I remember distinctly. The memory of these interconnected events is resonant with emotional meaning and depth for me. And memories of the hospital and suffering humanity were united with awareness of my father lying poised between life and death in a hospital bed at that moment. All of this was contained in the condensed symbolism of the black skull.

## Dreams, Memory, and Imagination

Dreams are often retrospective, opening a floodgate of memories and feelings long forgotten and submerged. In an essay on childhood amnesia, Ernest Schactel (1959) described how glimpses of the lost experiences of the past can emerge. The veil of amnesia lifts and lost experiences are recovered. A scene from childhood reappears as through it happened yesterday, with an air of incredible freshness and aliveness. For novelist Marcel Proust (1934), "the remembrance of things past" is the supreme satisfaction, carrying with it feelings of exhilarating happiness. Each recovery of forgotten experience, and of the person one was when having the experience, enriches us, adds to the light of consciousness, and widens the conscious scope of one's life. Dreams powerfully perform this function of memory retrieval. They evoke feelings and fragments of the distant past, of memories inscribed in our cells. Thus, dreams unify the former self with the present self and support our integration into a multifaceted whole. Dreams astonish us with their capacity to re-script memory and depict the co-presence of past and future.

In my black skull dream, there was a convergence of my father's impending death, my childhood awareness of poverty, illness, and infirmity, the reality of suffering, and the urge to revive the life force through Eros and excitation (B.B. King's manager with the pornographic magazines); my awareness of my animal nature, fierceness, and aggression; my vision of B.B. playing the blues onstage at the Apollo Theatre, rising above his childhood as a destitute sharecropper to triumph, glory, the spotlight of an individuated life. All of this varied emotional content was joined, sealed, and unified in an ecstatic moment, brought together by my black skull dream as a "uniting fact," a symbol of wholeness.

Dreams contribute to various cognitive activities such as information processing, problem solving, anticipation, learning, and the consolidation of memory (Hunt, 1993). Many examples in this book illustrate how dreams aid recovery and integration of memories. We recover not just memories but also the visceral feeling of remembered events. One theory about dreams, derived from theories of cognitive science, is that dreams are purely a memory-processing activity. There's some truth in this view. Our dreams about recent or distant past events help consolidate our memories and enrich them with new details. Dreams play a central role in the mechanism of memory processing in the brain. But can we reduce all dream content to the status of memory-processing?

Hunt noted that perceptual imagery is the core of dreams, which involve complex processes of mnemic (memory-based) and perceptual assimilation. However, dreaming isn't just a form of memory, for it also involves a symbolic capacity, utilizing imaginative recombination of mnemic and perceptual elements. Dreams are thus constructive, creative images, not just variants of remembering. While dreams do reflect our prior experiences, memory can't account for the vividness and intensity of dreams of phenomena we haven't actually experienced, such as dreams of flying or floating in the air, or dreams of extreme or perverse sexuality or aggression. Nightmares and lucid dreams (dreaming in a state of alert consciousness) also can't be explained in terms of memory processing. Thus, Hunt noted, dreaming is not only a process of sorting through perceptual and memory data but also involves the activity of a creative imagination. The way I'd state this is that in dreams, memory and imagination meet. In this meeting, the creativity of the unconscious is expressed in the spontaneous appearance of archetypes in synchronistic dreams.

## The Dream of the Walrus

Once when I was leading a group, a woman named Mindy reported a dream about a walrus. She had no idea what that meant. Carla, one of the other group members, said she had just spent the summer in Alaska and knew a lot about walruses. She said, "They're very rough during sex and can actually gore each other." Mindy found that quite interesting because she'd recently been processing memories of a traumatic sexual experience. She realized how much that episode had affected her mood, her self-confidence, and her capacity to trust. This detail about walruses suddenly brought up intense feelings. She started to have a deep catharsis in the group.

Synchronicities often occur when we tell a dream in the presence of other people. A dream will often be relevant to another person's experience, or someone present will be in a unique position to understand and interpret some detail of the dream. I wonder if that specific emotional content would have come to light that day had Carla not been present. And how did the unconscious know that the walrus would be a healing symbol?

What happened next was quite unexpected: Someone in the group said the dream reminded her of the Beatles song "I Am the Walrus." All at once, people began singing "I am the egg man, we are the egg men, I am the walrus, coo coo ca choo!" Mindy's face lit up with a smile, and she said, "That's the music I was listening to when I was a teenager. I felt so free then, and so in touch with my body. I remember how good sex felt." The same walrus image that represented sexual wounding also represented the original Eve innocence of her teenage sexuality. Mindy's dream had healing resonance.

## Synchronicity and Individuation: The Wisdom of the Parrot

A particular symbol or archetype may play a pivotal role in our individuation, and its appearance often occurs through synchronicities. As von Franz (1980b) stated, "[I]f a certain archetype is constellated in the collective unconscious then certain events tend to happen together" (p. 71). In this section, I discuss some ideas about synchronicity and individuation that emerged from contemplating a series of fairytales, dreamlike stories that have served for centuries as dreams for the collective. These stories provide treasures of meaning and delight for the imagination.

In 2003 I travelled to Costa Rica and returned home with a framed painting of a parrot, which I hung on my wall and gazed at. It seemed like a kind of trickster figure, but I wasn't sure what it represented. Around that time I began reading von Franz's *Individuation in Fairy Tales*, which discussed several Islamic fairytales featuring the symbol of the parrot. In one story, "The White Parrot," a witch exhorts a girl to send her brother to catch a certain valuable white parrot. "Whoever catches it will be rich all his life" (von Franz, 1977, p. 47). The boy is instructed by an old man where to find the parrot, and to wait until the parrot is completely asleep, with its head under its wing, before trying to catch it. Otherwise, he's told, the bird will escape and he'll be petrified, like many others who've attempted to catch the bird in the past. However, the brother tries to catch the parrot too quickly, it flies away, and the little brother is petrified.

The valuable parrot is a symbol of the Self as the source of deepest value. It represents the value of listening to the unconscious, which can influence our inner and outer realities, mysteriously changing our destiny. Trying to catch the parrot too quickly reminds me of haste, premature action, carelessness, not allowing things to ripen to the proper moment. von Franz (1977) analyzes "the petrification which occurs if one tries to snatch the parrot too soon" (p. 55). Petrification, a common theme in fairytales, represents book religions that petrify the truth, "religious mechanism devoid of inner meaning or inner experience." It also signifies being "psychologically petrified so that no more development is possible" (p. 57). We can't achieve individuation by merely following the letter of the law, moral codes, and collective attitudes. Nor can we remain stuck, frozen, rigid, and unyielding. We have to be willing to change, to become a different person. That's the meaning of the theme of the death of the king discussed in Chapter Nine.

In another story, *The Tuti-Nameh* ("The Book of the Parrot"), a young merchant who loves his wife very much is offered a parrot at a marketplace. It costs one thousand gold coins. When the merchant questions whether the parrot is really worth such a price, the parrot assures him:

> My heart is filled to the brim with pearl of wisdom and precious stones of knowledge. Of the truth, even the future is known to me and even the supernatural is understood by my intelligence. Whoever follows my advice moves on a path of happiness. (von Franz, 1977, p. 48)

The parrot's words inform us of the prescience of the unconscious, which reveals its foreknowledge of our development through prophetic dreams, hunches, and synchronicities.

To prove his value, the parrot gives the merchant a little tip, instructing him to purchase a certain spice that is about to increase in value and that will be very profitable. The merchant follows the parrot's advice and earns five thousand gold coins, so he's able to buy the parrot. The parrot then advises the merchant to make a voyage overseas for another business deal, and he decides to go, even though his wife is very sad about it. The merchant is away for a year, and eventually his wife falls in love with a young man and wants to have an affair, but she decides to seek the parrot's advice before going to meet the man. The parrot acts like he approves of her rendezvous with the young man, but then he tells her "she must be careful that it does not happen to her as it happened to So and So." The wife asks, "Oh, what was that?" The parrot launches into a long story that lasts all night, so that she's distracted and misses her chance to meet her prospective lover. This sequence of events repeats every night until the merchant finally returns home.

> Then the parrot tells the whole story and there is a general reconciliation and, as a favor for having saved the situation, about which naturally the wife is also glad, the parrot only asks to be set free and be allowed to fly about at will. So they live happily together forever after and the parrot visits them in a friendly way from time to time. (von Franz, 1977, pp. 49–50)

The parrot is a trickster figure who shows us the right path despite our conscious intention. By listening to the unconscious and following the way of individuation, we gain both practical and spiritual rewards, and the contentment that comes from knowing we've lived truly and fully. von Franz wrote: "[T]he Parrot in certain Arabic stories is a Hermes-Mercurius figure, a psychopompos, who speaks the truth" (p. 47). The Parrot represents morality, "fulfilling the will of God and a higher form of ethical realization" (p. 50).

> [T]he parrot is the spirit of truth, ... good is rewarded and evil is punished ... . [T]he Parrot ... is full of pearls of wisdom and precious stones, and the knowledge of the truth; ... it knows the future and supernatural things ... . [I]t is a symbol for the mysterious truth which the unconscious speaks. (von Franz, 1977, pp. 55–56)

In a third fairytale, called *The Secret of the Bath Badgerd* ("The Secret of the Castle of Nothingness"), the hero is Hatim-Tai, a cavalier or poet in the sixth or seventh century C.E., known as a very generous man, indeed, the ideal of generosity. The tomb of Hatim is analogous to the Grail, and plays the same role in Persian folklore as the Grail plays in Celtic and Germanic folklore.

In this story, "Hatim ... took as the seventh of many tasks ... the exploration of the Bath Badgerd, the Castle of Nothingness" (von Franz, 1977, p. 58). Along the way, an old man says to him, " 'Young man, what enemy sent you to the Bath Badgerd? Nobody knows where it is ... . [N]o one who ever tried to explore it ever came back.' ... But Hatim ... will not be put off his task" (p. 60). Whatever his destination is, this was already framed as a fool's errand, an impossible task. This is the way individuation often feels. We choose or undertake something that seems impossible, where we can only see insurmountable obstacles ahead of us.

Hatim ventures on and gets completely lost. He faces down a dragon that has been terrorizing the humble residents of a village, demanding that each year they offer him one of their daughters. Hatim tricks the dragon and incinerates him deftly. (Here Hatim honours and protects the feminine; he also shows courage.) In gratitude, "The King gives him a lot of gold and silver ... but in accordance with his generous nature he distributes it all to the poor, and after three days he goes on his way" (von Franz, 1977, p. 61). He travels on, getting lost again. His feet get cut up in a forest of metal, he encounters giant scorpions, and he keeps asking people where the Bath Badgerd is. Along the way he notices numerous stone statues and he wonders how they got there.

Eventually he comes to a castle, where a parrot calls to him that Hatim is a fool to enter here. "Why have you already finished with life?" Then over the doorway Hatim reads this inscription:

This place was enchanted by Gayomard, who, one day ... found a diamond which shone like the radiant sun and the gleaming moon. He ... showed it to his court and his wise men, asking if they had ever seen such a stone, and nobody had. So Gayomard said that he would keep it in a place where nobody could ever find it, and to protect it he brought about all this magic and built the Bath Badgerd. Even the parrot sitting in its cage is under its spell! Oh servant of God, with the castle on a golden throne are a bow and arrow, and if you want to escape from here you must take these and with them kill the parrot, and if you hit him the spell will be broken and if you miss him you will become a stone statue. (von Franz, 1977, p. 76)

von Franz says, "[H]e has to find something and he does not even know what it is." Slowly Hatim realizes he is reaching the goal of his life, "coming closer to the achievement of the thing for which he had been searching" (p. 76). He has to shoot the parrot. This is the moment of truth.

Hatim enters the castle, where he sees the parrot and finds the bow and arrows. Hatim picks up the bow and shoots the first arrow, but he misses the bird and his legs suddenly turn to stone. Hatim is very concerned! He shoots the second arrow, and misses the parrot again. Now he turns to stone up to his neck. Things are getting very serious. He knows what will happen if he misses with his final arrow.

> Anybody who does not hit the parrot gets petrified .... [H]itting the parrot really symbolically means either to get or miss the goal of his whole life. Then Hatim aims, shuts his eyes and shouting "God is great" he shoots. He does not concentrate his senses in a skilful, extraverted way towards the goal, but looks inside; and with his cry, "God is great," he really means, "My target is really Allah, and is what I must not miss or lose; He is great." Naturally behind this is the feeling-idea that probably he will miss again, and therefore he commits his soul to God before he is completely petrified. This is not so much a request for God's help as a declaration of his loyalty to God in what is probably the last moment of his life. In this way he turns away from the target, he gives up the attempt to shoot the parrot and concentrates entirely on keeping his loyalty to God and accepting his fate of even missing, if God has planned this for him ... . [T]hat was the moment when Hatim gave up all ego purposes ... . It is easy to give up one's ego obstinacy and what one wants if one has not worked for it for twenty years ... . [B]ut if you have to give up your ego obstinacy about the thing which you were looking and searching for many years, and for

which you had been through all those heroic adventures, that would mean a terrific sacrifice; and it is by shutting his eyes and saying, "Allah is great," that Hatim makes the sacrifice. He hits the bird. Then again there is a thunderous noise and a cloud of dust, and when that subsides he sees in the place of the parrot Gayomard's beautiful diamond, and all the statues which had been petrified come alive ... . The parrot is like a negative spell, veiling or hiding the sight of the diamond ... . [T]he diamond has always been a well-known alchemical symbol of the philosopher's stone ... , the immortal body, ... the *lapis philosophorum*, ... a symbol of the Self. (von Franz, 1977, pp. 112–113)

This story, like so many of our dreams, describes the commitment that individuation requires of us. The question each of us must ask is: What is my parrot? Where in my life do I need to shoot the arrow of my effort with full faith in the target? Individuation means living in accordance with inner truth, even if it means great risks and trials. With the help of the guide, the messenger, we can reach our destination. The parrot symbolizes the mercurial guide, the Self, the elusive messenger of dreams. The parrot is also the intuitive hunches that guide us to our next steps, through synchronicities. When we pursue our individuation without holding back, with full awareness that our task may be an impossible one, that is when we hit the bird. And that is when the diamond appears.

A synchronicity occurred the day I was writing this section. I ran into a colleague and told her about the parrot stories. She said, "That's so funny. I just had a dream about a blue and white macaw." For some reason, the parrot archetype was being constellated.

The following day I opened the *San Francisco Chronicle*, where I saw an article with the headline "Loquacious Parrot Splits Up Love Birds." The story described how a couple broke up after the husband heard his parrot repeating the name of his wife's secret lover.

"Hiya Gary" the parrot trilled flirtaciously whenever Chris's girlfriend answered her cell phone. But Chris, the owner of the parrot, did not know anyone named Gary. And his girlfriend, Suzy, who had moved into his apartment a year earlier, swore that she didn't either. She stuck to her story even after the parrot,

> Ziggy, began making lovely-dovey, smooching noises when it
> heard the name Gary on television. (Lyall, 2006, p. 2)

I noticed the connection between this story and "The Book of the Parrot," with its tale of the merchant's wife whose virtue was preserved by the parrot's inscrutable wisdom. Listening closely to the voice of the inner parrot of the unconscious assures our integrity is preserved as we navigate our personal and collective challenges. The parrot teaches us to "do the right thing." Doing what you know is right for you is a key to individuation.

Several days later, someone I had never met called me on the phone to say how much she enjoyed my book on spiritual apprenticeship—the same book I was so upset about some years earlier. She said, "You write about things that other people have said, but somehow the way you've said it is different. You write from direct experience. You aren't just parroting others." I curbed my fleeting instinct to squawk loudly, then to break up in laughter. Instead, what resonated inside me was a feeling of completeness, a peaceful sense that the labour of my task had been redeemed. Synchronicities are timeless moments of wholeness, when the light is so bright, you can't miss it.

Richard Tarnas (2006) described synchronicity as:

> a dawning intuition, sometimes described as having the character of a spiritual awakening, that the individual was herself or himself not only embedded in a larger ground of meaning and purpose but also in some sense a focus of it … . The phenomenon seemed to function, in religious terms, as something like an intervention of grace. (p. 51)

Like synchronicities, some dreams have the character of spiritual interventions and awakenings. In the next chapter we'll explore the spiritual nature of dreams and look at several more dreams that show us a glimpse of synchronicity, the sudden illumination of an archetype.

# CHAPTER TWELVE

# Spirit and the Body in Dreams

D reams are spiritual phenomena that awaken us. They are waves of spirit, ripples though the ocean of consciousness that disturb our complacent viewpoints and expand our awareness. Jung's writings showed the value of attending to the spiritual dimensions of the psyche, and taught that healing of the person results from contacting something within the unconscious that transcends and transforms the individual. This emphasis distinguishes Jungian dreamwork from approaches that look at dreams solely as expressions of personal, biographical contents such as memories and fantasies. Dreams are expressions and communications of spirit, the God within us, the Self, the wholeness that encompasses the ego. Their captivating images evoke in us a mood of contemplation, and become focal points for spiritual life, regardless of whether we adhere to any specific religious doctrine or tradition.

In this chapter, we adopt the attitude that Corbett (1996) called *the religious approach to the psyche*, which

> tries to approach the divine (or transcendent levels of reality) by locating it directly and deeply within ourselves ... . [T]he spirit can present to us something new and personal which cannot be

found in existing teachings but which is nevertheless needed by the individual. (Corbett, 1996, pp. 8, 55)

Corbett (1996) noted that spiritual revelation is not an event of the past that has ceased but is a process that continues inside us, and happens to us "as an unbidden gift" (p. 80). Dreams serve as vehicles for this ongoing process of revelation, conveying the experience of the *numinosum*, an astonishing, alluring, and fascinating presence. Jung called this "a dynamic agency or effect not caused by an arbitrary act of will ... . The *numinosum* is ... the influence of an invisible presence that causes a peculiar alteration of consciousness" (Jung, 1969 [1938/1940], par. 6). Corbett wrote:

> Rudolph Otto (1958) ... coined the term numinous from the Latin *numen*, meaning ... to nod or beckon ... . [T]he presence of the numinous is the crucial element of religious experience; it is felt to be objective and outside the self ... . The production— or the transmission—of numinous experience is an intrinsic function of the psyche ... . When an archetype is felt relatively directly within the psyche, its effect is numinous and it is felt as Other. Phenomenologically there is no difference between these experiences and those described as the experience of spirit in the religious literature. This overlap means that archetypal processes are not only of developmental but also of religious significance. (Corbett, 1996, pp. 8, 11, 60)

Numinous dreams have a momentous, electrifying, or captivating quality. A woman named Gina, who had recently become engaged, dreamed:

> *I saw a green fluorescent penis.*

Fluorescence represented the numinosity and sacredness of sex, which was a current locus of Gina's spirituality. It reminded her of the glowing wand wielded by Luke Skywalker in *Star Wars*, as he battled Darth Vader, and of the blessing "May the Force be with you." A wide variety of dream images possess spiritual, numinous qualities.

The religious significance of dreams derives from their capacity to gift us with our own spiritual visions and symbolism, and to reveal glimpses of illumined states of consciousness. Dreams convey images of our most exalted human experiences as well as of our complexes and shadow figures. In dreams, we may be touched by spirit as an illuminating message, as in the dream voice that told me, "God sees you" (Chapter Three). We feel it as a blessing, as in the Dream of Immersion and Spiritual Cleansing (Chapter Nine); or as a momentous intervention, as in the Dream of the Lost Wallet and the Border Crossings (Chapter Five), where a mysterious force helped Paolo cross borders, opening the gates like the Hindu god Ganesh, the remover of obstacles.

This chapter is a brief meditation on the archetype of spirit, its appearance in dreams, and its connection to the body. I'll discuss several dreams with spiritual imagery, and view them through the lens of yogic, Buddhist, gnostic, and alchemical ideas that enhance our understanding of spirit, dreams, and consciousness. I make no attempt to be comprehensive or philosophically airtight in this discussion. These are but sketchy brushstrokes, pastel traces of the beckoning mystery.

Ann Ulanov wrote:

> [W]e feel the Transcendent touching us, maybe even guiding us ... . Livingness comes from connecting to the center of reality, however we name it; it pours through us regardless of our degree, great or small, of health, wealth, wisdom; it makes us glad, filled with gratitude to be alive .... A certain autonomy associates with Spirit. Like the wind, it will blow or cease, come and go, according to its own law. We might hear it, but we cannot control it, or even direct it ... . When we invoke Spirit, we are calling on powers beyond the human ego to aid in the work of healing, and we are turning straight into its path (Ulanov, 2004, pp. 55, 73–75)

## The Archetype of Spirit

Spirit is an archetypal pattern of experience characterized by its energy, impetus, radiance, numinosity, its infinite creativity and imagination, and its appearance as the light of awareness. For Jung (1966 [1917/1926]), spirit is related to the primordial image of *energy*, found in "dynamistic religions whose sole and determining thought is that there exists a universal magical power about which everything revolves" (par. 108).

> This concept is equivalent to the idea of soul, spirit, God, health, bodily strength, fertility, magic, influence, power, prestige, medicine … . Among certain Polynesians *mulungu* … means spirit, soul, daemonism, magic, prestige; and when anything astonishing happens, the people cry out "Mulungu!" This power concept is also the earliest form of a concept of God … and is an image which has undergone countless variations in the course of history. In the Old Testament the magic power glows in the burning bush and in the countenance of Moses; in the Gospels it descends with the Holy Ghost in the form of fiery tongues from heaven. In Heraclitus it appears as world-energy, as "ever-living fire"; among the Persians it is the fiery flow of *haoma*, divine grace; among the Stoics it is the original heat, the power of fate. Again, in medieval legend it appears as the aura or halo … . In their visions the saints behold the sun of this power, the pleni-tude of its light. (Jung, 1966 [1917/1926], par. 108)

Spirit appears as a father image, wise old man or woman, magician, doctor, priest or priestess, teacher, professor, grandfather or grand-mother, animal, or any figure from whom "decisive convictions, pro-hibitions, and wise counsels emanate … . [I]t consists simply of an authoritative voice which passes final judgments" (Jung, 1969 [1948], par. 396). In this sense, spirit is an internal impetus for growth, an evolutionary force within the psyche. von Franz explained:

> One of the main ways in which we use the word spirit is in speaking of the inspiring, vivifying aspect of the unconscious … . [F]or the ego complex to get in touch with the unconscious has a vivifying and inspiring effect … . Jung therefore defines spirit … as *the dynamic aspect of the unconscious* … . One could say that composing dreams while one sleeps is an aspect of the spirit; some master spirit or mind composes a most ingenious series of pictures which, if one can decipher them, seem to convey a highly intelligent message … . [T]he unconscious energetically does something on its own, it moves and creates on its own, and that is what Jung defines as spirit … . Jung [says] that

spirit contains a spontaneous psychic principle of movement and activity; secondly that it has the quality of freely creating images beyond our sense perception ..., and thirdly, there is an autonomous and sovereign manipulation of those images. Those are the three characteristics of what Jung calls the spirit or the dynamism of the unconscious. It is spontaneously active, it freely creates images beyond sensual perception, and it autonomously and in a sovereign manner manipulates those images. (von Franz, 1980b, pp. 20–21)

All dreams express this vivifying, creative energy. There is no limit to its image-forming activity, nor does it refrain from forming images of itself. Jung called this the "self-representation of the spirit in dreams" (Jung, 1969 [1948], par. 396). In some dreams, spirit appears to represent itself as consciousness observing itself, freeing itself of objects and images, self-liberated into its own nature.

Mystics use the term *spirit* to denote the Absolute, the ground or source matrix of existence. In yogic traditions, spirit is described as pure consciousness without an object, beyond form and image. In some accounts, consciousness becomes obscured through its fascination with form—the physical, emotional, and relational structures that house consciousness and give it body. In Hinduism, spirit (Brahman, Shiva) emanates material forms as expressions of itself, and becomes identified with matter—lost in *maya* (illusion) and a sleep of self-forgetting. Spirit is concealed in the infinitely entertaining manifest realms of existence. But just as sleep is followed by waking, the concealed divine presence is eventually revealed in a moment of self-recognition, in which spirit rediscovers its innate freedom as eternal existence, infinite consciousness, and self-embodied bliss. The experience of spiritual self-recognition is the goal of meditation, and it may occur spontaneously in dreams.

## The Dream of the Karate Chop and a Flash of Light

I once dreamed:

> I'm in a meditation class. The teacher, a woman, gives me a quick karate chop to my back. I see and feel, in a flash, the white light of pure consciousness. Everything dissolves into nothingness and formless, blissful white light.

A karate chop is a decisive act, and a blow to the ego. This body blow jolts me out of a purely physical viewpoint. The chop leads to an experience that reminds me of a zen *satori*, a sudden spiritual awakening. The bright ray of blissful white light is an image of spirit as a flash of the numinous, a *mysterium tremendum*, a presence existing outside of ordinary reality that inspires awe, fascination, and humility (Corbett, 1996, pp. 12, 23). *Mysterium* refers to

> the feeling that one is in contact with something that is 'wholly other'—beyond the sphere of what is usual, intelligible and familiar, filling the mind with wonder and astonishment ... . The direct experience of spirit, or archetype, is always accompanied by ... the presence of intense affect ... . Spirit implies transcendence of the human, something which comes to us from beyond ego consciousness which is felt as other than myself. (Corbett, 1996, pp. 8, 12, 16, 113)

In the dream, I have no visible emotional response to this formless, blissful spiritual presence beyond the ego; there's only a statement that I can feel this consciousness. But an emotional response grows inside me as I contemplate and amplify this image. I feel an urge to love and venerate this inner light, to become part of it, to inwardly bow down before this nothingness and formless consciousness that is now paradoxically visible, and which is actively related to me. In religious terms, the dream is like a vision or revelation of the deity, and depicts the same spiritual light that poured into Job in his moment of self-offering to Yahweh (Figure 4). This self-disclosure of spirit is a primary archetypal event. Jung wrote:

> [T]he soul must contain in itself the faculty of relationship to God, i.e., a correspondence, otherwise a connection could never come about. This correspondence is, in psychological terms, the archetype of the God-image ... . Too few people have experienced the divine image as the innermost possession of their own soul. Christ only meets them from without, never from within the soul ... . [T]he soul possesses by nature a religious function, and ... it is the prime task of all education (of adults) to convey the archetype of the God-image, or its emanations and effects. (Jung, 1968 [1944], pars. 11, 12, 14)

In this book, dream images such as the sleeping wolf, the rose, the oval stone, the black skull, the steady firemen with their medallions, and the cathedral with stained-glass windows are equivalent to God-images, symbols of the Self, the wholeness that meet us from within. Also recall the image of light pouring in through windows in the Dream of the Church, the Pagan Altar, and the Sacrifice (Chapter Four). The numinous God-image appears in innumerable dreams conveying glimpses of spirit's energy, clarity, totality, and omnipresence.

## Spirit as Self-reflective Consciousness

We may also view the Dream of the Karate Chop and a Flash of Light as a representation of consciousness itself. Harry Hunt (1993) explained dreams of white light as evidence that human consciousness is self-reflective and has an intrinsic tendency toward self-reference. The psyche represents itself through dreams of white light, which reveal the most basic quality of visual-spatial perception, namely its luminosity (Hunt, 1993, p. 191). Just as an artist paints a self-portrait, consciousness portrays its own nature in dreams with mandala or white light imagery, where the luminosity of awareness is translated into tactile, kinesthetic patterns. From this I infer that this white light dream is a portrayal of spirit as self-reflective, self-illuminating awareness.

From the perspective of the Indian yogic philosophy of Kashmir Shaivism, dreams of white light can be understood as expressions of spirit's self-liberating movement, termed *visarga*:

> The *visarga* ... points to the inherently self-referential capacity of consciousness ... [and] represents the freedom of consciousness ... . [T]he *visarga* represents the basic component of the *sadhana* in which the finite consciousness is doubled back on itself. At first, ... consciousness simply encounters more and more of its own contents. Finally, a powerful moment of recognition (*pratyabhijna*) occurs when the beam of consciousness becomes conscious of itself and nothing else. (Muller-Ortega, 1989, p. 126)

In dreams, consciousness "doubles back," to reflect on itself and its current embodied condition. The spiritual dynamism of the unconscious expansively produces dream images that help us therapeutically and emotionally evolve the personality. At this stage, "consciousness simply encounters more and more of its own contents." But consciousness is also self-referential and becomes self-aware in dreams. The manifestation of spirit in dreams often brings about an experience of self-recognition that activates dormant energies within us.

The freedom of consciousness is also expressed in precognitive dreams, clairvoyant dreams, and telepathic dreams, shared dreams, out-of-body dreams, and lucid dreams. All of these are spiritual dream phenomena suggesting the movement of consciousness beyond the limitations of form and physicality, transcending the boundaries of space-time, into a field of pure awareness (Krippner, 1990; Krippner, Bogzaran, & de Carvalho, 2002).

## A Buddhist View of Dreams and the Space Beyond the Ego

The idea that dreams may open into a field of pure awareness is consistent with Buddhist doctrines. Tibetan Buddhism has long recognized dreamwork as a practice of spiritual yoga and unification. The Tibetan yogi Naropa taught that dreams undermine our belief in the exclusive reality of waking appearances, and reveal that waking reality is itself like a dream (Guenther, 1963, pp. 67–68). In Buddhist dream yoga, the practitioner learns to enter the dream state consciously through breath control, visualization, and "attending to the vibrations of the three mystic syllables (*om ah hum*)." A twelfth-century Tibetan text on the *Life and Teaching of Naropa*, stated:

> When a dream appears, his dream-life is particularly blissful and he ... transforms the unfolding into pure Buddha-realms and ... creates various enhancing situations. In some cases he will purify his former Karma, accumulated in the six forms of life; in others he will enter, stay in, and emerge from a great variety of meditative absorptions; or he will listen to the Dharma under the Buddhas of many and various realms. By practicing this dream state the bewilderment of holding as true what appears as an outer object in the waking life will be annihilated.
> (Guenther, 1963, pp. 68–69)

Working through the emotional, relational, and existential issues portrayed by dreams is a process of "purifying past karma" and creating various life-enhancing scenarios by amplifying dream symbols. We receive wisdom teachings from dream characters of many and various realms. And in some dreams we enter states of meditation, spontaneously glimpsing *dharmakaya*, the clear light of awareness—described as "a spread of light," "a soft glow," and "the primordial radiant light" (Guenther, 1963, p. 65). We saw this in the Dream of the Karate Chop and a Flash of Light, which may be viewed as a glimpse of spiritual realization. This was explained to me by Buddhist psychologist Rick Amaro:

> Your dream of nothingness portrays the emptiness and space of the *dharmakaya*. According to Longchenpa (2001), the ultimate authority within the Tibetan Nyingma lineage, dharmakaya represents the emptiness nature of awareness, which is vast as space. The phenomenal space around us is inseparable from awareness. "Nothingness" is eternal, timeless awareness, constantly emanating from out of itself the play of phenomena. In the dream, "everything dissolves into nothingness." This shows how all that arises in the realm of phenomenal appearances, including dreams, is encompassed by awareness—the formless clear light. Your dream depicts the process of relaxing into dharmakaya and merging with space, beyond duality. This is a nondual experience beyond what we typically call consciousness, which implies the presence of an object and a self. This dream shows that the true nature of awareness is egoless, inseparable from space. There's no self-reference, and no numinous deity that we characterize as "other." There's only self-aware space. (Rick Amaro, personal communication)

The karate chop symbolizes the principle of cutting through our individual story line, our personas and shadows, to reveal the self-luminous nature of awareness. The karate chop cuts through the dualistic mind and initiates me into non-egoic awareness. The dream reveals a perspective beyond self-reflectiveness and self-referentiality—a space antecedent to the ego. Spiritual dreams portray a viewpoint outside the ego complex altogether, beyond memory and imagination.

The bewilderment of waking life is annihilated in the dream where "everything dissolves." This is also a vision of impermanence, which is intrinsic in nature. The insubstantiality of phenomena, a basic tenet of Buddhism, is evident in the evanescent quality of dreams, which are delicate like a hummingbird's wing, shimmering with electric colour; the vision only lasts a fleeting moment. Dreams are maya, illusion, fantasy, mirage. They allow us to reach our hands through a veil beyond the visible world, like a curtain leading to the other side of reality. We saw an image of this in the Dream of the Lace Curtain (Chapter Eight). This is reminiscent of Naropa's teaching about recognizing the dreamlike quality of phenomena. Dreams show us the non-solidity of conditioned perceptions, the fluidity of complexes. We are changeable and mercurial, a moving center.

## The Dream of Two Snakes and a Flame

Helena, a divorced woman who had started dating again, had this dream:

> I felt a powerful current of male-female energy running inside my body in the form of two snakes that were matched but not fused. Suddenly, they joined together and ignited a flame inside me. I felt soft liquid fire spreading throughout my body.

"Liquid fire" aptly conveys the feeling and intensity of spirit noted by Corbett (1996). This is an exquisitely sensuous description of spirit. The imagery is consistent with yogic descriptions of *kundalini*, the serpent power; *tapas*, the inner heat of transformation; and *tummo*, the Tibetan term for mystic heat and the yoga of inner fire. All of these terms describe transformation of sexual energy. The two snakes form the *caduceus*, a living vortex of energy within our awakened body. It's significant how this soft liquid fire spreads throughout the body, the vessel. Spirit's movement within us needs to be lived through the body.

## Matter, Earth, Body, Gnosis, and the Alchemical Mercurius

Ann Ulanov noted:

> Spirit ... must inhabit a body to become real in time and space. Otherwise it just wafts upwards into ethereal realms, the stuff

of dreams or inflations, or superstitions. To be real, Spirit must step over into concrete reality, into time and space … . The body, whether it is our own or the body politic, … is the only way Spirit can be seen—in the flesh, in definite form and shape, limited but real. (Ulanov, 2004, p. 78)

Spirit forms a pair of opposites with the archetype of matter, or earth, which represents physicality, groundedness, incarnation, and embodied life. Earth is evident in the lush imagery of the Dream of the Rundown Shack and the Cosy Cottage (Chapter 9): "a roaring fire … a fresh pot of tea … a soft chair … an amazing garden with vegetables, fruit, vines. Everything is in full bloom." Earth dream imagery reminds us to enhance sensation and our full presence in nature and physical embodiment. A question I like to ask is, "How am I embodied in this dream?" Recall the image of a man's distended belly in the Dream of the Condoms (Chapter Three); the fearful, frozen body of the Dream of the Wall; and the resurgent instinctual body evident in the Dream of the Sleeping Wolf (both in Chapter Two). Also consider how the condition of the body is portrayed in the Dreams of the Pig; the Flightless Bird; the Shivering Child; the Pregnant Horse; the Kung Fu Fighter; the Walrus, and many others. These dreams are portrayals of what John Conger (1988) called *the body as shadow*—"the body as 'character,' the body as bound energy that is unrecognized and untapped, unacknowledged and unavailable" (p. 108). This is what Wilhelm Reich (1970) termed the "secondary layer" of biopsychic structure that needs to be liberated to access "the deep biologic core of one's selfhood" (p. xi).

> As reflected in the body, Reich saw the secondary layer as rigid, chronic contractions of muscle and tissue, a defensive armoring against assault from within and without, a way of shutting down so that the energy flow in the afflicted body was severely reduced. Reich worked directly on the armored layer in the body, in that way releasing the repressed material. The body as the shadow refers, then, to the armored aspect of the body … , expressive of what is repressed by the ego. (Conger, 1988, pp. 110–111)

Each of the dreams just noted can be viewed as attempts of the unconscious to release bound energies, to dissolve the armored layers of the body, to make accessible our untapped energy. Dreams portray the emotional assaults that have hardened into defences that perpetuate our affliction. Recall the Dream of Mother and the Grisly Murders (Chapter Two), and the Dream of the Bunker and the Psychotic Killer (Chapter Seven). Dreams also liberate repressed material that is held in the body. They are a flowing stream that revitalizes the body.

This was evident in the Dream of the Sleeping Wolf (Chapter Two), which helped an ex-priest resolve the Christian emphasis on denial of the flesh—a viewpoint rooted in ancient gnostic dualism. The relationship of spirit and matter was a central theme of gnostic myths, which described how sparks of light descend, assume material form, and long to be liberated from the body, through ascetic spirituality. Gnosticism expressed the alienation of embodied spirits and a longing for liberation from physicality. My own reading is that gnostic myth portrays embodiment as a necessary phase or condition of spirit's evolution. Spirit is eternally wedded to matter, earth, and body. Sparks of light need to be housed in a body, in a specific place and time; indeed, one can gradually form a body of light.

This is the perspective of alchemy, which uses the language of transforming matter and the body. Stephen Hoeller explained:

> Jung held that in human life we possess two sources of Gnosis, or salvific knowledge. One of them is *Lumen Dei*, the light proceeding from the unmanifest Godhead, the other is *Lumen Naturae*, the light hidden in matter and the forces of nature. While the Divine Light may be discerned and appreciated in revelation … , the Light of Nature needs to be released through alchemy before it can become fully operative. God redeems humanity, but nature needs to be redeemed by human alchemists, who are able to induce the process of transformation which alone is capable of liberating the light imprisoned in physical creation. (Hoeller, 1988, p. 37)

Dreamwork is a powerful technique for modern alchemists striving to extract gold from base metals, to liberate their total human potential. Dreams induce transformation of the embodied personality and can reveal the spiritual light concealed in the body and in nature itself. Aniella Jaffe wrote:

> Matter for the alchemists was a source of numinosity. They saw it as the vessel of a captive, divine spirit from which it had to be liberated ... . This spirit or divine presence in the mystery of matter was named Mercurius ... . In the alchemical opus it is not man who is in need of redemption but matter, or the Spirit, imprisoned in matter, in the darkness of physical nature. (Jaffe, 1984, pp. 59, 63–64)

The alchemical *Mercurius* is "the secret 'transforming substance'" (Jung, 1968 [1944], par. 30), the catalyst of alchemy, and represents the source of all opposites. According to Jaffe (1984), his polarity comprises masculine-feminine, good-evil, light-dark, conscious-unconscious, and the unity of matter and spirit. Mercurius is "a symbol of the unconscious itself ... [and] the opposites that are inherent in it ... . [H]e is both a material and a spiritual being" (p. 69). Mercurius appears in two forms, crude or ordinary quicksilver and the spirit Mercurius. "For the alchemists quicksilver meant the concrete, material manifestation of the spirit Mercurius" (Jung, 1969 [1950b], par. 5). Dreams are expressions of the psyche as Mercurius, liquid quicksilver, shape-shifting intelligence, agent of personal alchemy and unification. The Dream of Two Snakes and a Flame portrays this.

## The Dream of Radiance: A Vision of the Unus Mundus

I conclude this chapter with a dream that had the character of a synchronistic, visionary experience and revelation of spiritual mystery. It occurred one night in 2001 after I stayed up late studying a passage in a book by one of my teachers, the philosopher-sage Dane Rudhyar, who had died sixteen years earlier. The passage read:

> [T]he fundamental goal of evolution is the consummation of the "divine Marriage" of spirit and matter within a human being. In this union of opposites, the all-encompassing meaning of Wholeness is revealed in a moment of Illumination ... . The union must be contained within a form that can resist the

union's intense "heat" and not be shattered by it. This form
is the mind of wholeness— ... the mind illumined by spirit.
(Rudhyar, 1983, pp. 159–160)

That night I dreamed:

*I was visiting a house. Somebody informed me that Rudhyar had just
died, and asked, "Would you like to see the body?" I climbed a staircase
and entered a room. Rudhyar was lying on a couch on his right side,
with both arms reaching over his head. His eyes were wide open, gazing
into the radiant luminosity of the infinite. He was looking directly into
the Light. This image was incredibly vivid, and I was jolted awake by
that luminosity.*

The dream depicts an ascension to the upper floor of a house, where
radiance breaks through from the unconscious into conscious awareness. It depicts death and rebirth, the body and the luminosity of
spirit; and the presence of the teacher, spiritual guide, the wise old
man serving as the vehicle of initiation. The dream juxtaposed death
of the body and rebirth in the spirit. Rudhyar was dead, but he was
also *alive*. His eyes were gazing into the Light, and also revealed
it. The dream had the quality of a *hierophany*, an appearance of the
*numinosum*.

This dream has several parallels to a hermetic text described by
Mahe (1998). In the "Discourse on the Ogdoad and the Ennead,"
Hermes Trismegistus led his student through

an initiation into the divine mysteries of the Ogdoad and
the Ennead, so that he may be born again and become a new
man, being directly inspired by God's intellect ... . The [text]
begins with a prayer by Hermes and his disciple to the Invisible God, who is one and threefold at once, i.e., Unbegotten,
Self-Begotten, and Begotten. Then the two partners, drawing
attention to their spiritual nature, ask for the favor of contemplating the Ogdoad and the Ennead. Once they have said this
prayer, they kiss each other. At that very moment, the Power
that is light comes down to them. Both of them are lifted up in
ecstasy. The teacher explains to the disciple that they have just
seen the Ogdoad with the souls that are in it ... . In the second
century A.D., when our text was written, the words Ogdoad

and Ennead would have evoked astrological ideas, namely the
eighth and ninth heavenly spheres .... Soaring up to the Ogdoad
means first of all getting rid of the influence of the seven planets
and having access to the superior world, the abode of Divinity.
(Mahe, 1998, pp. 79–81)

Just as the prayer of Hermes and his disciple was answered by their
joint vision, my dream revealed the meaning of the passage I was
contemplating. In the dream, I proceed up the stairs, which is like
ascending the lower spheres of planetary influence to gain access to
the abode of divinity, the Ogdoad. In the Discourse, Hermes and the
disciple perceive the Unbegotten One beyond the planetary spheres.
Here, Rudhyar is "gazing into the radiant luminosity of the infinite."
He has reached a higher level of consciousness, the Ennead, and is
perceiving the One beyond. It should be noted that Rudhyar was the
originator of humanistic astrology, which gives additional meaning
to this vision of the realm beyond the planets. In the dream, Rudhyar has become the mind of wholeness, "the mind illumined by
spirit." He's like the man who stepped out of Plato's cave, emerging
out of the shadows into the light of the Real. This image made a lasting impact. I can still see, and feel, that luminosity.

   The imagery of this dream reminds me of gnostic texts describing visions of the *pleroma*, the mystic's journeys into formative,
angelic, spiritual realms—the realms of splendor and radiance. This
was described by Jung in his own gnostic visionary text, *The Seven
Sermons to the Dead*:

> Nothingness is both empty and full ... . This nothingness or full-
> ness we name the PLEROMA ... . The pleroma is both beginning
> and end of created beings. It pervadeth them, as the light of the sun
> everywhere pervadeth the air ... . We are, however, the pleroma
> itself, for we are a part of the eternal and infinite. But we have
> no share thereof, as we are from the pleroma infinitely removed;
> not spiritually or temporally, but essentially, since we are distin-
> guished from the pleroma in our essence as creatura, which is
> confined within time and space. Yet because we are parts of the
> pleroma, the pleroma is also in us. Even in the smallest point is
> the pleroma endless, eternal, and entire ... . It is that nothingness
> which is everywhere whole and continuous. (Jung, 1961, p. 379)

Dreams reflect our existence as *creatura*, helping us evolve as individuals. Dreams also restore our connection to our spiritual ground of being, the eternal and infinite that pervades our existence. Dreams are thus emotionally, spiritually, and somatically unifying. The Dream of Radiance was an experience of mystical union, a vision of what Jung referred to as the *unus mundus*, "the original non-differentiated unity of the world or of Being."

> [T]he idea of the *unus mundus* is founded on the assumption that the multiplicity of the empirical world rests on an underlying unity … . But this much we do know beyond all doubt, that empirical reality has a transcendental background. (Jung, 1963 [1955–1956], par. 660)

Stephen Hoeller observed:

> Jung envisions a great psycho-physical mystery to which the alchemists of old gave the name of *unus mundus* (one world). At the root of all being, so he intimates, there is a state wherein physicality and spirituality meet in a transgressive union. Synchronistic phenomena … appear to proceed from this unitive condition. (Hoeller, 1988, p. 38)

The Dream of Radiance reveals a glimpse of the transcendental background of reality, the undivided, unitary field beyond duality. In the dream, the body is the container of the unified reality; it's the orb of infinity. It's the chalice, cauldron, and crucible. The dream invites me to *see the body* and the light pouring through it. The body transforms into the diamond, the *lapis*, the reflective gem of consciousness extending its pervasive ray.

There are several synchronistic features of this dream. The inner event of my dream closely paralleled the outer event of reading Rudhyar's words about a moment of illumination. The relationship between these events was not necessarily acausal; I believe the dream was clearly shaped by the passage I read about the mystic marriage. But the two events were connected by their unified meaning. The psyche was telling me, "These ideas you read were not just words but a living bread for the soul." What also makes this dream synchronistic is its unveiling of a timeless archetype—the *coniunctio*, the divine marriage. In another sense, the dream is a symbol of synchronicity itself—a realization of the unity of spirit and the body. von Franz explained:

> The most essential and certainly the most impressive thing about synchronistic occurrences, the thing which really constitutes their numinosity, is the fact that in them the duality of soul and matter seems to be eliminated. They are therefore an *empirical* indication of an ultimate unity of all existence, which Jung, using the terminology of medieval natural philosophy, called the *unus mundus* ... . [T]his concept designates *the potential preexistent model of creation in the mind of God*, in accordance with which God later produced the creation ... . [The *unus mundus*] proliferates into a multitude of forms, but nevertheless remains always one ... . Gerhard Dorn, a pupil of Paracelsus, saw the completion of the alchemical work in a union of the individual with this *unus mundus* in the mind of God ... . Dorn describes the experience ... as the opening of a "window on eternity" or of an "air-hole" in the eternal world. (von Franz, 1975, pp. 247–248)

The Dream of Radiance is a window into the eternal world—an image of this original template of reality in which body and spirit fuse into luminous life, mystery everlasting. In another sense, the Dream of Radiance is a vision of death, showing that death can be radiant. The dream's message is to accept death, and to see beyond death. This prefigured my experience, several years later, as I sat with my father during his last weeks of life. He went in and out of consciousness, spending long periods when he was apparently sleeping, but with his eyes wide open, gazing upward into the top of his forehead. His eyes looked like bright suns, and he seemed to be reaching out into some realm beyond his physicality. The sun king and sun queen must one day die, yielding to that encompassing intelligence and love, that unnameable order of being that is seeking to enfold us within itself.

Throughout this book, we've seen that dreamwork is a basis for emotional process work and gradual self-unification. Dreamwork is also a spiritual practice, a form of prayer, a mode of spiritual seeing. Dreamwork strengthens the ego, supporting our social adaptation. It validates the contradictions of each individual, urging us from within to live our unique polarities. It also connects us to the spiritual realms beyond ego. Dreams show us visions of our wholeness and possibilities, guiding us through a multitude of regenerative passages.

Through the wisdom of dreams, an inevitable *enantiodromia* leads us from spirit back to the body and the realm of sexuality. Commenting on the fifth of Jung's *Seven Sermons to the Dead*—a text written in the voice of the gnostic sage Basilides—Stephen Hoeller wrote:

> Basilides begins his discourse by saying: "The world of the gods appears in spirituality and sexuality. The heavenly gods appear in spirituality, the earth gods appear in sexuality." Thus we have represented a great duality which is at once cosmic and personal, divine and human. Matter or body ... is represented by sexuality, while spirit ... is represented by the quality derived from spirit, namely spirituality. (Hoeller, 1982, pp. 133–134)

Having taken a brief journey into the upper spiritual spheres, it's only natural that we now return to earth and come full circle, back to the topic of dreamwork as a means to enhance our human relationships. Let's turn to a final example of the kind of therapeutic dreamwork with which this book began. I hope that reading these stories of transformation strengthens each reader's connection to the deep center from which the healing images of dreams emerge.

# PART III

## CASE STUDY

## CHAPTER THIRTEEN

# Taming Wild Horses: A Study of Animal Symbolism and Male Sexuality

To conclude this volume I've selected a final example that illustrates the principles of therapeutic dreamwork and self-healing. In this chapter I explore relationship themes that emerged in my dreamwork with David, a gay man in his late forties. David was in a long-term, long-distance relationship with a man named George, and he was grappling with a recurring pattern of having affairs during periods when he and George were separated. He had a series of dreams that were catalysts for therapy exploring his fear of commitment, a conflicted relationship with his father, and his tendency to engage in sexually compulsive behaviour. David encountered five animal dream symbols—horse, camel, snake, alligator, and buffalo—representing different facets of his sexuality. These dreams had a profoundly healing effect and became an active guiding factor. We'll note how an animal dream image—in this case, a horse—can evolve and transform over a series of dreams, reflecting the individual's growth in consciousness. This is a story of a person who developed more emotional maturity in the course of working with his dreams. One dream depicted a man wrestling with an enormous snake, an image depicting the eternal hero myth, heralding a process of transformation and emotional rebirth. David's story illustrates the clinical usefulness of working with dreams and archetypal symbolism—in this case aiding the resolution of Oedipal conflict, which had previously inhibited satisfaction of central life aims. This study contributes to our understanding of human sexuality from the perspective of Jungian depth psychology.

## The Dream of the Wild Horses

My new client David wasted no time in telling me about a central concern. During an early therapy session he told me, "Recently I had unsafe sex during an anonymous encounter at a bathhouse. It was foolish and a lapse of judgment, and I feel a lot of guilt." David then reported this dream:

> I was with friends (all men) in the country. Wild horses saw us and ran toward us. My friends stood aside but I ran to hide inside a truck. The horses ran over to me and reared up on their hind legs. They seemed agitated; smoke was coming out of their nostrils. They reared up, and their hooves came down and dented the hood of the truck and cracked the windshield. The owner of the horses, an older man, came outside and was angry, saying we had caused the horses to run wild.

David's associations to the horses were that they represented freedom, galloping, instinct, being on a rampage, stampeding. I explained to David that when some figure in a dream is pursuing us, chasing us, or confronting us, it may indicate the emergence of shadow material. Something excluded from our conscious viewpoint is trying to come into consciousness. I suggested that David ask the horses, "Who are you? Why are you in my dream? What part of me do you represent?"

David's horses replied, "We represent strength, energy, and power—uncensored, unbridled. Our message to you is be yourself. Follow your instinct. Don't be afraid."

I asked David to imagine standing inside the body of the horses. "What does that feel like?"

"They are large, strong and proud. I've let other people's view of me diminish my pride in myself. My father was ashamed of me for being a sissy and unathletic, for being more interested in playing with dolls than in sports. My father lost interest in me, and he was never proud of me. I'd like to have more pride in myself."

I said, "I think the horses also represent your issues about having anonymous sex. Horses remind me of 'feeling your oats.' I think the dream is asking you, 'Does this wild part of myself feel corralled, or does it need to be corralled?' Wild horses remind me of unbridled sex, passion, abandon, galloping, feelings of sexual vigour, strength, and excitement. In the dream there's a sense of freedom but also of danger. The question is, 'Is this energy destructive?' And what does it mean that the owner of the horses is angry with you? He seems like a symbol of the superego, the judge, the inner principle of constraint. He doesn't want the horses to run wild. The owner held you in contempt, expressing disapproval, just like your father did. Unfortunately, in our society gay people sometimes do face contempt from others. It's something you've dealt with all your life. It also becomes something internalized that you feel toward yourself."

David replied, "When you described being treated with contempt, it sent shivers through me. That is exactly how it felt. And just like in the dream, I was blamed for something that wasn't my fault. Being gay isn't my fault. It's just the way I am. I'm realizing through our work here how important my dad's lack of involvement with me really was. His lack of approval caused me to feel flawed. And my sexuality is tied up with this sense of deficiency."

## The Dream of the Low-Flying Bomber

At his next session David reported that the night after our last session he had an intense dream:

> I was at George's Ranch. Some kind of war was being fought. Small planes flew overhead but high enough so I thought we were safe, but still I felt threatened. Doors and windows were wide open. A plane flew overhead very low. This time I was worried that the house was visible from that low elevation. Was it safer to be in the house hidden, or out in the open? The plane dropped a bomb as well as firing bullets. The house reverberated strongly. I woke up feeling vulnerable and worried, like something bad was going to happen.

David said, "George's ranch reminds me of George's family. A war being fought reminds me of George's struggles with his dad, who's an alcoholic and a sex addict." David and I noted the relevance of this detail about sex addiction, given his own presenting issue.

Then I asked David, "How are you at war in your life?"

"There's a war inside me trying to reconcile or come to grips with my dad. It's a war about my sexuality, and feeling I have to overachieve to compensate for some fundamental flaw."

"So the war reminds you of not being accepted for who you are."

"The dream also reminds me of how I'm scared of how at work I feel unwanted by some people in the company because of my sexual orientation. The planes dropping bombs remind me of violence, coming under attack, my fear of gay bashing. I remember being a kid and feeling that I didn't know how to defend myself. The bombs remind me of feelings of urgent fear and threat, and the fact that recently I had unsafe sex, and my fear of AIDS infection."

Later, David said, "Your question about what wars are going on inside me reminds me of my desires to have sex outside of my relationship. I feel torn. I get attracted to other men. Being with George makes me restrain myself most of the time, and I fear damaging that relationship. Yet I have a strong desire to act on those impulses."

"We're still dealing with your dilemma about taming wild horses."

"I'm scared."

"You're torn between your sense of honour and obligation to George, and your feelings of desirousness—the part of you that feels driven by compulsions, wild horses. Jung said when we are torn between a pair of opposites, we have to bear the tension and wait until a third factor emerges that resolves the conflict. So we'll have to wait and see what emerges." We would not have to wait long for an integrative symbol to emerge from the unconscious, through a dream that conveyed an image of wholeness.

### The Dream of the Horse, the Judge, and the Camel

As our session continued, I told David, "The earlier dream image where the horses are agitated suggested the presence of inner conflict; there was fire in their eyes."

"Yes, smoke was coming out of their nostrils."

"How are you agitated?"

"Because I feel desire, and I don't know what to do with it. I want to act on it, and I'm fearful of acting on it. And it's hard keeping it hidden."

"In that dream you couldn't hide from the horses."

"Yes, they ran after me."

"Perhaps the dream is asking you, 'How much can this energy be let loose and out in the open?'"

At that moment, David spontaneously recalled that two months earlier he had another horse dream ("the day after the *previous* time I had unsafe sex"):

> *At an arena I saw a horse and a woman who appeared to be a judge of a horse show. The horse looked like she was going to do harm to the judge. She leaped forward, kicking her leg, and knocked the judge down. She pawed at her a few times. Some people shooed the horse away. The horse went to the other side of the arena, near where I was. She broke through the fence, ran away from the arena. I saw the horse's profile. Her body was extra long, and she had two humps in her back like a camel.*

The arena suggested containment, a defined space. The horse breaks out of containment. The fact that the judge was a woman and the horse was also female suggests that the dream was addressing a problem or issue of the feminine. David said, "The judge reminds me of the judge in me, the judge of my own behaviour. My mom was always the moral authority figure in our family. I never had a sense of my mother as sexual. She made derogatory remarks about people who were sexy or who dressed suggestively. She was very prudish."

"Maybe there's a prudish judge in you that internalized some of her attitudes."

"Yeah, in her eyes, being sexual is not good."

I said, "In the dream the horse harms the judge, kicks her, and paws at her. That reminds me of how sometimes your sexuality can overpower reason—your restraining judgment. But what do the humps and the camel remind you of?"

"A camel reminds me of quiet strength, quiet endurance, fortitude. A camel has persistence, can endure long periods without water and food."

"Like the desert of enduring periods without sex."

David said, "Yes. A camel can endure."

"It's significant that in the dream the horse turns into a camel. Perhaps you are both the horse *and* the camel. You've shown that you can break out of the pen like the wild horses. But a camel accepts being tethered, tamed, kept on a leash. You don't think of stampeding camels! The camel represents a more austere attitude, the ability to contain or channel your desires."

The shift from wild horses to a camel reflected a significant internal shift for David. A reorganization and transformation of energy was under way within the unconscious. The union of the horse and the camel is an example of *coniunctio,* which Edinger (1994a) described as the creation of consciousness through the union of opposites (p. 18).

## The Dream of the Circuit Breaker and the Manufacturer's Representative

David's next dream occurred several months later, right after a session when he had discussed thoughts of ending therapy. This dream had the effect of considerably deepening the therapy.

> *I'm in an open, rural space. There's a problem with a circuit breaker on a thing tripping too readily. The manufacturer's representative for the circuit breaker arrived in a late 1960s or early 1970s mint condition car. I was surprised that the manufacturer's rep showed up for such a small problem. I compliment him on the car's condition and guessed the date and year. He was impressed with my knowledge of cars. I got in and we drove somewhere. We stopped. There was no top on the car. Was it a convertible or was the top missing?*

The 1960s/1970s car reminded Dave of his adolescence, and his denial and repression of sexuality during his adolescence in the 1960s. "At age fifteen and sixteen I was attracted to other boys but was too uncomfortable to act on it." The car in the dream evoked David's memory of how his budding sexuality got put on hold. The 1960s–1970s reminded him of an era of sexual liberation, gay pride, and sexual freedom. But perhaps the dream was also saying something about the limits of sexual freedom.

In the dream a circuit breaker trips too readily. A circuit breaker stops something from going wrong. It provides protection; it's a "prophylactic measure." It suggests being overly cautious; here it is triggered too soon. "Mostly my sexuality has been on the cautious side rather than the dangerous, unsafe side. I've engaged in a lot less promiscuity than some other people. I could have had a lot more sex than I did. Often I put the brakes on, exercising caution. I'm glad there was a circuit breaker. Otherwise I'd be dead now."

The "mint condition" car suggested innocence, being virginal. David said, "It reminds me of my preadolescent sexuality." The convertible car reminded David of having fun, being sporty or adventurous, taking an "outing," coming out, "being out in the open about who I am." It was a symbol of freedom, mobility, independence.

I said, "The innate Self, the essence of who you are, is unfolding its integrity from the beginning, like the acorn becoming a tree, realizing its potential. You are unfolding perfectly, exactly as you were made, in mint condition, exactly the way you came off the manufacturing line, just as the Creator made you." David thanked me for this comment.

The open-top car implied being exposed, revealed, not hiding things. This dream afforded us the opportunity to discuss David's feelings about therapy, and whether he felt he could be completely open with me. We discussed his feelings about whether he would be more comfortable working with a gay-identified therapist. He was aware that there were things he was hiding, not talking about. He felt embarrassed talking about intimate sexual details with me. I said it was important for him to be able to talk openly with me about sex. The open-top car allowed us to have this conversation, and David said he felt he could be more open with me. Indeed, he felt maybe it could be deeply healing for him to have a therapeutic relationship with a straight man who accepted and affirmed him.

The manufacturer's representative was a specialist sent to help solve, troubleshoot, or diagnose a problem. David said, "I think maybe it's you, Greg, helping me explore my sexuality." In the dream, the manufacturer's representative provided conscientious service. David commented on how attentive I was to his feelings. The manufacturer's representative symbolized an attentive, nurturing male, a positive father figure. Working with this dream revealed that Dave was forming a positive transference and had favourable feelings about therapy. He felt renewed commitment to his inner work.

## The Dream of the Swamp and the Snakes

David's next dream contained powerful animal symbolism:

> *I'm in a lowland area, a swamp, but the water was not murky. I was on firm land next to a tree at water's edge. It occurred to me that alligators might be present so I climbed up a few feet on the tree trunk to be out of harm's way. A man was in the water, up to his knees. Snakes of all sizes were swimming around and he wanted to catch a large one. A ten-inch-wide, eight-foot-long snake was circling around his legs. It raised its head. The man grabbed its mouth and held it open, one hand on each jaw, so it couldn't bite him. He tried to disable the snake by tearing its mouth open.*

A swamp is a transitional place between water and land, between two states of being. It is a place of life, but also of rot, decay, decomposition. The watery swamp suggested activation of the unconscious and the feeling function. I viewed the alligators as an image of reptilian drives and instincts.

David's associations were that alligators are dangerous, stealthy; they creep up on their victims. Stealth reminded David of "how I'm dealing with having sex outside of my relationship."

I said, "I wonder if the dream is implying that there's a connection between stealthy sexual encounters and something that could bite you or injure you. The alligators suggest strong sexual drives that you want to act on. Could that be dangerous?"

"I could contract AIDS or other diseases. Or I could meet someone at the bathhouse who knows me and George; that could definitely be a danger."

The tree at the water's edge suggested safety, refuge. The tree implied life, growth, individuation. Climbing the tree implied ascending, finding an elevated vantage point. "That's why I'm coming here for therapy," David said. "I think the man in the water is me." The dream vividly portrayed David's encounter with the instinctual forces of the unconscious.

In the dream, snakes of all sizes are present, which reminded Dave of "immersing myself in sexual possibilities. I've been checking out lots of guys recently." The image of the man with the snake wrapped around him reminded Dave of "my desire for a sexual encounter."

In the dream, disarming the snake was connected to doing something for other people's entertainment and holding it up like a prize or a trophy. "In my twenties and thirties I was wrapped up in whether whomever I was going home with was a prize or conquest. People would be impressed by what a great-looking guy I was going home with."

"You sought to affirm your self-worth by taking home a trophy guy."

Disarming the snake was a striking image. Tearing open the snake's mouth suggested ferocious oral craving. In a deeper sense, the dream represented the archetype of the hero grappling with the sea monster, symbol of the great mother, from whom the archetypal male hero must extricate himself. This was the central mythic theme that fascinated Jung in *Symbols of Transformation* (Jung, 1956 [1911–1912]). In the eternal myth of the hero, the hero slays the dragon, monster, gorgon, or serpent through a primordial act of self-assertion. Marduk slays the dragon Tiamat. Zeus slays the serpent Typhon. The hero must engage with the monster, fully encountering its power, without being engulfed, consumed, or devoured by the monster. The heroic masculine principle is triumphant over the primal, primitive energy of the Serpent. David had been enveloped in a regressive union with the energies of the unconscious. His dream portrayed the heroic masculine principle of consciousness grappling with the instinctual "reptilian psyche" (Edinger, 1994a, p. 96). It's important to be able to experience our instinctual life force, without being consumed or overwhelmed by it. Jung wrote:

> [The God] appears at first in hostile form as an assailant with whom the hero has to wrestle. This is in keeping with the violence of all unconscious dynamism. In this manner the god manifests himself and in this form he must be overcome. The struggle has its parallel in Jacob's wrestling with the angel at the ford Jabbok. The onslaught of instinct then becomes an experience of divinity, provided that man does not succumb to it and follow it blindly, but defends his humanity against the animal nature of the divine power. (Jung, 1956 [1911–1912], par. 524)

I told David, "The dream suggests that you're wrestling with an immense titanic power. The man in the dream is merging with this

*Figure 8.    The hero and the serpent, illustration from Maier (1618).*

power, grappling with the great serpent deity, like the timeless myth of the hero wrestling with a dragon or monster. The dream reflects the way you're grappling with the urgency of your sexual energy, as well as portraying its intensity and its numinosity. The image of the snake circling the man's body also reminds me of the *ouroboros*, a symbol of the regenerative power of the life force."

As I noted in Chapter Nine, the dragon eating its own tail signifies unifying mind and body, intellect and instinct, and all the pairs of opposites. The ouroboros represents joining the poles of the psyche—conscious and unconscious, male and female, king and dragon, father and son. Earlier, I also noted how the transformation of the king into an ouroboros suggests that the perspective of the king or father is transcended and transformed. For David, this implied that a dominant attitude of ego consciousness was being challenged and deposed (Edinger, 1985, p. 148). Sometimes this involves humbling of the ego through defeats, or revisiting our primal woundedness. The ouroboros is portrayed as a dragon with wings, suggesting a capacity for visionary flight or transcendence through acts of the imagination—as in this highly evocative dreamwork. The coiled energy of the ouroboros represents the intensification of inner life through encountering the unconscious itself (see epilogue to this chapter). David's snake dream called forth this archetypal pattern of regeneration and emotional rebirth. In another sense, the snake was a symbol of his own libido struggling to liberate itself from the prohibitions of the father, an issue pointedly raised by the unconscious through David's next immense and potent dream.

## The Dream of the Blind Date and the Shy Weightlifter

David's next dream seemed quite important to me, but it took much effort to understand its meaning. Discussing this dream occupied us for three full therapy sessions.

*I'm rollerblading by myself down a sidewalk. I come to a playground area covered with pine needles, leaves, and debris. I think, "I should bring a brush to sweep it off." I continue, and come to a covered pavilion where kids are playing. I go in and perform a few tricks on my blades and go out. I was to meet someone on a blind date. The date was set up by my mother and this young guy who wanted his older brother to meet me. An old Cadillac, a limo or hearse, drove down the street and I realized it was carrying my date. The young guy, his brother, and my mother were in the car. Then all of us were in my house. The young man's brother was shy and socially uncomfortable. Finally, my date comes over to engage me in conversation. He asks how close is my house to the water. I bring him to the kitchen window and say water is just behind the rocks outside my yard. At that moment a large wave crashes on the rocks and onto my house. Another wave crashes into the house. Then my father is there. I feel like I have to justify living in a house so close to the water where this would happen, like I didn't do my research enough so the house wasn't a good purchase. My date and I sit in the living room. His shirt is off, and I notice how nicely built he is. He's a weightlifter, shy, and doesn't know how to engage in conversation.*

Rollerblading reminded David of "fun, gliding graceful, movement, being by myself, being content in myself." Kids playing reminded David of having friends, people to play with; this evoked his sense of loneliness. Indeed, David said, loneliness was one of the feelings that often compelled him to seek sexual encounters during periods of separation from George. The playground brought up childhood memories of feeling ostracized and not fitting in with his peers. He said, "This was potentially a great place for rollerblading if it was swept up."

I asked, "What needs to be swept away and cleaned up?"

David replied, "My hidden feelings about George's drinking." David was troubled by his perception that George often drank too much and sometimes embarrassed David in public. This bothered David immensely, but he had kept quiet about it because he didn't want to upset George and was afraid George would leave him. David said, "It's in my court to do something to clean this place up."

"Performing a few tricks" suggested a desire to be seen or noticed; it reminded me of the natural exhibitionistic strivings of children—the way a child says, "Mommy, Daddy, look at me!" It suggested a need for mirroring and affirmation of the emergent self, which David didn't receive from his father. Performing tricks also implied his sexual escapades, as in "turning tricks."

Being set up on a date reminded David of anxiety, uncertainty, and a sense of obligation. That reminded Dave of "feeling obligated to remain silent about George's drinking, out of fear of losing his love."

The old limo-hearse reminded David of something eccentric, "retro," a person trying to be cool by being bizarre. "That's how I acted in my late teens and twenties. I adopted a cool persona." A hearse also reminded David of death. He said, "The paint on the car had faded. That reminds me of the feeling that the shine and newness of our relationship is gone; it isn't so glossy and shiny anymore. It also reminds me of the end of youth, and growing older."

Waves hitting the house implied that the tide of the unconscious was rising, bringing waves of emotions. The house was a symbol of David's personality. Water outside the house symbolized close access to the unconscious. Father's presence in the dream reminded David of having to justify his identity, his choices, and his life to his father. Now David was able to state some core themes of his father complex: "I felt judged and criticized by my father. I was always second-guessed about my decisions and my sexual orientation, like I was on trial." It was striking to me that purchasing a house too close to the ocean reminded David of his father berating him. Something about his closeness to the ocean of his feelings, to his feminine nature, to the unconscious itself, drew his father's inner criticism.

I asked David about having a date with the weightlifter, which implied a need to integrate whatever this figure represented. David said, "People who are way into weightlifting I view as shallow. It's like they are trying to cover up their flaws by having the perfect body. That's an ideal I can't attain." The man's shyness reminded David of his own social awkwardness, and feelings of unworthiness and inadequacy. The man's shyness suggested a deflated, collapsed position. But the fact that he was a weightlifter suggested having an inflated sense of male beauty and potency, a grandiose, idealized male persona.

The weightlifter who enhances his physique reminded me of a godlike hero image, like Hercules, the archetype of male strength. To David it suggested "self-development, meeting challenges, becoming strong." This figure has a slightly grandiose quality, as if such a man is trying to be like a superhero, like Superman. My own association to the weightlifter was that he reminded me of someone vain and self-involved who wants attention. It reminded David of how he compared himself to other men. The dream image suggested that David had a tendency toward idealization, and perhaps exhibited what Heinz Kohut called a *merger-hungry self* (Kohut & Wolf, 1978). In such a personality, there's a longing for merger with an idealized person who will enhance the sense of self-worth. The weightlifter was an image of a good-enough, potent, beautiful self, in contrast to the diminished, inadequate sense of self David felt in relation to his critical, rejecting father.

The weightlifter suggested to me idealization and admiration of the perfected male form. When I asked David if that reminded him of anything, he replied, "I used to try to be very masculine so I wouldn't be seen as gay. I tried to be a mainstream male. I didn't want my masculinity called into question. I became a carpenter and drove a truck so my sexuality wouldn't be dismissed."

I said, "I think the dream is about your life path, your personal truth. It contains an image of an inner marriage; and your partner in the divine marriage is a man like you. It suggests that you're seeking self-love, through loving someone who matches your masculine ideal. Here your image of the beloved is a strong but sensitive man, the shy weightlifter. Your date with a man who is shy like yourself implies the need to develop self-love, the self-love you couldn't learn from your father because he couldn't validate you."

The theme of seeking union with someone like himself reminded me of the theme of the *union of similars*, which was sometimes mentioned in alchemy. As Howard Teich (1983) put it, "Jungian perspectives on men's relationships usually revolve around Jung's contrasexual archetype of the feminine, or anima. But the male-male union emerges as a critical step in all men's individuation process— and as the final step for some" (p. 137).

It occurred to me that David's dream, with his mother and father both present, presented an image of his oedipal situation. In the dream, mother orchestrates the date, which suggested an unconscious merger or identification with his mother. When I asked David what came to mind about mother orchestrating the date, he said, "I was her favourite. I felt I had to take care of her. One day when I was five years old I found her very sad. She was singing, 'You are my sunshine, my only sunshine.' I realized she had a lot of sorrow, and I felt I truly was her only sunshine."

"You felt you had to take care of her and make her happy. How did you do that?"

"By being cheerful, good, and polite. By not causing problems and being a good boy." I pointed out that this was exactly how David was acting now, regarding George's drinking; he was remaining silent, trying to be a good, compliant partner.

I said, "In the dream, your mother is able to affirm who you are. In a sense, mother is 'giving away the bride.' Perhaps this represents her acceptance of you." The dream seemed to affirm a positive inner connection with the mother.

I sought consultation on this dream from Robert Hopcke (1989), author of *Jung, Jungians, and Homosexuality*, who analyzed this as follows:

Because gay men are attracted to men, a characteristic they share with heterosexual women like their own mothers, many gay men feel close to the archetypal feminine aspects of their own experience. Here the mother is ushering David into the realm of intimacy. It is as if, in the dream, the mother is bringing him into relationship with the father. David had a bad experience with his father and became wary of intimacy with him. The weightlifter symbolizes the narcissistic masculine ideal that he seeks. He sees himself as inadequate, while the weightlifter is the good-enough, beautiful, empowered male self he seeks. The weightlifter's shyness, and David's own shyness, reflects the fact that he hasn't been affirmed by the father, so that he feels his masculinity is wounded. As a result, he holds men at a distance. Instead of moving in with George, David has maintained a long-distance relationship, expressing an underlying ambivalence around intimacy. Avoiding true intimacy with his lover and continuing to have compulsive, anonymous sex has been a way of continuing to project the ideal outward. David has been identified with the inadequate self and projecting the idealized, good-enough self onto beautiful strangers (Robert Hopcke, personal communication).

## The Dream of the Domesticated Horse

Exploring these dreams brought forth a prodigious amount of material to be explored in therapy. Months of sessions passed. David and George went to couple's therapy where David confronted George about his drinking, saying this was one reason he'd been ambivalent about living together. They made progress in communicating about a number of other important issues and eventually made plans to live together. The week that George moved in, David had this dream:

> I'm with a horse. I lead him down a corridor near stalls and onto a long, open path. His lead rope wasn't attached to the halter, so he wasn't completely under my control. Later, another horse with rider came up the path.

David's association to the dream was that this was a domesticated, tame horse, and that he, too, was becoming domesticated. This was a familiar horse, a friend, not a wild horse. It represented his becoming more open, honest, and intimate with George. I said, "The horse isn't running wild anymore. You and George are domestic partners now."

David said, "In the dream, I'm riding on a long path. Maybe the relationship is the long path. It has been a longer road together than I expected." The fact that the horse in the dream wasn't completely under his control reminded David of fear of losing his freedom now that he was making a commitment to George. Yet he seemed to be in harmony with the horse, which wasn't totally out of control, as in earlier dreams. He realized that the horse might cooperate of its own accord, without coercion. This insight provided the basis for further conversations about monogamy and fidelity.

Several more months passed and David again assessed what was happening as a result of ongoing therapy. He said, "I think I've accomplished a tremendous amount here, especially identifying the wounding with my father and realizing that there's nothing fundamentally wrong with me. I don't feel so lonely anymore. My relationship with George is in a renewed place. I'm speaking the truth authentically. I feel more like a man now. I used to feel like a child in a man's body. I feel like I've grown into myself, and filled out my body. I belong to myself."

### The Dream of the Buffalo Hide

David persisted with therapy, and several months later he reported this dream:

> I picked up an animal hide that I put on as a jacket. It was fresh and there was blood on the hide. Then I saw a buffalo on a range. It was a large animal with a huge back and shoulders.

A buffalo reminded David of independence, freedom, strength and self-sufficiency, being part of a herd, having a sense of community. "This raises the question of where in my life can I feel this connection, where I'm part of something."

"That would be an antidote to the loneliness you often feel."

"Buffaloes flock together. But they also tend to stand by themselves. They remind me of solitude in togetherness, and how I live my life, in a herd but separate." He noted that buffaloes are migratory creatures; they roam the plains. Roaming reminded David of "migration, seasonal movement, finding nourishment and satisfaction of needs."

"Your basic needs are being satisfied—in your work and career, and in your relationship with George."

The buffalo's huge back and shoulders reminded David of "power and strength, where I am now. I have power and strength and community."

"In many cultures, slaying an animal is a symbolic mark of manhood and coming of age. Wearing an animal's hide suggests male initiation, conquest, bravery, mastery. It's a mark of initiation, manhood, and passing through ordeals."

David said, "This morning when I got up I said to myself, 'Today I feel like I know what it feels like to be a man.' At age forty-nine, I'm in solid middle age. I feel like I have gone through an initiation."

"You've faced down your father and gotten full-on married to George. That's the initiation. You've claimed your life and chosen your partner. You've gone through a rite of passage into manhood."

"I feel integrated and whole."

"The buffalo is a symbol of your power, claiming the relationship you want without shame or fear of disappointing your parents."

Then I revealed to David a significant fact—that several months earlier I myself had a dream that I was wearing an animal skin. I had recently explored this symbolism and discovered that the Greek god Dionysus was said to appear wearing an animal skin. I said, "Dionysus represents freedom, being uninhibited, liberating our ecstatic life energy. Dionysus is the god of libido, not the god of silent reflection (Apollo). He's the god of ecstasy, drunken inebriation, overcoming inhibition and embarrassment, joining in the feast and dance of life."

David said, "That's so funny. This weekend was Halloween. We went out to a party and wore costumes and I was incredibly uninhibited and dancing. Everyone said we were the life of the party. Someone said, 'Who let David out of his cage?!?'"

The fresh blood on the hide suggested the alchemical stage known as *rubedo*, the reddening, a stage in which we're enlivened by desire, through free movement of our libido, feeling a sense of unimpeded vitality. Red denotes passion, lust for life. In animistic religions, blood was sacred, numinous, full of *mana*. This dream evoked the experience and symbolism of initiation rites. In tribal cultures a youth proves his manhood through killing an animal and donning its hide, becoming one with the animal and assuming its power.

"The dream is telling you that you are involved in a process of coming of age. You've received the mantle of power. You're in the state of a warrior. You've arrived. Wearing this animal hide is a mark of maturity. You possess its *mana* (its life energy), and its power."

David said, "This is the nature of my beast."

David's inner work continued. Exploring the animal intelligence of his dreams helped David access charged feelings and memories, deepened our therapeutic alliance, and allowed him to fully embrace a nurturing relationship with George. The wisdom of the wild and domesticated horses, the austere camel, man and snake locked in their eternal embrace, the stealthy alligator, and the proud buffalo—each of these archetypal patterns of transformation influenced David's development in ways he and I never could have anticipated, contributing to tangible therapeutic gains and positive personal evolution.

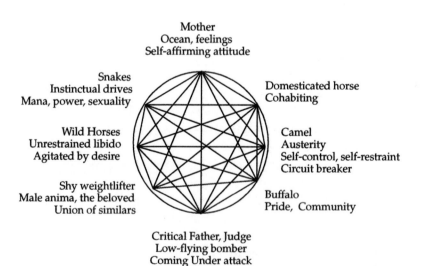

Mother
Ocean, feelings
Self-affirming attitude

Snakes
Instinctual drives
Mana, power, sexuality

Domesticated horse
Cohabiting

Wild Horses
Unrestrained libido
Agitated by desire

Camel
Austerity
Self-control, self-restraint
Circuit breaker

Shy weightlifter
Male anima, the beloved
Union of similars

Buffalo
Pride, Community

Critical Father, Judge
Low-flying bomber
Coming Under attack

*Dream Mandala: Taming wild horses*

# EPILOGUE

While working with David, I was inspired by these words from Jung's *Commentary on The Secret of the Golden Flower:*

> Here and there it happened in my practice that a patient grew beyond himself because of unknown potentialities, and this became an experience of prime importance to me ... . When I examined the way of development of those persons who quietly and, as if unconsciously, grew beyond themselves, I saw that their fates had something in common. The new thing came to them out of obscure possibilities either outside or inside themselves; they accepted it and developed further by means of it ... . In no case was it conjured into existence through purpose and conscious willing, but rather seemed to be borne on the stream of time ... . What did these people do in order to achieve the development that liberated them? As far as I could see they did nothing (wu wei) but let things happen. As Master Lu-tsu teaches in our text, the light rotates according to its own law, if one does not give up one's ordinary occupation. The art of letting things happen, action through non-action, letting go of oneself, ... became for me the key opening the door to the way.

We must be able to let things happen in the psyche ... . The Hui Ming Ching is introduced with the verse:

*If thou wouldst complete the diamond body with no outflowing,*
*Diligently heat the roots of consciousness and life.*
*Kindle light in the blessed country ever close at hand,*
*And there hidden, let thy true self always dwell.*

These verses contain a sort of alchemistic instruction, a method or way of creating the 'diamond body', which is also meant in our text. 'Heating' is necessary; that is, there must be an intensification of consciousness in order that the dwelling place of the spirit may be illumined. But not only consciousness, life itself must be intensified. The union of these two produces 'conscious life.' (Jung, 1962 [1931], pp. 91–92, 93–95, 98)

Dreamwork is a practice that furthers this heating and intensification of conscious life. We let things happen, seeing where the unconscious leads. We experience the dynamic forces set in motion as "the light rotates according to its own law."

# CONCLUSION

Dreamwork is a personalized yoga of the unconscious, a direct link to inner truth and guidance. Anyone can practice it. There are no prerequisites, and there's no limit to how far this path can take us. Dreamwork offers one of the most dynamic ways to transform our lives. It allows us to revisit points of maturational stress, to resolve them, to free up energy for change. Dreams clarify our feelings, magnifying and transforming them. They stir resonant intentions and initiatives that well up within us like gushing springs. Dreams facilitate social adaptation, reveal our shadows, and unite the opposites within us. Dreams add perceptual and emotional nuance and depth to waking life events, to our feelings and relationships. Like all great spiritual practices, dreamwork can awaken powerful energies within us. We need to be prepared to respond with full commitment to each dream's provocative messages.

The perceptual gestalt of a dream is always shifting. If we look at it from one angle, it has one meaning; from another angle the dream is something else entirely. The dream's limitless and simultaneous meanings open up dimension after dimension of pulsating evolutionary lessons. Jung wrote, "It is precisely the spontaneity of archetypal contents that convinces" (Jung, 1968 [1944], par. 19).

That spontaneity of dreams lights up something unexpected inside us. Dreams are a helpful and creative evolutionary force.

Dreams are an ever-expanding spiral, an axis of new consciousness. No matter what the nature of our particular emotional or spiritual malaise, dreams can guide us, expand our perception, excite our sense of possibilities. The process begins when we write down any dream fragments we recall, even if they don't seem to make any sense. We can be infinitely creative in unfolding these condensed messages, these inner cartoons of the imagination. I say to my own unconscious, "Tell me another dream." I'm always eager to hear another.

I invite you to follow the procedures demonstrated in this book. Be a dreamkeeper. Preserve records of dreams and the stories and feelings they evoke. Name the characters and complexes that appear. Expand your associations to each dream image. Draw dream mandalas to clarify conflicts and the tension of opposites in your life and personality. Unfold the healing symbols of the unconscious. Amplify each dream, and polish it to a gem. Then the dream becomes a philosopher's stone, the refracted light of an infinite sun.

# REFERENCES

Allen, M.L., & Sabini, S. (1997). Renewal of the world tree. In: D. Sandner & S. Wong (Eds.), *The Sacred Heritage: The Influence of Shamanism on Analytical Psychology* (pp. 214–225). New York: Routledge.

Arguelles, J., & Arguelles, M. (1995). *Mandala.* Boston and London: Shambhala.

Beebe, J. (2001). The anima in film. In: C. Hauke & I. Alister (Eds.), *Jung and Film: Post-Jungian Takes on the Moving Image* (pp. 208–225). Philadelphia: Brunner-Routledge.

Bennet, E.A. (2000). *What Jung Really Said.* New York: Little Brown.

Bogart, G. (1995). *Finding Your Life's Calling: Spiritual Dimensions of Vocational Choice.* Berkeley, CA: Dawn Mountain.

Bogart, G. (1997). *The Nine Stages of Spiritual Apprenticeship: Understanding the Student-Teacher Relationship.* Berkeley, CA: Dawn Mountain.

Bogart, G. (2002). *Astrology and Meditation: The Fearless Contemplation of Change.* Bournemouth, U.K.: Wessex Astrologer.

Campbell, J. (1983). *The Way of the Animal Powers.* New York: Alfred Van Der Marck.

Conger, J. (1988). *Jung and Reich: The Body as Shadow.* Berkeley, CA: North Atlantic.

Corbett, L., & Rives, C. (1991). Anima, animus, and self-object theory. In: N. Schwartz-Salant & M. Stein (Eds.), *Gender and Soul in Psychotherapy* (pp. 251–260). Wilmette, IL: Chiron Books.

Corbett, L. (1996). *The Religious Function of the Psyche.* London: Routledge.

Eliade, M. (1959). *The Sacred and the Profane: The Nature of Religion.* New York: Harvest.

Eliade, M. (1979). *The Forge and the Crucible: The Origins and Structures of Alchemy.* Chicago: University of Chicago Press.

Edinger, E. (1985). *The Anatomy of the Psyche.* La Salle, IL: Open Court.

Edinger, E. (1992). *Ego and Archetype: Individuation and the Religious Function of the Psyche.* Boston: Shambhala.

Edinger, E. (1994a). *The Mystery of the Coniunctio.* Toronto: Inner City.

Edinger, E. (1994b). *The Eternal Drama: The Inner Meaning of Greek Mythology.* Boston: Shambhala.

Fabricius, J. (1994). *Alchemy: The Medieval Alchemists and Their Royal Art.* London: Diamond Books.

Fordham, M. (1990). *Jungian Psychotherapy: A Study in Analytical Psychology.* London: Karnac.

Goldwert, M. (1992). *Wounded Healers: Creative Illness in the Pioneers of Depth Psychology.* New York: Rowman & Littlefield.

Guenther, H. (1963). *The Life and Teaching of Naropa.* New York: Oxford University Press.

Hall, J. (1983). *Jungian Dream Interpretation.* Toronto: Inner City.

Henderson, J., & Oakes, M. (1963). *The Wisdom of the Serpent: The Myths of Death, Rebirth, and Resurrection.* New York: Collier.

Herdt, G. (1982). *Rituals of Manhood: Male Initiation in Papua New Guinea.* Berkeley, CA: University of California Press.

Hill, G. (1992). *Masculine and Feminine.* Boston: Shambhala.

Hillman, J. (1978). *Revisioning Psychology.* New York: Harper & Row.

Hillman, J. (1979a). *The Dream and the Underworld.* New York: Harper & Row.

Hillman, J. (1979b). *The Puer Papers.* Dallas: Spring.

Hoeller, S.A. (1982). *The Gnostic Jung and the Seven Sermons to the Dead.* Wheaton, IL: Quest.

Hoeller, S. (1988). C.G. Jung and the alchemical renewal. *Gnosis,* 8.

Holmes, J. (1993). *John Bowlby and Attachment Theory.* New York: Routledge.

Homans, P. (1979). *Jung in Context: Modernity and the Making of a Psychology.* Chicago: University of Chicago Press.

Hopcke, R. (1989). *Jung, Jungians, and Homosexuality*. Boston: Shambhala.

Hunt, H. (1993). *The Multiplicity of Dreams: Memory, Imagination, and Consciousness*. New Haven, CT: Yale University Press.

Jacobi, J. (1942). *The Psychology of C.G. Jung*. London: Routledge & Kegan Paul.

Jaffe, A. (1984). *Jung's Last Years*. Dallas: Spring.

Jonas, H. (1958). *The Gnostic Religion*. Boston: Beacon.

Jung, C.G. (1956) [1911–1912]. *Symbols of Transformation, C.W.*, 5, R.F.C. Hull (Trans.). Princeton, NJ: Princeton University Press.

Jung, C.G. (1966) [1917/1926]. *On the Psychology of the Unconscious, C.W.*, 7, R.F.C. Hull (Trans.). Princeton, NJ: Princeton University Press.

Jung, C.G. (1966) [1928]. *The Relations between the Ego and the Unconscious, C.W.*, 7, R.F.C. Hull (Trans.). Princeton, NJ: Princeton University Press.

Jung, C.G. (1962) [1931]. *Commentary on the Secret of the Golden Flower: A Chinese Book of Life*, R. Wilhelm (Trans.). New York: Harcourt Brace Jovanovich.

Jung, C.G. (1966) [1934a]. *The Practical Use of Dream Analysis, C.W.*, 16, R.F.C. Hull (Trans.). Princeton, NJ: Princeton University Press.

Jung, C.G. (1969) [1934b]. *A Review of the Complex Theory, C.W.*, 8, R.F.C. Hull (Trans.). Princeton, NJ: Princeton University Press.

Jung, C.G. (1976) [1935]. *Tavistock Lecture II, C.W.*, 18, R.F.C. Hull (Trans.). Princeton, NJ: Princeton University Press.

Jung, C.G. (1969) [1936]. *The Concept of the Collective Unconscious, C.W.*, 9(i), R.F.C. Hull (Trans.). Princeton, NJ: Princeton University Press.

Jung, (1969) [1938/1940]. *Psychology and Religion (The Terry Lectures), C.W.*, 11. Princeton, NJ: Princeton University Press.

Jung, C.G. (1969) [1939]. *Conscious, Unconscious, and Individuation, C.W.*, 9(i), R.F.C. Hull (Trans.). Princeton, NJ: Princeton University Press.

Jung, C.G. (1968) [1944]. *Introduction to the Religious and Psychological Problems of Alchemy, C.W.*, 12, R.F.C. Hull (Trans.). Princeton, NJ: Princeton University Press.

Jung, C.G. (1969) [1948]. *The Phenomenology of the Spirit in Fairytales, C.W.*, 9(i), R.F.C. Hull (Trans.). Princeton, NJ: Princeton University Press.

Jung, C.G. (1966) [1946]. *The Psychology of the Transference, C.W.*, 16, R.F.C. Hull (Trans.). Princeton, NJ: Princeton University Press.

Jung, C.G. (1969) [1950a]. *Concerning Mandala Symbolism, C.W.*, 9(i), R.F.C. Hull (Trans.). Princeton, NJ: Princeton University Press.

Jung, C.G. (1969) [1950b]. *A Study in the Process of Individuation*, C.W., 9(i), R.F.C. Hull (Trans.). Princeton, NJ: Princeton University Press.

Jung, C.G. (1969) [1954]. *On the Psychology of the Trickster-Figure*, C.W., 9(i). Princeton, NJ: Princeton University Press.

Jung, C.G. (1969) [1955]. *Mandalas*, C.W., 9(i), R.F.C. Hull (Trans.). Princeton, NJ: Princeton University Press.

Jung, C.G. (1963) [1955–1956]. *Mysterium Coniunctionis*, C.W., 14, R.F.C. Hull (Trans.). Princeton, NJ: Princeton University Press.

Jung, C.G. (1959). *Aion*, C.W., 9(ii), R.F.C. Hull (Trans.). Princeton, NJ: Princeton University Press.

Jung, C.G. (1961). *Memories, Dreams, Reflections*. New York: Viking.

Jung, C.G. (1988). *Nietzsche's Zarathustra* (J.L. Jarrett, Ed.). Princeton, NJ: Princeton University Press.

Jung, E. (1981) [1957]. *Animus and Anima*. Dallas: Spring.

Kohut, H., & Wolf, E.S. (1978). Disorders of the self and their treatment. *International Journal of Psychoanalysis*, 59: 413–425.

Krippner, S. (Ed.) (1990). *Dreamtime and Dreamwork*. Los Angeles: Tarcher.

Krippner, S., & Waldman, M. (Eds.) (2000). *Dreamscaping: New and Creative Ways to Work with Your Dreams*. Chicago: Lowell House.

Krippner, S., Bogzaran, F., & de Carvalho, A.P. (2002). *Extraordinary Dreams and How to Work with Them*. Albany, NY: State University of New York Press.

Levinson, D. (1978). *The Seasons of a Man's Life*. New York: Ballantine.

Longchen Rabjam (2001). *A Treasury Trove of Scriptural Transmission: A Commentary on the Precious Treasury of the Basic Space of Phenomena* (R. Barron, Trans.). Junction City, CA: Padma Publishing.

Lyall, S. (2006). Loquacious parrot splits up love birds. *San Francisco Chronicle*, January 18, p. 2.

Maguire, A. (1987). Jung's first dream. In: L.C. Mahdi, S. Foster, & M. Little (Eds.), *Betwixt and Between: Patterns of Masculine and Feminine Initiation* (pp. 60–66). La Salle, IL: Open Court.

Mahe, J.P. (1998). A reading of the discourse on the Ogdoad and the Ennead. In: R. Van den Broek & W. J. Hanegraaff (Eds.), *Gnosis and Hermeticism from Antiquity to Modern Times* (pp. 79–85). Albany, NY: State University of New York Press.

Maier, M. (1618). *Atalanta Fugiens*. Oppenheim, Germany: Johann Theodor de Bry.

Mansfield, V. (1995). *Synchronicity, Science, and Soul-Making*. La Salle, IL: Open Court.

Metzner, R. (1998). Journey to the place of vision and power. In: *The Unfolding Self* (pp. 223–248). Novato, CA: Origin Press.

Mindel, A. (1982). *Dreambody: The Body's Role in Revealing the Self*. Santa Monica, CA: Sigo.

Moore, R., & Gillette, D. (1994). Four male archetypes: King, warrior, magician, lover. In: R. Frager (Ed.), *Who Am I?* (pp. 125–131). New York: Tarcher/Putnam.

Muller-Ortega, P.E. (1989). *The Triadic Heart of Siva*. Albany, NY: State University of New York Press.

Otto, R. (1958). *The Idea of the Holy*. New York: Oxford University Press.

Proust, M. (1934). *Remembrance of Things Past*. New York: Random House.

Rank, O. (1978). *Will Therapy*. New York: Norton.

Reich, W. (1970). *The Mass Psychology of Fascism*. New York: Farrar, Straus, & Giroux.

Roob, A. (2001). *Alchemy and Mysticism: The Hermetic Museum*. Koln, Germany: Taschen.

Rudhyar, D. (1983). *Rhythm of Wholeness*. Wheaton, IL: Quest.

Russack, N. (2002). *Animal Guides in Life, Myth, and Dreams*. Toronto: Inner City.

Schactel, E. (1959). *Metamorphosis*. New York: Basic Books.

Stein, M. (1998). *Jung's Map of the Soul*. La Salle, IL: Open Court.

Stern, D. (1985). *The Interpersonal World of the Infant*. New York: Basic Books.

Stevens, A. (1990). *On Jung*. New York: Penguin.

Stevens, A. (2003). *Archetype Revisited: An Updated Natural History of the Self*. Toronto: Inner City.

Storr, A. (1973). *C.G. Jung (Modern Masters)*. New York: Penguin.

Storr, A. (1983). *The Essential Jung*. Princeton, NJ: Princeton University Press.

Symington, J., & Symington, N. (1996). *The Clinical Thinking of Wilfred Bion*. Hove and New York: Brunner-Routledge.

Tarnas, R. (2006). *Cosmos and Psyche: Intimations of a New World View*. New York: Viking.

Teich, H. (1993). Homovision: The solar/lunar twin-ego. In: R. Hopcke, K. Carrington, & S. Wirth (Eds.), *Same Sex Love and the Path to Wholeness* (pp. 136–150). Boston: Shambhala.

Ulanov, A. (2004). *Spiritual Aspects of Clinical Work*. Einsiedeln, Switzerland: Daimon Verlag.

von Franz, M.L. (1964). The process of individuation. In: C.G. Jung, M.L. von Franz, J. Henderson, J. Jacobi, & A. Jaffe, *Man and His Symbols*. New York: Dell.

von Franz, M.L. (1970). *The Problem of the Puer Aeternus*. Dallas: Spring.

von Franz, M.L. (1975). *C.G. Jung: His Myth in Our Time*. New York: C.G. Jung Foundation for Analytical Psychology.

von Franz, M.L. (1977). *Individuation in Fairy Tales*. Dallas: Spring.

von Franz, M.L. (1980a). *Shadow and Evil in Fairytales*. Dallas: Spring.

von Franz, M.L. (1980b). *On Divination and Synchronicity: The Psychology of Meaningful Chance*. Toronto: Inner City.

Whitmont, E. (1969). *The Symbolic Quest*. Princeton, NJ: Princeton University Press.

Whitmont, E., & Perera, S. (1989). *Dreams: A Portal to the Source*. New York: Routledge.

Williams, S.K. (1976). *The Jungian-Senoi Dreamwork Manual*. Berkeley, CA: Journey Press.

Wolff, T. (1956). *Structural Forms of the Feminine Psyche*. Privately printed paper for the Students Association, C.G. Jung Institute, Zurich.

Woolger, J., & Woolger, R. (1994). The goddess within: A Jungian typology for women. In: R. Frager (Ed.), *Who Am I?* (pp. 116–124). New York: Tarcher/Putnam.

# INDEX

295